Mental Health and Wellbeing for Journalists

This book offers a first-of-its-kind, practical and person-centred guide to managing and contextualising journalists' emotional wellbeing and mental health.

Drawing on the author's experience as a storyteller, journalist and media safety consultant, the book combines significant lived personal experience with reflections from an international network of journalists and mental health experts to collate industry good practice and guidance. It takes readers through a history of mental health discussions in the industry, moving from a focus on war correspondents and post-traumatic stress disorder to considerations of vicarious trauma, moral injury and the impact of online harm on journalists. It shows how pressures already faced by those in the sector have been exacerbated by the global pandemic, giving rise to the prospect of a mental health crisis in the media if these issues remain unaddressed. As a counter to this concern, Storm shares insights from experts on what leaders can do to create safer workplaces and processes, how they can channel the empathy that is core to healthy journalism to promote the health of its people, and how they should consider mental health as intersecting with other issues such as physical safety, diversity and inclusion. Insights from science shed light on resilience levels, how our brains and bodies respond to trauma, and strategies that can be adopted to help us recover from challenging experiences. While acknowledging that some news organisations are starting to take note, Storm shows how others need to do more, offering ways in which newsrooms can learn from the lessons of recent years to bring about long-lasting change.

Mental Health and Wellbeing for Journalists is written for news media professionals, educators, and students, as well as anyone interested in promoting more sustainable journalism through supporting the industry's most precious resource: its people.

Hannah Storm is a media consultant specialising in journalism safety, mental health and leadership. She is the founder and co-director of Headlines Network, a community to improve mental health conversations in the news media. She is the former CEO and director of the Ethical Journalism Network and served as director of the International News Safety Institute. She began her career at Reuters, and has spent more than two decades working internationally across diverse forms of media, including broadcast, print and digital.

Mental Health and Wellbeing for Journalists
A Practical Guide

Hannah Storm

NEW YORK AND LONDON

Designed cover image: © Getty Images

First published 2024
by Routledge
605 Third Avenue, New York, NY 10158

and by Routledge
4 Park Square, Milton Park, Abingdon, Oxon, OX14 4RN

Routledge is an imprint of the Taylor & Francis Group, an informa business

© 2024 Hannah Storm

The right of Hannah Storm to be identified as author of this work has been asserted in accordance with sections 77 and 78 of the Copyright, Designs and Patents Act 1988.

All rights reserved. No part of this book may be reprinted or reproduced or utilised in any form or by any electronic, mechanical, or other means, now known or hereafter invented, including photocopying and recording, or in any information storage or retrieval system, without permission in writing from the publishers.

Trademark notice: Product or corporate names may be trademarks or registered trademarks, and are used only for identification and explanation without intent to infringe.

Library of Congress Cataloging-in-Publication Data
Names: Storm, Hannah (Former journalist), author.
Title: Mental health and wellbeing for journalists : a practical guide / Hannah Storm.
Description: New York : Routledge, 2024. | Includes bibliographical references and index.
Identifiers: LCCN 2023051614 (print) | LCCN 2023051615 (ebook) | ISBN 9781032382463 (hardback) | ISBN 9781032382456 (paperback) | ISBN 9781003344179 (ebook)
Subjects: LCSH: Journalism—Psychological aspects. | Journalists—Mental health.
Classification: LCC PN4771 .S76 2024 (print) | LCC PN4771 (ebook) | DDC 070.4—dc23/eng/20240108
LC record available at https://lccn.loc.gov/2023051614
LC ebook record available at https://lccn.loc.gov/2023051615

ISBN: 978-1-032-38246-3 (hbk)
ISBN: 978-1-032-38245-6 (pbk)
ISBN: 978-1-003-34417-9 (ebk)

DOI: 10.4324/9781003344179

Typeset in ITC Galliard Pro
by Apex CoVantage, LLC

Contents

Preface	*vii*
1 Introduction	1
2 The evolution of mental health conversations in journalism	5
3 Averting a mental health crisis: a clarion call for change	21
4 Culture, coping and conditioning	34
5 The journalist's brain	44
6 Post-traumatic stress disorder (PTSD)	54
7 Vicarious trauma	67
8 Moral injury	80
9 The mental health impact of online harm	93
10 Journalists and burnout	109
11 The pandemic and a perfect storm of pressures	121
12 Self-care and supporting others	135

13 Managing with empathy, and effective leadership 152

14 Conclusion: When journalists thrive,
   so does journalism 165

   Index 178

Preface
The author's story

I became involved in the conversation around journalism and mental health because of my own experiences of being injured through my work.

In late 2019, I was diagnosed with post-traumatic stress disorder (PTSD) after a series of traumatic experiences, related to my journalism. These included incidents that occurred during repeat visits to Haiti in 2004 and 2010, which coincided with periods of deadly political and gang violence, and the aftermath of a devastating earthquake which killed tens of thousands of people. They also included two serious sexual assaults, one of them a rape, by men I met related to my work in Haiti, and an abusive relationship with someone who, again, I met through my journalism.

It took me many years to realise my mental health had also been impacted negatively by the cumulative toll of the graphic images, interviews and accounts I was exposed to simply by being a journalist. I was also affected by the behaviours of certain colleagues who abused their positions of power and subjected me to harassment. From the start of my career, the cultures within which I worked conditioned me to behave in certain ways, even where this made me feel uncomfortable.

I first spoke publicly about my PTSD in 2020 in an article for Poynter.org, the website of the US-based media institute. Over the years, I have formed a fuller picture of my story, and writing this book has allowed me to better understand my experiences and how the cumulative nature of my trauma exposure, coupled with an environment that rewarded certain behaviours and repressed others, impacted my mental health. In this chapter, I'll share something of my perspective, which I hope sheds light on why I am writing this book.

Some of what follows may not make for easy reading.

It's tempting to work chronologically, to show how things built up over time, but one of the things I have learned about mental health is that things are rarely linear. Recovery is not – that's certain. And when we try to unravel our stories and understand the sources of our traumas, we find they aren't linear either. It makes sense to me to start from the bottom and work up, because it was only by hitting the bottom that I was able to find a way back towards the light, and a sense of purpose.

In April 2018, I was at the International Journalism Festival in the Italian city of Perugia to moderate a series of panels, including one on #MeToo in the media. It was six months after the hashtag went viral and became a global cry against sexual harassment. There had been allegations made against several high-profile journalists, some of whom had lost their jobs in the wake of the movement, but many colleagues I spoke with believed that some news organisations continued to protect the perpetrators, while those who were harassed and assaulted had been conditioned to put up with, and shut up about, these unacceptable behaviours.

At this point, I had never spoken openly about my experiences of sexual harassment as a journalist. I'd never mentioned the sources who'd invited me back to their homes; the news boss who had done the same, told me his marriage was failing and that only I understood him; the older married colleague who seduced me with similar sentiments; and those who suggested strongly that if I wanted to be part of the team, I join them at the lap-dancing club. I'd never mentioned the hands on my legs, waist, bum, the sexual comments from colleagues, interviewees, strangers in the crowd, bosses. Like many of my colleagues, I had been conditioned to assume they were part of my job. Over time, there were so many incidents that, to this day, I sometimes remember experiences of harassment that I had completely forgotten.

I had kept quiet too about the sexual assaults I had suffered, perpetrated by men I met through my work. Instead, I had spent years advocating for survivors and teaching reporting on gender-based violence for the United Nations, and I'd co-authored a groundbreaking book, which, more than a decade after its 2012 publication, is still an important reference in newsrooms in terms of the safety of women journalists.

Ostensibly, *No Woman's Land: On the Frontlines with Female Reporters* was published in response to the change in conversations around the safety of women journalists after the rape of CBS correspondent Lara Logan in Egypt's Tahrir Square. But my own experiences provided a subconscious motivation as I collated the stories of our 40 women contributors, even as I kept my own a secret. In retrospect, the book helped me process some of my trauma, but it also added to my emotional load, even if not all the stories featured harassment or assault.

By the time I got to Perugia in 2018, I had been working at the International News Safety Institute (INSI) for eight years and its director for more than half that time. Much of my work saw me liaising with news teams from around the world, sharing fast-moving safety information from front lines and fault lines and coordinating safety conversations, as well as collating the casualty figures of the dozens of news media workers who died doing their work every year.

During that time, I was also exposed, as many colleagues were, to the weaponisation of social media and a ratcheting-up of online violence, including the use for propaganda purposes by the Islamic State of a horrific video showing the murder of the American journalist James Foley in Syria.

In my personal life, the years preceding 2018 had brought an accumulation of distressing experiences, including the legacy of the abusive relationship that I had fled years previously and the traumatic birth of my second child.

Back in Italy, though, I was also moderating a panel on a recent study I had co-authored into moral injury in the media. Walking through the cobbled streets of the Umbrian university city to that panel, a concerned colleague took me aside. I remember her warning that I was heading for a crash, and that I could either apply the brakes and slow down to reduce the impact or ignore the signs and hurtle headlong into serious harm. Either way, it was going to happen, and it was probably going to hurt. I only half heard her at the time, but I now know how important her words were, and I am very grateful to her for them.

That evening, I attended a dinner organised by the Dart Center for Journalism and Trauma. Sitting with a colleague, feasting on delicious Italian food and copious wine, we bonded with the intensity that comes from knowing how it feels to live on the edge. During that meal, we shared some of the most intense moments we had experienced as journalists – the sights, sounds and smells we would never be able to shake, the people whose faces were seared into our minds, the things we had done or failed to do, the memories, decisions and behaviours we felt nobody else but those who belonged to our journalism tribe could really understand.

I fell into my bed, drunk and depleted, waking the next morning from nightmares, twisted in sweat-drenched sheets. I panicked as I tried to escape the clutches of my chaotic dreams, trapped inside the bedding and my past. I thought the room was shaking. Perugia is, after all, on a fault line and has a history of earthquakes, even if it is thousands of miles from Haiti. I managed somehow to drag myself out of bed, and continue through the rest of the conference, only just holding it together.

I knew I could not carry on in this vein, but I also felt I had no option but to do so. I made the decision that day to ask for help, though it took more than 18 months for me to get a diagnosis. I would reach the point of considering suicide on more than one occasion, even after I confided in colleagues. But, looking back at that time in Perugia, in April 2018, this was when everything changed.

Through another colleague I met during that conference, I arranged to write publicly about my sexual assaults and my experiences of being conditioned to behave in certain ways, which became the 2020 piece for Poynter.org. I received an outpouring of support, but I wasn't prepared for the mental health crisis that ensued. Putting my words out into the world had made my experience real, even if I could not yet acknowledge its psychological impact.

I felt intense shame. I questioned my decisions and behaviours that had preceded the assaults. I remembered being told by one of the perpetrators that nobody would believe me. I blamed myself for not being able to identify the other man who assaulted me. I thought about all the women whose stories I'd been privileged to share as a journalist and I constantly compared myself with them, telling myself that my trauma wasn't valid because they had endured worse. As a woman working in the predominantly male environment of journalism safety, I also feared that speaking about my experiences would be an admission of failure, that those who thought my work was 'no place for a girl' would have been right all along.

My mental health deteriorated. I had intrusive thoughts frequently. Reminders of my traumas would ambush me: sounds, smells or places that made me feel as if I was trapped. I avoided crowds, lifts and public transport, restrooms with doors that locked to the ground. I became intolerant to loud noises, and found certain sounds extremely distressing, such as cars backfiring, low-flying planes, jackhammers, drills at the dentists. I felt myself panicking every time things shook around me, such as when a heavy vehicle passed or when the ground vibrated because of an underground train. I became hypervigilant to men with similar accents to my attackers. I struggled to concentrate. My memory was poor. I was irritable, most of all with those closest to me. But I was also terrified something awful would happen to those I loved. I drank too much alcohol, exercised to excess, ate too much sugar, skimped on healthier foods. I struggled to sleep, often scared to close my eyes because of nightmares. My body was inevitably affected. I had gastro-intestinal issues, which repeated visits to nutritionists failed to diagnose. Some nights I itched all over. My hair grew thin. I was always cold, apart from when I relived certain experiences, when my body would break into intense sweating.

The journalistic environments in which I worked enabled me to mask some of my behaviours because others were doing similar, especially in terms of the drinking. Even as the director of a journalism safety organisation, I did not feel safe to share my experiences, which saddens me now. PTSD brought huge guilt and shame and a sense that I did not have the right to speak about my experiences because there were so many others out there, journalists and those whose stories we covered, who had it so much worse. Somehow, I managed to keep on working, even as I kept my symptoms from colleagues and concealed certain behaviours from those closest to me. For years, I felt ashamed and alone.

It took repeated visits to the doctor, seeking help for other symptoms, many of them physical, before I was told I was suffering from burnout. I was signed off work but didn't get better. Without mental health support at work, I was advised to self-refer and did so through the National Health Service in England. I got as far as an initial chat with someone who asked for my history, before I realised that they were completely the wrong individual and had no clue about journalism, what motivated us or our ways of working. I'd had previous experiences of unsuitable therapists and it, once again, felt like an uphill struggle at a time when I was going downhill fast.

It was clear to me that what I was experiencing was something other than burnout. I had to return to my job, but by then I knew recovery would only begin when my INSI role ended. I took another job as director of the Ethical

Journalism Network, where I did not have to deal with journalism safety issues on a daily basis. I started to confide in people who understood where I was coming from, some of whom had been injured by their work. I finally got an appointment to see a therapist.

I was diagnosed with PTSD just before the Covid pandemic, in the late winter of 2019, a result that confirmed my long-held suspicions. My own PTSD stems not from one experience but from many. In diagnostic terms (and a diagnosis that isn't always seen as distinct from PTSD), I have complex PTSD, something I was not aware existed. However, the more people I speak with, the more I realise trauma can be cumulative, especially in journalism. To me, it felt like a skein of interconnected threads, hard to unravel. I was, however, determined to unravel them, before they were able to do the same to me.

I began therapy as the pandemic began. Sessions with my therapist happened across Zoom. I was reticent about seeing him because I had found most previous therapeutic interactions made things worse. But I decided to stick with it, and during the weird early weeks and months of Covid, he was another connection with the outside world. Early on, I admitted I didn't want to cry because I was scared of what might happen if I did. I used the analogy of an emotional flak jacket with him, and he told me that a flak jacket serves no purpose if it is hiding an injury. He said that if keeping the body armour on meant we prevented ourselves seeking treatment for something, the injury would simply get worse. I understood this analogy, from places where I had worn physical flak jackets, where we would don this protective equipment proactively. In order to get help for PTSD and to really embark on the road to recovery, I had to take off my ill-fitting flak jacket and allow things to get worse before they got better.

Covid brought challenges to therapy. I was in lockdown with my family, facing my fears and speaking about them through a screen with someone I had only met once in person. I worried that my family would be able to hear some of my horrible experiences. Instead of having me speak about them, my therapist encouraged me to write down my experiences, in the present tense. Time and again, I focused on one specific incident, writing and re-writing it until I could remember more clearly. PTSD had messed with my memories, leaving big gaps in my history but reminding me repeatedly about other parts. Over time, I began to piece together the jigsaw pieces of my past. For years, my inability to clearly remember my assaults exacerbated my shame. But through this therapy, I learned to safely unpack the boxes where my memories had been wrongly stored, to safely relive those experiences and then put the memories back in their rightful boxes.

Writing and therapy allowed me to move forwards. I found other things that helped me too. I benefited from speaking with friends and colleagues, and spending time outside. Running was a great exercise, a way to feel grounded and with nature. Gradually, I became able to write publicly about my mental health experiences. It was the start of my mission to use my mental health journey to help others. I have since written a collection of flash fiction, with several stories inspired by my experiences. After being recognised for my writing with awards and nominations, I began working on a novel about a journalist who, in the course of her work, makes a difficult ethical decision that has devastating consequences.

I have launched a company called Headlines Network to promote more open conversations about mental health in journalism. Working with my colleague, John Crowley, as well as with clinicians, mental health experts and other journalists, we deliver workshops and develop practical resources for the news industry. We also host a podcast, hearing from celebrated journalists about the stories that have affected them and how they manage their mental health. The conversations have confirmed to me the power of storytelling, not only as a tool for journalism, but also as something that could benefit journalists' mental health.

I recognise we are often told that we must not become the story and that we're conditioned to keep on going, often at the expense of our mental health. Things are changing, though, and conversations are becoming more commonplace – I welcome this. But there are still far too many people who are fearful of sharing their experiences because they are genuinely worried about negative repercussions. My own career was punctuated with times when I felt ashamed to speak about my experiences. Looking back, I was conditioned to behave in a certain way, and keep quiet about my distress.

Beginning with my first role as a graduate trainee journalist at Reuters in 1999, many of our conversations in the pub provided a place for us to confide in each other. We shared stories we felt only we could understand. This continued for the next decade or so, even as I changed jobs, with regular visits to drinking holes where we would debrief and let our hair down after particularly difficult stories. In those times, I felt part of a tribe, sharing a unique language. I remember the secrets we swore would stay with us, the things that happened on tour that we agreed would stay on tour, the affairs that grew from alliances formed quickly in dangerous places, the black humour that helped us process painful things.

Early in my career, I remember a colleague, in his early twenties, drinking throughout the night, sleeping in the office toilet, and then appearing at his desk the next morning in the same clothes. Others applauded his stamina. Later, from afar, I watched his mental health collapse, saddened that his seniors had not provided the support he needed.

The interview for my second journalism job took place in a bar on Fleet Street, the spiritual home of journalism in London. There was just me, aged 24, and a veteran journalist from the Home News desk, who was probably twice my age, and the interview process seemed to involve assessing how much wine I could consume before I became too drunk to hold a conversation. Days into my role at that news organisation, one of the editors yelled and swore at me for a reason I can't remember. Nobody expressed their support for me, and I kept my crying for the bathroom. I now know this editor's reaction was less about me and more about his inability to cope with the stressors of his work. Not that I condone his actions. As a young journalist, it hurt me and showed me that bullies could make it big in newsrooms. Fortunately, he no longer works in newsrooms.

In my subsequent job, I was on the desk of a British TV newsroom when I was asked by someone more senior than me to view a live feed of images from one of the news agencies. I was to decide what was too graphic to show our audiences on a nightly news programme. It was 2003 and the first night of the bombing of Baghdad by the US-led coalition. I was given no training, not told what I was likely to see, not asked how I was, or reminded of the purpose of my work. I was a junior in a newsroom and the glory and attention went to those who were out risking their lives in the field.

I saw images I still remember decades on. Shortly afterwards, I began having nightmares, drinking too much, engaging in risky behaviour. I began to question why I was doing my work and struggled to equate what I had seen with my work environment in a London newsroom, where there was no risk of bombs falling from the sky, destroying buildings and lives. A few months later, I moved overseas to be a journalist in the field, where I hoped that I would finally get noticed, like the men, for the most part, who had been in Iraq. I didn't yet recognise that I would also be exposed to other kinds of trauma. I did not know then that vicarious trauma is trauma.

March 2003 marked the first time that the work I was doing in journalism really impacted my mental health, despite my earlier exposure to the toxic management styles that had conditioned me to put up and shut up. The vicarious trauma aspect was not something I considered until many years later, when I was running INSI and once again found myself dealing with graphic images.

I mentioned these early experiences in passing to a colleague at an awards dinner shortly before the 20th anniversary of the Baghdad bombing, and they reminded me that whoever tasked me with this work was probably also incredibly young and not equipped with the tools themselves to know how to limit exposure to potentially distressing content. This is not an excuse, but I hope it shows that some things have changed and that now most line managers would be able to support their colleagues to avoid the risk of vicarious trauma.

Our mental health can be affected whether we are exposed directly or remotely to distressing events. In 20 years of working in journalism, I have seen this too often. More recently, I have questioned why I did not spot the signs that another older male colleague was suffering. He died by suicide years after we covered a traumatic story together, and after a career covering an accumulation of difficult and dangerous news events. Of course, I don't know the full picture in terms of what he was enduring, but I remember asking myself if I could have done anything differently and feeling confused by how the newsroom responded to his death. They applauded his work and I wondered if anyone had actually taken the time to do that when he was alive, to ask him how he really was. Had there been fewer taboos around talking openly, might his story have ended differently?

Too many journalists have ended their lives during my own career. I fear for others. We must do more to normalise conversations about mental health, because – even now, a generation on from when I started my work – journalists are still breaking. I feel fortunate to have survived, though there were times when I felt I might not, when even getting through the day felt like an insurmountable challenge, only managed by coping strategies and support from others.

I still find myself reliving aspects of my trauma sometimes. I still have really dark days too. When I was most unwell, intrusive memories would floor me, but now I am more aware of my reactions, of what helps and what does not. Now I am more aware of how much I need to pace myself, say no, take time alone, listen to my body. There are days when the sun seems to stubbornly sit behind the cloud, but these are days I know will pass. I know my story is just one person's history, from her perspective, but I hope that some of it will resonate and that others will take from it a recognition of the small part we can all play in sustaining the people who keep journalism alive.

1 Introduction

The costs of not addressing mental health are great. Also great are the costs of not ensuring that conversations around wellbeing are positioned front and centre in our work. Where journalists are not safe, they will take greater risks at work, their journalism will suffer, and so will their journalism colleagues. Where journalists are not safe, journalism will see reduced performance and productivity, rising presenteeism, problems with retention and increasing costs in terms of sickness and injury, as well as increased pressure and payouts related to staff turnover.

Good journalism relies on journalists being well, and yet the mental health of news media workers has simply not been a priority for many in our industry. This book seeks to make the case for why we need to take the mental health of our journalists seriously, for their sake and for the sake of journalism.

Like physical security, psychological safety in journalism has often been seen through a narrow Western lens. Conversations have been dominated by those who make up the status quo in newsrooms – straight, university-educated white men – further marginalising those who do not see themselves represented in these discussions. Although some stigma exists almost everywhere, in some countries where there are significant societal taboos, conversations about journalism and mental health may be almost non-existent. Furthermore, a focus on mental health can seem a privileged perspective, when you live in an environment that frequently exposes you to physical danger, or where your job as a journalist is regularly insecure and unpaid.

I spoke with more than 40 people from more than a dozen countries when writing this book, and I hope their diverse insights will offer new and more nuanced and inclusive perspectives. The aim is to provide practical insights into the connection between journalists' work and our mental health, and to consider the ways in which both the stories we cover and the environments in which we work affect us. It offers tips from people who recognise the realities of our work: journalists, clinicians who have treated people in the media, and other experts at the intersection of journalism and wellbeing. They share measures taken to support their own mental health and steps they have seen taken by individuals, institutions and the industry.

DOI: 10.4324/9781003344179-1

The book begins by charting the history of research in this field and how conversations have evolved across time and cultures. It considers key moments that spurred change, sparking a recognition of the need to consider mental health in all forms and across our industry. But it also shows there are still significant taboos and stigmas in parts of the world and facing certain communities.

It also details the barriers within our industry that prevent conversations about mental health from becoming commonplace and how the environment of the newsroom has often conditioned the people working in it to keep quiet. The book therefore offers suggestions for creating more inclusive and open newsroom cultures, where people feel safe to speak without fear of repercussions.

While the issue of mental health in journalism has historically been seen through a narrow lens, this book shows there's a move towards considering how mental health exists across a wide spectrum. We all have mental health, as we all have physical health, and we experience it in different ways. The book draws out specific examples of systemic stressors, as well as highlighting hostile environments that have a greater impact upon certain people because of their identity, and calls for greater awareness in newsrooms of how identity-based violence and inequity can hurt specific communities.

Several chapters mention mental health conditions and include descriptions of how our bodies and brains typically respond to stress and trauma. Trauma, for the purposes of this book, derives from the Greek word for 'piercing' or 'wound' and refers to a distressing or disturbing experience, as well as the emotional response to such an event. However, this is not a science publication, nor am I a scientist. Mental health is still a contested field in many ways, and though I recognise that labels, names or diagnoses may be helpful for some, the focus of this book is on people, not pathology.

Throughout this book are reminders that it is normal for the body and brain to react in certain ways when exposed to terrible and traumatic things. As we would expect to make time for, and benefit from, support and resources for recovery from physical injury, psychological recovery also benefits from us being able to find support and resources. That might be through self-care, from friends and family, or via more specialised support from medical professionals; and our needs may vary over time.

If this book is about people, it is also a reminder that the skills that help make us good journalists can also help us from a mental health perspective. Empathy allows us to walk alongside those whose stories we amplify. We can also use it to promote our own wellbeing and that of others. One chapter shows the value of empathy in leadership. Without compassionate leaders walking the walk and talking the talk, newsrooms will not be able to normalise conversations around mental health.

During my research for this book and in my wider industry work, I have heard frequent expressions of good intent. People do care. Many recognise the importance of conversations about mental health, and the need to invest in them. But many also feel unable to do so, juggling the relentless demands of journalism and diminishing resources, emerging from a global pandemic with extra pressures in their personal lives and a blurring of the boundaries between work and home. This book offers a clarion call. Investing in journalism and investing in journalists are not mutually incompatible.

We must take these conversations more seriously. There is an economic, emotional, ethical and efficiency cost to not doing so, for newsrooms and our news makers. Journalists are journalism's most precious resource and unless we invest in them, we risk losing them to ill-health, to burnout, stress. This book is dedicated to those of my colleagues who feel and have felt alone in their experience of mental health.

Those I interviewed come from all over the world: from Ireland to India, Pakistan to the Philippines, Mexico to Lebanon, Kenya to the United States, Germany to Canada. Some are journalists, while others are clinicians or work to promote more open conversations around journalism and mental health. Their collective wisdom is wide and shows there is no one single conversation around mental health, even within their own countries. Through their generous insights, therefore, they demonstrate there can be no singular approach to supporting the mental health of journalists; good practice differs depending on the context, just as there is no singular experience of mental health.

I have been humbled by how many of these individuals agreed to speak on the record to me. Unfortunately, I could not include everything I was told, but I have used all I learned to shape this book. For the purposes of consistency across my interviews, I asked colleagues versions of the following questions: how did you become involved in the field of mental health and journalism; how have you seen conversations change; what do you see as the most significant challenges; what does good practice look like?

My colleagues' insights are incorporated throughout the chapters, and in several instances, I share their stories at greater length, with their permission. Their experiences show that many aspects of mental health overlap, and therefore their inputs are integrated throughout the book, with some crossover of themes.

Although this book is based on a diverse group of interviews, I would have liked it to include more geographic breadth. I spent months trying to arrange conversations with many other people, but sadly could not secure as many as I would have liked. I do know that some people may still feel uncomfortable speaking openly with strangers about their mental health – even more reason for me to write this book.

We are all different, but we are all human. And sometimes, in the clamour to feed the news beast, I fear we forget this. Speaking with these individuals has reminded me that we all have that in common. My first question to all my interviewees was about how they became involved in the conversation around journalism and mental health. Many told me they were driven by their own personal experiences of being hurt. This is a testament to their empathy and compassion and an indictment of how often action is left to individuals rather than institutions or the industry. I hope hearing this multitude of diverse voices, many of them united by a common desire, will act as a call for collaborative action.

It has been a privilege to hear other people's stories. As journalists, our work centres on listening to and amplifying the stories of others. We are conditioned to not become the story. But those I spoke with told me frequently that hearing the stories of others can help, can enable them to feel less alone. At the heart of this book is an invitation to empathise, an invitation to remember the skills we have as storytellers, to listen actively, to do so non-judgementally, and to create and hold spaces where people share their authentic selves.

The following work is my attempt at a nuanced look at the history of conversations about the mental health of journalists, by considering the key challenges faced in this field by our industry, institutions and individuals and sharing examples of good practice. It cannot be entirely conclusive, but it is as comprehensive as possible. Without journalists, there would be no real journalism. We need to protect the messengers in order to protect the message, to ensure we can continue bearing witness. It is this mission that often motivates us to become journalists in the first place and it can be one of the most powerful protective measures for our mental health.

My own experience of journalistic injury brought me to the bottom, a place where I felt so alone and ashamed that I believed there was no way out and nobody who could help me. But there was, and during my recovery I committed to ensuring I did all I could so others did not suffer as I did. I know this is a lofty ideal, that people will continue to hurt, but I also recall someone messaging me after I first spoke about my PTSD, thanking me and telling me they had heard something of their experience in mine. I can only ever speak from my perspective. I shared more of my story in the preface and am profoundly grateful to those – some of whom I interviewed for this book – who walked alongside me during my darkest days.

2 The evolution of mental health conversations in journalism

> The question that troubled me was: she was very smart, so why had she not reached out for help when she realised that she was getting into difficulties? And she said to me, 'Well, you don't understand this profession. If I told my editors I was feeling this way, they would never send me out in the field again.' This was 1999. And I thought this was pretty punitive.
>
> —Professor Anthony Feinstein[1]

In journalism, there is often a thin line between risk and reward. Although the physical dangers inherent in our work have been understood for a long time, actual discussions about journalism safety are relatively new. In order to understand how conversations developed around the psychological impact of journalists' work, it is necessary to consider the evolution of those around physical safety.

In the United Kingdom and the United States, home to some of the most well-resourced and long-standing newsrooms, initiatives involving physical safety really gained traction in the late 20th century. In 1981, the Committee to Protect Journalists[2] (CPJ) was founded, with its head office in the United States, in response to the harassment of the Paraguayan journalist Alcibiades González Delvalle. A little later, around the same time as the Balkans wars in the 1990s, the advent of cable television opened up the opportunity for continuous news and increased the pressure on journalists.

Around 140 journalists were killed[3] after the break-up of Yugoslavia. One of them was the BBC journalist John Schofield, who was fatally shot in August 1995, close to the Bosnia–Croatia border. 'John Schofield was killed, and that really changed the dial in terms of our whole industry, looking at safety in general – you know, physical safety,'[4] said Sarah Ward-Lilley MBE, a former managing editor of BBC News. 'His tragic death really kick-started the whole hostile environments training and then we had the Gulf Wars coming soon after that,' she added.

At around the same time, the first Hostile Environment and First Aid Training (HEFAT) courses were launched in the UK. By the end of the 1990s, courses were being offered to local journalists too, via the Rory Peck Trust, an

DOI: 10.4324/9781003344179-2

important advocate for the safety of freelance journalists, launched after the death in Moscow in 1993 of cameraman Rory Peck.

HEFAT courses were run mainly by former special forces soldiers and aimed to help journalists understand the risks they might face in hostile environments and how they might respond to those risks. However, the early courses paid little attention to mental health and trauma, as highlighted by Stuart Hughes, a BBC producer who has spent many years advocating for better awareness of mental health in the journalism industry, after his own experience of PTSD:

> At most, in those days, it was a short lecture at the very end, maybe half an hour, 40 minutes. And it was just after three or four days of all the other stuff. There was half an hour before we paid our hotel bar bills and went home, where they said, 'By the way, some people go to war zones and get fucked-up. Here's a video of a botfly being pulled out of someone's arm. Please pay your bills and go home.' That was the extent of it.[5]

By the turn of the millennium, the conversation was still dominated by Western newsrooms and focused on physical safety and war zones. Still, there was a small but passionate group advocating that newsrooms needed to consider more than just the physical impact on journalists of working in dangerous places. Two of those advocates were John Owen and Mark Brayne, who had helped deliver a HEFAT course in Kosovo for journalists in the 1990s. At the time, Owen was the Europe director of the Freedom Forum and a former head of news at CBC in Canada. He had spent time in hostile environments and seen for himself the impact of trauma on himself and colleagues. Brayne was the BBC World Service's European regional editor and was also training to be a psychotherapist, later setting up Dart Centre Europe. Both men recognised the need for the news industry to do more to combine conversations around physical and emotional safety.

In 2003, shortly after the US-led invasion of Iraq, the International News Safety Institute (INSI)[6] was founded, bringing together some of the world's leading newsrooms to prioritise the safety of journalists. INSI, along with the CPJ, is one of a handful of media safety and press freedom organisations to publish an annual record of journalists killed doing their work, underpinning the dark reality that, even with stringent safety protocols, journalism continues to be a dangerous job. In addition to those killed, there are countless others who are hurt and harassed, and whose lives and livelihoods are attacked.

If the importance of journalism safety has become more widely recognised, it is still not universal. It is largely the same countries who have topped the grim league table of those most dangerous for journalists over the last two decades. Syria, Iraq, Mexico, Afghanistan, Pakistan, the Philippines and Brazil are frequently among the deadliest.

Unfortunately, in many of these countries, the conversation around safety is limited; impunity is rife, with perpetrators often going unpunished. Frequently, the insecurity faced by journalists is compounded by the demands of those who run newsrooms, who pay little heed to the dangers they insist their colleagues face daily. Journalists often have limited job security and poor – or sometimes non-existent – salaries, no access to safety training or equipment and no choice but to do their work.

In 2012, the United Nations launched its action plan on the safety of journalists and the issue of impunity.[7] More than a decade on, and despite it being unlawful under international humanitarian law to target journalists, safety is still a preserve of the privileged in many parts of the world.

It is important to understand this context of physical safety, because it has become increasingly accepted that physical and psychological safety issues intersect, a thread that will run throughout this book. Where there is a lack of discussion about the former, there is almost certainly little consideration of the latter.

The first research was conducted into this area around the turn of the millennium, and while the subject matter of this research informed the discourse, so too did the status quo of newsrooms. Hence, when discussions began, they were predominantly focused on Western journalists who covered conflicts overseas.

This has changed over time, to incorporate conversations about other sources of trauma and stress for journalists, and the ways in which people might be impacted differently. Of course, conversations are still at varying stages around the world, shaped, advanced and stymied by cultural, local and newsroom-specific influences.

Some newsrooms have started to acknowledge the ways in which physical safety and mental health are interconnected, which is encouraging. In those that take physical safety seriously, with policies, training and equipment available to protect journalists, there is more likelihood that mental health will also be considered. Yet the two are rarely afforded the same resources or investment or reach the same level of conversation.

In most countries, there are taboos in society around mental health, which shape the awareness of and appetite to talk about it in newsrooms, but even in places where there is significant stigma, there are signs that things are shifting. Colleagues in Lebanon, Kenya, India, the Philippines, Sri Lanka and Mexico told me of conversations taking place in these countries, with many noting the Covid pandemic as having played a significant role in the growth of the topic.

Although there is often an appetite among journalists to talk about their mental health, the appetite may not be as strong on the part of management and news leaders. One of the most recurrent concerns I hear, no matter where journalists work, is that talking about their mental health will negatively impact their reputation or role. This is exacerbated for people who belong to communities traditionally marginalised in newsrooms. Writing during a time of economic uncertainty in many countries and newsrooms, I have seen how much this stigma tends to become more pronounced during times of financial insecurity.

Anthony Feinstein is a professor of psychiatry at the University of Toronto and a neuropsychiatrist. He is one of the world's leading experts on the impact of journalists' work on their mental health and has conducted studies globally for more than 20 years. He led the first research into the mental health of journalists, prompted by a referral to him of a female journalist, suffering a severe stress reaction after she returned to Canada from covering conflict and crises in East Africa.

> The question that troubled me was: she was very smart, so why had she not reached out for help when she realised that she was getting into difficulties? And she said to me, 'Well, you don't understand this profession. If I told my editors I was feeling this way, they would never send me out in the field again.' This was 1999. And I thought this was pretty punitive.[8]

He could find no research pertaining to the experiences of this journalist, although trauma literature existed in relation to other industries. Professor Feinstein's grant application to the Freedom Foundation, an organisation dedicated to free press and free speech, and whose European arm was directed by John Owen, led to it funding the first ever study of journalism, conflict and war. Owen recalled

> I had been very involved in the journalism safety movement, along with Chris Cramer of the BBC and others, and I'd helped get safety training courses going, underwriting them through the Rory Peck Trust, and put on local safety journalism training courses in Kosovo. And this seemed like a natural outgrowth of that. You know, you're dealing with preparing people the best you can to not make foolish 'courage' decisions, to make rational decisions, and reflexively know what to do. But we weren't really dealing with what Chris Cramer said was your 'head laundry' after you came back. That was his wonderful expression. You come back from an exhausting trip, and you take care of your laundry, and you try to get yourself back together, but you don't do much with your head.

Cramer would become a pioneer in the field of physical safety and one of the first news leaders to speak openly about his PTSD.[9]

The research, authored by Feinstein, John Owen and Nancy Blair, was published in 2002.[10] In their study of 140 war journalists, they found the lifetime prevalence of PTSD for the group – the proportion who at some time in their life would develop PTSD – was 28.6%: the percentage was similar for combat veterans. More than a fifth of these journalists had major depression and one in six were abusing substances. Alcohol consumption was significantly higher in these men and women than in the general population. This group had far greater psychiatric difficulties than journalists who did not cover war, and the rate of major depression was greater than that seen in the general population. However, the conflict reporters were not more likely to have received psychological help than their colleagues. 'These results [. . .] should alert news organizations that significant psychological distress may occur in many war journalists and often goes untreated,' the authors wrote.

A generation on, we know most journalists will never develop PTSD or major depression. However, they are more likely to do so than the general population because of the nature of their work. Still, research has also shown that journalists are resilient. Professor Feinstein reminds us that 'resilient doesn't mean immune': we need to ensure journalists have access to support systems and coping strategies.

The notion of resilience, and whose responsibility this is, will be considered in more detail in other chapters, which will also reflect on the warning issued by this early research, of 'significant psychological distress', and whether it has been sufficiently heeded.

Early on in his research, Professor Feinstein was invited by Tony Burman, then editor-in-chief of the Canadian public service broadcaster, to discuss his work at an annual gathering of foreign CBC correspondents in Ottawa. 'There were a couple of journalists sitting in the front row, and they basically started to heckle me while I was talking,' recalled Feinstein:

> [They said], 'This is psychobabble. This is nonsense. This is all mushy head psychiatrists, kind of manufacturing problems that aren't there.' I wish that meeting had been recorded, because they shamed an entire room into silence. I said, 'You let me finish my presentation – I'd be happy to answer questions.' They couldn't even contain themselves to let me finish. They were just kind of throwing comments at me.

Feinstein later received an apology, but he believes this episode, and the wider hostility he faced, was prompted by the discomfort many journalists felt about an issue so close to home.

It was becoming difficult to ignore the fact that journalists' work was having an impact upon them. At around the same time as this groundbreaking research, two experienced journalists were killed in Sierra Leone. The deaths in 2000 of Kurt Schork, a Reuters journalist, and the Associated Press's Miguel Gil profoundly affected attitudes towards safety, shattering the notion that journalists were somehow immune from injury. A year later, there was another watershed moment for many newsrooms: the attacks of September 11, 2001, in the United States.

In his book *Journalists Under Fire: The Psychological Hazards of Covering War*, Professor Feinstein wrote of the 'halcyon pre-September 11' days when the world seemed safe and less fraught',[11] later going on to research the effects this event had on journalists. He was not alone in noting this pivotal moment, particularly in US newsrooms. Bruce Shapiro is the executive director of the

Dart Center for Journalism and Trauma,[12] an organisation launched in 1999, initially to improve the ethical reporting of traumatic events and then to raise awareness of trauma experienced by journalists, including through a fellowship programme:

> First it [9/11] did unleash a generation of war that all news organisations needed to cover, but more particularly, people who had thought about mental health in journalism at all had thought about it as an issue facing war reporters. And instead, here you had a whole generation of local journalists in and around New York City, people who you would never have thought of as being profoundly trauma exposed, who were in the middle of it. On September 11, 2001, some of the first reporters to show up at the site were actually fashion reporters from all over the world. It was Fashion Week and they all rushed downtown with their notebooks. Newsrooms in New York, those that were downtown, were exiled. Every newsroom either lost people or lost family members of people.[13]

David Schlesinger was Reuters' Editor for the Americas at the time:

> It was incredibly stressful and hard and emotionally wrenching for the New York and Washington newsrooms. In particular, because these were their cities. They weren't just journalists on a foreign assignment. These were their cities that had been attacked, these were their neighbours, many of their contacts, in many cases, their friends who died, and the scars on the city lasted for months and months. And they had to continue to report everything, not just the aftermath of 9/11. They had to report the bond market, the stock market, the mayor's office, the dog show, whatever else. They had to report these things as if nothing had happened. And yet something had happened. And so, it was very clear that you couldn't put mental health somewhere to the side; it couldn't just be an adjunct of the human relations department, it couldn't just be something that the company paid lip service to. It had to be something that you tried very, very hard to deal with more effectively: an integral part of what you did as an editorial department.[14]

Schlesinger, who played an important role in launching Reuters' first psychological support programmes for journalists, began his career in 1987, and remembers the heavy-drinking and macho culture in his early days based in Hong Kong. Like many I interviewed for the book, his commitment to mental health came from personal exposure to traumatic experiences in his work.

In 1989, he was sent to report on the Tiananmen Square protests, which resulted in the Chinese government violently suppressing the country's student-led pro-democracy movement, and an unknown number of deaths, which some estimated to be in the thousands. Returning to Hong Kong from Beijing, the only support Schlesinger was shown by his editor was the offer of a few extra taxi rides on expenses.

> It was totally unacceptable to me, what happened to me and to my colleagues – and, believe me, I still have friends who also covered Tiananmen Square, who are affected to this day. So it was a very devastating, important event in so many people's lives, in so many journalists' lives, that was basically not dealt with. At such an early stage of my career, it was such a defining moment that I became personally very aware of the mental toll. I was aware that I personally, David Schlesinger, couldn't do it with cigarettes, drugs, alcohol – the way others might – that's just not my style. And I personally was so aware of how inadequate the advice to take a few taxi rides on expenses was.

Shortly after this, Schlesinger attained his first bureau chief role in Taiwan. There, in what he described as a 'smaller, much more family-type atmosphere', he processed his response to his experiences in China and Hong Kong, and started to consider how to support his colleagues. More than a decade on, and after 9/11, Schlesinger was Reuters' global managing editor and then editor-in-chief, and he was committed to ensuring the organisation really considered the impact of trauma on its workforce.

In the early part of the millennium, those working at Reuters were affected by the deaths of several of its journalists. During our interview, Schlesinger listed each of those colleagues, as well as their place and year of death. It is clear these experiences took their toll on him and fuelled his commitment to advance conversations around safety.

> There were so many deaths during the time that I was involved in senior editorial management and, of course, that's what first sparked my interest in journalists' safety. That's when I got involved in INSI, when I got involved in the CPJ. That's when I got involved in trying to lobby the Defence Department in the US. And so journalists' safety became a huge part of my life and what I did as an editor. But more than simply journalists' safety: it's one thing to try to keep people safe in the field. It's another thing to try to educate defence departments in the United States, or in Israel, about what a journalist does. But then you also had to deal with the effect of these deaths and the effect of these incidents and the effect of these wars on the whole newsroom.

Looking back at the early years of the 21st century, these people – Schlesinger, his Reuters colleague Stephen Jukes, who was then global head of news, and Professor Feinstein – were at the forefront of conversations about journalism safety and mental health. So too were John Owen, mentioned earlier, and

Mark Brayne, who spent the latter part of his BBC career on attachment with the corporation's High Risk Team at Television Centre:

> The leaders of that department were willing to hear me say that we needed to do something in advance of the Gulf War, because we were clearly going to war, and it was going to involve emotional stuff. With support, I did a bunch of small lunchtime seminars, not really knowing too much at the time myself about PTSD and trauma. I guess that for all my training in psychotherapy – where I was already an accredited practitioner – like so many of us at the time, I was learning about trauma as I went along.[15]

In November 2002, Brayne travelled to the annual conference of the International Society for Traumatic Stress Studies (ISTSS), attending a Dart Center retreat where he met many of the world's luminaries of trauma, including psychiatrist Bessel van der Kolk, and Jonathan Shay, the man responsible for coining the term 'moral injury'. Shay introduced Brayne to a team from the British Royal Marines that was working on trauma risk management, including Neil Greenberg, a specialist in this field and Cameron March:[16]

> Jonathan said to me, 'Mark, you're doing this BBC thing and emotional wellbeing – you need to talk to these guys.' So he introduced me to Neil Greenberg and Cameron March. I listened to them talking and I thought, wow, that would be just the programme for the BBC, because journalists, being the tough nuts that they are, just might take the Marines seriously.

Brayne's meeting with Shay, Greenberg and March led to the first formal trauma training at the BBC in early 2003. Since then, Professor Neil Greenberg, who is cited later, in Chapter 14, has become one of the world's leading experts on the organisational management of traumatic stress. Brayne's former colleague Bruce Shapiro, who still runs the US arm of the Dart Center for Journalism and Trauma, reflected on how the need to consider the mental health of journalists was prompted by a series of high-profile, difficult news events that happened in swift succession:

> Afghanistan, Iraq – you also had in 2005 Hurricane Katrina, you had the Boxing Day tsunami, other events around the world, which had a profound impact on all the journalists and newsrooms who covered them and at the same time, thanks to the work of some of our friends and colleagues, a language for talking about this in journalism was beginning to emerge.

His Dart Center colleague Professor Elana Newman agreed, noting that journalism was starting to become more open to first-person accounts, with several renowned journalists sharing their stories of PTSD. One of them was Chris Cramer, referenced earlier by John Owen. Cramer was a former BBC and CNN International executive, who was chair of INSI when I joined it in 2010.

He was passionate about journalism safety for very personal reasons, having developed PTSD after being held hostage in 1980, during a siege at the Iranian Embassy in London. Cramer was one of the most high-profile journalists to share their experiences, although in the early 2000s there were others, including Allan Little, Fergal Keane and Jeremy Bowen, all of them BBC correspondents.

The sharing of stories can help in tackling stigma and shame, normalising conversations and showing those who experience distress that they are not alone. It takes immense courage to speak about one's mental health. Those mentioned above – pioneers of these conversations – are notably all Western white men, many of them experienced in covering overseas conflict and war. They are confronting taboos that often prevent men from feeling able to speak about their mental health. However, it is worth noting that each of these individuals also reflect something of the white male status quo in newsrooms, which may afford them a degree of privilege and platform that others do not share.

Throughout this book, various journalists share their stories of how their work has impacted their mental health. Hopefully, these individuals, from different countries and different backgrounds, will help to normalise conversations for many other people.

The familiarity of the names of the journalists referred to above reinforces how the early conversations about the psychological toll of journalism were predominantly focused on foreign reporters working in conflicts. There had been little consideration given to how journalists living and working amid constant uncertainty and danger were faring. Subsequent to his initial research into journalists, Feinstein was approached by UNESCO. The United Nations agency was worried about the safety of journalists in Mexico, having long been one of the most dangerous places in the world for our profession. Feinstein travelled to Mexico on several occasions to speak with those who regularly faced the threat of death: 'It was the first research into local journalists, and it showed very clearly that if you wanted to silence a journalist, you silenced their families,' he explained. His findings showed that 25% of journalists had stopped working on a drug-related story because of threats to their relatives or themselves. Years on, threats against journalists' families and loved ones are one of the most insidious forms of attack, designed to instil fear in the journalist, and can take a significant emotional toll, as discussed in Chapter 9, which deals with online harassment.

Although conversations around mental health have become more commonplace, in Feinstein's view the stigma persists and can be even more entrenched in certain countries:

> You've got to step out of our world, the West, [and] when you go to other countries, there is no discussion of this [. . .] this is not even on

their radar screen. I think there's just not a culture of it. It's really informative to have a look at the World Health Organization map of mental health expenditure, see which countries are spending, how much of the healthcare budget goes towards mental health. You'll see countries, like Canada, which are at the top of the scale, that are still underspending relative to what the World Health Organization recommends. When you go into Africa, you have countries there that are spending less than 1% of the budget on mental health. So there isn't even a discussion; it's not a priority for them.

It's not a priority for them, because often the focus is on daily survival.

As a trauma and mental health consultant, Dr Khaled Nasser works with journalists predominantly in the Middle East and Africa who are frequently exposed to trauma and danger. He found they needed a different kind of support from that traditionally espoused by Western medicine:

With time, I changed the way I dealt with journalists. Because when you study how to do therapy, you're studying it from a Western perspective that focuses heavily on the individual, focuses on you taking care of yourself, disregarding the context around you, because there is this assumption [that] the context is really in order [stable].[17]

This is a perspective that we could do well to learn from in our approaches to safety around the world, a perspective that recognises how conversations concerning mental health benefit from a variety of starting points.

In the Philippines, one of the most dangerous countries in the world for journalists, many community newspapers don't pay their reporters. 'So, they definitely don't, and will not, provide for a mental health programme,'[18] said Weng Paraan, the former head of the National Union of Journalists of the Philippines (NUJP). 'And then there's the stigma, still, of being perceived as weak if you are being traumatised by an experience, so there are a lot of challenges. I think newsrooms still have to develop that programme, so they will be able to respond to their staff.'

The NUJP has led physical safety conversations to help support journalists at risk, which have blended into a consideration of psychological impact, as Paraan explained:

In the safety programme, which is done regularly by the NUJP, one major component of the module is recognising and dealing with trauma. Putting it there is very good because the statement that you're making is that physical security is important, but mental wellbeing is also important, and a press freedom issue, so they [come] together and should not be looked at separately.

One way Paraan has helped tackle the stigma was by identifying individuals to champion the issue, such as the executive director of the Philippine Press Institute:

> This is an organisation of publishers and editors in print, and because he organises a series of seminars for their member publications, when people hear about it, they ask how come they're not invited, and so on. It's a slow process. But I think a lot has changed from the time when we started talking about it in 2005.

Amantha Perera began his career in Sri Lanka and is now based in Melbourne as a PhD researcher, training journalists across the region as the project lead for Dart Centre Asia Pacific.

> I think the way the conversation has evolved is there is more space now to talk about trauma. But the conversation in Asia, in the part of the world that my work is centred on, is happening within the community. So now, it's easier for me to go and talk to colleagues like journalists, and those who do the reporting. For a long time, trauma remained a topic that was peripheral at best in the conversation: not any more. The difficulty, or the kind of resistance, is still there when you want to talk about the industry, meaning [from] those who either manage or own media [. . .] they don't want to acknowledge that it probably refers back to resources, that if you talk about this then you have to acknowledge that you do [need to] put resources in place to deal with this. And it also translates to diverting funds. So yes, we have progressed, but there is more work to be done.[19]

Colleagues in Africa, Asia, South America and the Middle East have said that societal stigma often prevented conversations about mental health from progressing. Some of their insights will be shared across this book.

Since his Mexico research, Professor Feinstein has studied the mental health of journalists in countries including Iran, Afghanistan and Kenya. By early 2023, his database included more than 1,100 frontline journalists who covered conflict, crises and civil unrest. Others have undertaken research too, some of which will be referenced throughout this book. However, Feinstein's work has been instrumental in shaping the mental health conversation. His findings helped move the focus from frontline foreign reporters to local journalists, and to user-generated content and moral injury, areas which will be detailed in subsequent chapters. As the research evolved, conversations did too. Where journalists started to speak about their experiences, there followed something of a cultural shift in newsrooms.

Much of this was driven by individuals like Schlesinger, motivated to prioritise the mental health of their colleagues, either because of these leaders' experiences or because their colleagues had died or been severely emotionally affected by their work. Schlesinger himself has noticed a real change during his career.

> When I started in '87, you couldn't admit that events had shaken you. You are a professional. You covered plane crashes and market crashes and deaths in the street – just the ordinary part of the day. So, this wasn't really done, to admit that it had shaken you personally. That would have shown too much personal involvement in the story, which of course was always the great taboo of journalism. But I think that at least has gone, and it's easier to have conversations with people. People are much more willing and much more ready to talk about how they were personally affected by the story, perhaps because journalism in general has moved off the purist objective stance into much more [of a] realisation that every story has something of the reporter in it to a greater or lesser degree.

Over the years, the conversation in newsrooms has also expanded beyond the impact on journalists of their work, to a broader recognition that work environments are capable of affecting people's mental health, as well as acknowledging that personal stressors can affect our ability to be well at work.

Kate Nowlan, a psychotherapist and former CEO of the CiC employee assistance programme, who began working with Reuters in 2006, discussed this shift:

> I think the conversation has changed in that there's much more openness to discussing the whole topic of mental health. One of the things that has really changed is that the global support programmes were initially designed for correspondents and photographers working in conflict zones and very much trauma focused. To begin with, they worked with the news organisation to provide Reuters journalists with a free 24/7 phone line accessible across the globe, in order that individuals (including stringers) could speak to an experienced professional clinician in their language with cultural understanding.
>
> Stress and resilience workshops were also delivered in bureaus to help prepare those working in hostile environments. In 2015, CiC helped Reuters launch a peer support programme, making it one of the first news organisations to do so. CiC worked closely with Reuters to select and train volunteers within the company to provide support to their peers. As we became more integrated into the organisation, people began to use the confidential service to talk about stress levels impacting their families, workload and burnout, and domestic issues, which weren't necessarily to do with being in a conflict zone.[20]

The past few years have brought a broadening of the conversation around mental health, and a generation on from the first research, there has also been a shift in perceptions and expectations, with many younger journalists showing far greater literacy around mental health than their older colleagues.

Mar Cabra, founder of The Self Investigation, expanded on this:

> Another variable that has been affecting or influencing is the generational change. I think that millennials and Gen Z, outside of journalism and in journalism, have been saying mental health and wellbeing are important aspects for me, and they need to be taken care of if you want to keep me, so that's part of how the conversation is changing with all these variables.[21]

This means the conversations need to adapt to that change. Dr Cait McMahon, the founding managing director of Dart Centre Asia Pacific, agreed:

> We're getting young people now coming into our programmes who are already far advanced in terms of understanding stress and trauma and self-care. So our conversation has to be far more advanced and more nuanced than it used to be when we did what I'd say was Trauma 101.[22]

As well as younger journalists and journalism students speaking more openly about issues such as trauma, depression and anxiety orders, there is a greater overall recognition that hostile environments are different for different people, situations can impact people in diverse ways, and that mental health isn't homogenous, just as people aren't. With seismic news events renewing the focus on systemic and societal inequity, particularly of a racial and gendered nature, it is clear conversations need to recognise that some people are more vulnerable and need to be better supported, in order that journalism can ensure it remains diverse and representative. 'There is far more awareness of trauma and other mental health issues tied up in your work,' said Shapiro. 'And there's a far higher expectation of a duty of care. So that's been a really dramatic change in the last couple of years.' He continued:

> There's also a dramatic change in newsrooms in the willingness of identity affinity groups in news to talk about their particular emotional burdens. Journalists of colour, in particular, have led the way in this, as have women in journalism. But it's more widespread, and that, too, is a really new conversation in which journalists have been willing to say, 'There are particular emotional burdens associated with who I am that come into my work.'

As the conversation expands, it becomes clear that a much more diverse, sensitive and nuanced approach is needed to mental health. Elsewhere in this book, there will be further consideration of how events of recent years have brought a renewed focus on the emotional toll borne by certain journalists, and why news organisations need to recognise these and develop flexible support systems to cater to different people's needs.

At the Dart Center for Journalism and Trauma, there is a growing demand for training that looks at all aspects of stress and trauma. 'We used to have to beg people to listen, when we started,'[23] said Elana Newman, Dart's research director, and a professor of psychology at the University of Tulsa. 'I used to have to explain to people why journalists were in the line of fire [. . .] and now it's no longer surprising to people.'

If conversations have evolved in the past 20 years, so have the stressors faced by journalists. At the same time, a language of mental health is available to journalists now – but these changes present their own challenges. 'I think that we're confusing two areas: one is the prevention of mental health disorders, two is promoting optimal functioning, and those two are getting merged,' said Professor Newman. 'So I think there's the wellness, which we need to be doing, and the mental health. And they seem to be being talked about in the same breath. And that worries me, because it's an oversimplification.'

Professor Feinstein welcomed this greater focus on mental health in journalism, but said work is still needed. 'I think education is absolutely pivotal. You have just got to educate journalists through sessions, education sessions, going back, reminding them about what's good emotional health, you know, what is PTSD, what is moral injury, what to look out for, what's healthy drinking, all those kinds of things.'

One way that news organisations and media support bodies can ensure they are responding in the best way possible to changing needs is through collaboration. 'We should be sharing best practice and coming together as often as we can to talk about some of the challenges and to help each other find solutions,'[24] said Joyce Adeluwoye-Adams MBE, Editor, Newsroom Diversity at Reuters, where mental health falls within her remit.

Using a model developed at INSI, where I convened news organisations to share good practice around physical safety, I launched a regular industry conversation in 2020. This enabled news leaders to collaborate and address issues related to mental health via confidential sessions in which they shared challenges and solutions, connecting with peers in ways that would help them support their colleagues and themselves.

At the same time, similar conversations in education are more commonplace, with some journalism and media courses now integrating mental health into curricula, as well as broader conversations between teaching institutions.

Sarah Ward-Lilley received her MBE – an order of the British Empire award – for her services to mental health in journalism. For decades, she supported colleagues at the BBC and beyond, observing significant changes across the industry. She noted that most reputable organisations recognise that their duty of care extends to mental health as well as physical safety and to provision of relevant resources.

> Some parts of the media industry don't appear to have moved very far; others have moved in leaps and bounds. It's just patchy, both

internationally and even within the UK, I think. My view on this veers between a feeling that we're on a good road somewhere to, oh my God, we've only just started.

She added that, by and large, there have been improvements: 'We've got resources for journalists going to hostile environments, which has definitely changed. And we've got the development of resources at the beginning of people's careers, which I think is a good move.' She welcomed more individuals sharing their stories, explaining that this increases the expectations placed on managers in terms of their responsibilities to people's emotional welfare.

The past few years have seen a welcome rise in cross-industry approaches, and a recognition that when it comes to safety and mental health, this is a space where collaboration is more favourable than competition. Despite this, Ward-Lilley noted:

> It is still a very competitive industry. There's still a lot of focus on foreign correspondents and war reporting, where a lot of the awards are still focused. [And while there is also] much more focus on good interviews, scoops, exclusive coverage and specialism [. . .] there's still a slight tendency towards the 'bang-bang' and stuff like that. So, [there's] a sense that in order to get noticed, get famous, progress in your career, you may need to put yourself in harm's way, and that sense of, 'If I admit I'm having an issue with the story, I won't get deployed on a good story, whether it's a war zone or any other difficult story.' I think there's still a sense of feeling that will be career limiting.

A generation after conversations began, we return to the issue of stigma – a regular refrain in this book. Globally, it prevents journalists from feeling safe in speaking about their experiences; it is an obstacle that stops them doing their best work, as well as a barrier to journalism's ability to thrive.

Notes

1. Author interview with Professor Anthony Feinstein, July 2022
2. Our History – Committee to Protect Journalists. Available at: https://cpj.org/about/history/
3. Balkan Insight (2018) 'Last despatches: remembering the journalists killed in the Balkan Wars'. Available at: https://balkaninsight.com/2018/12/12/last-despatches-remembering
4. Author interview with Sarah Ward-Lilley MBE, September 2022
5. Author interview with Stuart Hughes, September 2022
6. https://newssafety.org/
7. UNESCO. UN Plan of Action on the Safety of Journalists and the Issue of Impunity. Available at: https://www.unesco.org/en/safety-journalists/un-plan-action
8. Author interview with Professor Anthony Feinstein, July 2022
9. Sadly, Chris Cramer passed away in 2021
10. Anthony Feinstein, John Owen and Nancy Blair (2002) 'A hazardous profession: war, journalists, and psychopathology', American Journal of Psychiatry 159(9): 1570–5. Available at: https://pubmed.ncbi.nlm.nih.gov/12202279/

11 Feinstein, *Journalists Under Fire* (The Johns Hopkins University Press, 2003, 2006)
12 https://dartcenter.org
13 Author interview with Bruce Shapiro, August 2022
14 Author interview with David Schlesinger, February 2023
15 Author interview with Mark Brayne, August 2023
16 Major Cameron March served with the Royal Marines and helped devise the Trauma Risk Management (TRiM) peer support system in the British Armed Forced in the 1990s
17 Author interview with Dr Khaled Nasser, October 2022
18 Author interview with Weng Paraan, February 2023
19 Author interview with Amantha Perera, November 2022
20 Author interview with Kate Nowlan, January 2023
21 Author interview with Mar Cabra, February 2023
22 Author interview with Dr Cait McMahon, August 2022
23 Author Interview with Professor Elana Newman, August 2022
24 Author interview with Joyce Adeluwoye-Adams, MBE, January 2023

Reference list

Balkan Insight (Balkan Investigative Reporting Network) (2018) 'Last despatches: remembering the journalists killed in the Balkan Wars'. Available at: https://balkaninsight.com/2018/12/12/last-despatches-remembering-the-journalists-killed-in-the-balkan-wars-12-11-2018

Feinstein, A. (2006) *Journalists Under Fire* (Johns Hopkins University Press, Baltimore MD)

Feinstein, A., Owen, J. & Blair, N. (2002) 'A hazardous profession: war, journalists, and psychopathology', *American Journal of Psychiatry*, 159(9): 1570–5. Available at: https://pubmed.ncbi.nlm.nih.gov/12202279/

UNESCO. UN Plan of Action on the Safety of Journalists and the Issue of Impunity. Available at: https://www.unesco.org/en/safety-journalists/un-plan-action

3 Averting a mental health crisis
A clarion call for change

Around the world, many of our colleagues have to work within a news environment that leaves them feeling hung out or wrung out. The global pandemic has left a legacy of exhaustion and burnout, and our coping mechanisms continue to be compromised by the cumulative stressors placed upon us as individuals, and upon our industry. According to Professor Anthony Feinstein:

> The pandemic has been huge. But the pandemic is running like a thread against the background of the collapse of Afghanistan, war in Ukraine, mass shootings in the United States, George Floyd, racial protests, Black Lives Matter, climate change. There's so much that journalists have been hammered with and they're having to do their job in the midst of a pandemic.[1]

In competition against other content creators for legitimacy, journalists are no longer regarded as the privileged Fourth Estate. They are coming under increasing assault in person and online, yet at the same time resources are ever more stretched and the potential for breaking news seemingly endless, as highlighted by Phil Chetwynd, Global News Director of Agence France-Presse (AFP):

> What people haven't understood is that in a real-time, social media-driven world, there is no limit to the amount of work you can do, because things don't shut at a certain time. So the whole process of trying to control the quantity of work people do, and their levels of interaction, became really challenging. I think that has certainly contributed a lot to mental health pressure, and also to people who were already in trouble. The context was certainly there before the pandemic, and then when you get this exceptional event, which – as has been widely said – opened up a lot of questions for a lot of people about what they're doing, where they are, what's happening, plus all the anxiety, [. . .] it did bring this whole issue to the fore.[2]

DOI: 10.4324/9781003344179-3

Over the past few years, several high-profile journalists have stepped down from their positions, citing the impact their work was having on their mental health. Stacy-Marie Ishmael resigned as executive director of *The Texas Tribune* in March 2021. Writing on Twitter[3] about her decision, she described spending 'the last year operating at a relentless and breakneck pace to ensure that our journalism could rise to the demands of the moment. It did. We did,' Ishmael went on. 'And in the process, I *totally* burned out.' Later that year, Jaden Edison wrote a piece for Poynter.org, headlined, 'Why Stacy-Marie Ishmael doesn't see leaving a job as failure'.[4] The article's subheading speaks volumes about the state of our industry: 'Working through one crisis after another presents questions about sustainability, not just burnout.'

Edison explained how Ishmael, a Black woman from Trinidad, was not party to the same privileges afforded to those who see themselves more frequently represented in management roles in journalism. 'People like Ishmael don't get days off,' he wrote. 'The expectations from self, audiences, colleagues and superiors are high. The empathy is low. They're always in situations of performance. They aren't provided the same room for error as white people in their shoes.'

Ishmael became exhausted by the professional pressures of managing through the pandemic, while worrying about being separated from loved ones overseas. According to Edison, 'There were a lot of workdays Ishmael finished with nothing left in the tank. She would lie down on the floor to recover from hundreds of microdecisions.' Ishmael later took on a new role. However, her experience may resonate with other journalists who have left their jobs, taken time off or turned to freelance work.

In September 2022, Ed Yong, science writer for *The Atlantic*, who covered the Covid crisis, wrote a Twitter thread, which began:

> Some personal news: I'm taking a 6-month sabbatical, starting now. These past 3 years have been the most professionally meaningful of my life, but they've also deeply broken me. The pandemic isn't over, but after a long time spent staring into the sun, I need to blink.[5]

He continued, 'Persistence matters, but it has limits, and I've long since reached mine.' Persistence does matter. Sadly, I know too many colleagues who have little left to give in an industry that makes them feel undervalued, and in a society where journalism's reputation has diminished.

The psychological burden is often significantly greater for non-white journalists, women, and those from the LGBTQI+ community, as well as others who are historically under-represented in newsrooms, leadership and news content. These individuals often come from communities who face social inequity and who regularly experience attacks against their identity. This burden may translate to them experiencing poor mental health and leaving their jobs, unable to continue in an environment where they feel unsupported by news leaders to do their jobs to the best of their ability. Losing such people threatens the diversity of our newsrooms and news content. It risks deepening the disconnect felt by under-represented audiences and entrenching the sense that journalism is run for and by an elite minority.

While Yong and Ishmael made the difficult decision to step away, albeit temporarily, others remain in their jobs, stuck for various reasons: struggling to practise journalism to the best of their abilities and feeling uninspired, unmotivated, unsupported, undervalued and under threat. This cannot be good for productivity. If news organisations cannot retain talented, diverse journalists, because they do not offer them the support they need to experience good mental health, these institutions are unlikely to be the kind of places that can help individuals reach their potential. Without pipelines in place to develop the careers of diverse people, newsrooms are incurring costs in terms of resources and reputation. They are also likely to find it more difficult to recruit journalists who do not see themselves represented.

From the conversations I have had with colleagues, I sense many of them see their news organisation as two different companies: the one perceived by the outside world, reflected in editorial guidelines or principles, which espouse accountability, accuracy, inclusivity and humanity; and the one reflected in the ways in which the company cares for its journalists – or fails to care, ultimately overlooking these same values.

This has led to many journalists feeling overwhelmed and disenfranchised, as if the environment in which they work is at odds with the mission-driven reasons they became journalists. Tanmoy Goswami, founder of Sanity, an independent, reader-funded mental health storytelling platform, has seen this:

> There was this moral wounding that was happening, I think, where a lot of journalists felt that [in terms of] the values that they stood for, their employers weren't necessarily walking the talk [sic]. And they could not live with that sort of duplicity and hypocrisy. A lot of people would come to me and say, 'You know what, this is not why I wanted to be a journalist.'

Goswami's concerns remind me of my own work around moral injury, expanded upon later in Chapter 8, as well as conversations I've had since the start of the Covid pandemic, with colleagues who express a similar sense that their mission and beliefs are no longer aligned with those who manage their newsrooms.

Many of those I interviewed cited that a lack of education and resources for young journalists can negatively impact their mental health in later years. Journalists are starting out with limited understanding of what their jobs might entail and the impact that their work might have on them. Goswami explained: 'One of the big cognitive dissonances I see is that people join this industry expecting something very different. And I think that becomes too much of a disconnect for young people; they get disillusioned very rapidly.'[6]

Today's generation of young journalists, though, may vote with their feet. 'You've got journalists leaving the profession because it's just too stressful,'[7] said Dean Yates, an Australian journalist and workplace mental health trainer. 'I think the younger crowd are realising this and deciding: "I'm getting out of this profession, I'm going to go and do something that's less stressful."'

For many younger journalists, mental health is not an afterthought but as critical as physical health. 'I think younger people are a lot more aware of the importance of their mental health than my generation was, and they're just not going to put up with this shit,' Yates said. 'And I think that's going to drive away really good journalists from the profession. I think it also reduces the quality of journalism. No one can do their best work when they're not in a good state of mind.'

Journalists are the industry's most precious resource, but this seems to have been overlooked often in the endless rush for content. Expected to do more with less, with limited breaks, after immense stress in their professional and personal lives, many of them are frayed. And if we are frayed, we cannot do our jobs well. If we cannot do our jobs well, we cannot connect with our audiences. They lose faith in us. It becomes a vicious cycle. Even when managers see this, they are often unable to apply the brakes, or to take action to radically overhaul the ways of working of those they manage.

We need to make mental health part of our regular conversations and integrate support and resources into the workplace as we would any other programmes and policies meant to improve our journalism. Doing this proactively will prevent the costs of inaction – of illness, presenteeism, employee turnover – from spiralling. Of course, it is hard to argue for investment when budgets are tight, and when jobs are so insecure.

At the time of writing this chapter, in early 2023, Buzzfeed had recently closed its news division, gal-dem ceased publication after eight years, and Vice Media filed for bankruptcy in the United States. Digital and non-legacy outfits weren't the only ones to suffer, with job cuts at NewsCorp, NPR and Reach to name a few more, and 3,340 jobs[8] cut, or announced to be cut, at Press Gazette in the first quarter of the year in the UK, US and Canada.

Financial insecurity has hit many countries, with a cost-of-living crisis not only impacting personal budgets but also exacerbating the stigma around mental health: it is hard for people to speak openly when they are worried about losing their jobs. In an industry that is notoriously low paying, it is unsurprising that journalists' mental health is under greater pressure against the backdrop of this economic uncertainty.

Current pressures in the industry are intense, and something will inevitably give: at the moment, it is likely to be the mental health of our journalists. The argument in favour of breaking news cannot stand if the cost of that is the breaking of journalists. In fact, it is not a contradiction to say that the economics of the industry requires investment in mental health conversations, as argued by Professor Feinstein: 'I think management now realises that it's in their best interests to have people who are psychologically healthy and well, because it's good for your organisation to be employing people who are not overwhelmed, or going off sick the whole time.' He added, 'There's obviously a level of this whereby it is good for business to keep people well, otherwise companies will be haemorrhaging money.'

Spending on mental health saves money. It also saves time in the long run. It's good for people and it's good for business. Professor Elana Newman, research director at the Dart Center for Journalism and Trauma, agreed:

> There's a great expense when people leave, when there's absenteeism, when there isn't good quality of work. We don't have a lot of data to support this at this point, but I do think that [if] people will stay in the profession longer, will make better news choices, health care costs will go down. Again, that may not be pertinent in every country, but all those things are really important. And people will tell better stories.[9]

While not specific to journalism, the professional services company Deloitte produced a report[10] in April 2022, showing that for every £1 invested in staff wellbeing, UK companies saw a return on investment of £5.30. The same research noted the cost of poor mental health to UK employers had climbed to £56 billion in 2020–21 compared with £45 billion in 2019, prior to the pandemic.

In some countries, however, any discussion around wellbeing is a privilege. Kiran Nazish is the founder of the Coalition For Women In Journalism, an organisation that supports groups around the world, many of which exist outside mainstream conversations, without access to support, and unaware of available mental health resources. She pointed to the huge discrepancy between those who are talking about mental health and those who aren't:

> I would say the majority of those journalists, like 60 to 70%, would be local journalists working in cities, smaller cities that don't have access to some of the most critical resources available to the mainstream. Meanwhile, these smaller groups maintain their own cultures, and they develop intricate methods to deal with their own problems. Often, mental health is not seen as one of the problems. They're in small Spanish bubbles, or Arabic bubbles, in their own bubbles, trying to solve their problems or figure things out their own way. And there's a huge mental health crisis in that area, [yet] they don't talk about this at all.[11]

It does not cost much to thank someone for their work or acknowledge the toll a story may take or may have taken. It does not cost much for a manager to show empathy. News leaders should recognise that by supporting the mental health of their staff, they will create cultures where people feel more motivated. It's not just in the best economic interest of our industry to do so, but also in the best interests of journalism.

Of course, it does cost money to develop mental health policies and resources, to build peer networks, give people time off work, or enable them to cover different stories after challenging ones. It costs money to maintain an employee assistance programme, or a newsroom focal point for wellbeing, but these are all areas of good practice that will improve the mental health of our people and profession. It is a balancing act. It requires commitment and a substantial degree of strategic thinking, whereby managers step away from the fray and consider the bigger picture, to try to understand how we might move from 'churnalism' to something more sustainable.

The nature of news means this is not easy; arguments for investment need to be accompanied by a reality check.

One of the pressures facing journalists is the public nature of their work itself. Phil Chetwynd has noted how journalists 'are increasingly overwhelmed by the real-time, intense nature of the job, often exacerbated by criticism and commentary on social media,' adding:

> A lot of people find that very hard; you're in a difficult environment, where [the public] don't have great opinions of journalists and let them know that. That is challenging, because you can't instantly change what people think of journalists, you can't instantly stop the abuse coming from outside, you can't instantly change the way people work. And something I've always linked to that is the economics of the industry. It's an industry where, however much we try, we're always scrambling for resources, aren't we? We're always struggling to keep up, and we know that even if we put significantly more resources in, we'll still be in the same position, in a way. [Over] the last ten to 15 years, everybody has been under that much more pressure.[12]

Chetwynd explained that a lot of time has been spent at AFP trying to figure out how to lessen some of the pressures on journalists by streamlining processes for news-gathering:

> There has got to be a more efficient way to enable us to follow the news and break the news and rumours [. . .]. There's got to be a more institutional and clever way to do that which will allow us to tell our staff to do it less, because at the end of the day you have so many hundred journalists all spinning in circles. You see this all the time, people thinking I can't do this, or I can't do that, because something [bad] might happen, so we are trying to plunge more deeply into that. Are there better processes we can have? Can we centralise certain tasks? And then we could actually say to people, 'Stop now, you don't have to.'
>
> For example, off the top of my head: in the Middle East, could we create one unit somewhere that after 7/8 pm will be monitoring breaking news in every single Arab market? So, the bureau in Tunis or Dubai can just say to its journalists, 'Turn off, because there's a unit somewhere following everything; if there's something important, I'll give you a call.'

At AFP, another important area is bolstering management training alongside more frequent proactive use of personal coaches for first-time managers, rather than after people have already begun to struggle. As Chetwynd stated, 'I see so much going on, people being overwhelmed all the time. Somebody steps up for the first time and takes responsibility and then is plunged into, "God, it's limitless and it's all on my shoulders and what if, what if, what if."'

This management issue is explored further in Chapter 13, but leaders play a significant role in the mental health equation and, where they show empathy to themselves and others, there is a greater likelihood others will follow. As an industry, we are used to running from story to story, crisis to crisis. We are less adept at harnessing institutional learning and planning, at adopting lessons from what went well and what did not. We thrive on spontaneity. It is the very nature of news.

Therefore, it requires a significant reset to acknowledge that the pandemic took away a lot of our ability to be spontaneous, meaning we now need to be more intentional. We have the opportunity to realise that rather than slipping back into old ways of working we can adapt to the positive aspects of change and adopt practices that make it easier for us and our mental health. Both journalists and organisations need to learn to determine what we really *need* to do, and what we can let go. As individuals, we must be more systematic, more conscious of what we commit to, less afraid to say no, and be better at creating and sustaining boundaries. Self-care is not a selfish thing.

On the other hand, we may no longer have valuable pre-pandemic 'water cooler' moments. I worry when colleagues have no breaks in their schedules, bouncing from one virtual meeting to another. If one overruns, they spend the rest of the day playing catch-up because their schedules are filled back-to-back. It is as though the lack of physical interaction has forced us to stuff every possible space in our virtual calendars, affording us no time to reflect, and little opportunity to action everything we have agreed to do or that has been delegated in those meetings, many of which may well be unnecessary.

Pre-pandemic, when more of us worked in physical offices, commuting gave us time between our work and home lives. We moved between offices, a natural break between meetings. Hence we need to build intentional spaces, breaks and bridges into our calendars, as well as time to reflect and time for action. It is difficult when others have access to our agendas, but it is necessary. Part of this is putting in place processes that help us establish boundaries, so we are more conscious about how we connect. A way of doing this is to use some of the tools that emerged during the pandemic. Some of these are identified elsewhere in this book, while Chetwynd pointed to the use of conference tools in helping 'humanise management', noting that AFP has used the same tools for training:

> Our vision previously, in terms of training, was always very much about, 'Oh, you know, we'll have to do a seminar somewhere and get people

together and it'll be a two-day thing.' It was all very heavy and very complicated. But we're understanding now that there's so much you can do, small and big stuff, around mental health projects that work through video conferencing and so on. It's not a sort of light bulb moment; we had these tools before, but we just didn't use them in that way.

These platforms might have downsides, but used intentionally, they offer opportunities to be more flexible, inclusive and accommodating, to create more open cultures and to better support journalists' mental health. However, this needs to be combined with some of the benefits of the in-person connection, to regain a sense of community that was lost during the pandemic, and which was so valuable for our mental health. In this way, perhaps we can find the best of both worlds. Professor Elana Newman described it in this way:

> What we've lost, particularly post-Covid, and with everybody telecommuting, is community. It's not in the newsroom any more. It's all virtual. And we've lost social support, which is a real problem, because we know that being part of a group and remembering your mission keeps you strong. Now, there aren't that many newsrooms where there's truly a newsroom and a community you [are part of] every day. I think we need to combine some of the flexibility of virtual working with some in-person connection, or you need to figure out how to create a community online, reminding people of their purpose, reminding people of the good work they do often. That's all that needs to be done – and not bullshit, like, 'Yeah, you did a good job', but, 'Hey, you did a great job!' – really reinforcing the importance of what people do and their value.[13]

This brings us back to the fact that journalists are human beings, not cogs in a machine. Anna Blundy, psychotherapist, and founder of The Mind Field, expressed concern about today's generation of journalists, believing many to be frightened, isolated and insecure. She grew up 'surrounded by crazed drunk journalists war correspondents'[14] until her journalist father David Blundy was shot dead in El Salvador when she was 19:

> Everyone I speak to who comes in as a patient is always in a terrible panic about their job, even when they have a great job. Because they're not getting on with their foreign editor, or whatever it is, and they're under so much pressure. I think it's actually harder. And I've now decided that I think they're more ill than the mad old drunks of my father's generation.

Blundy said she believed today's journalists work harder with fewer resources than their predecessors, and with less of the social support that was boosted by evenings spent drinking in the bar:

I think now it's much more corporate. So they probably feel technically cared for. I'm sure they have better health insurance and better medivac organisation and stuff like that. However, I think the loneliness is worse because you're being sort of processed by a big organisation, rather than loved, very genuinely loved.

This is a damning indictment of our industry. As mentioned earlier in this chapter, the stresses exacerbated by Covid have led journalists to leave their jobs in unhealthy newsrooms. Some have moved into freelance work. But the risk here is that the exposure to isolation and insecurity felt by those working for news organisations and highlighted by Blundy is even more intense for freelance journalists. Many are dealing with the accumulation of years of stressors and exposure to trauma, compounded by financial pressures and isolation, amid demands to do more with less. They often lack institutional and financial resources to access mental health support. Noting this, organisations like the ACOS Alliance,[15] an industry coalition focused on developing standards to better protect freelancers, and the Rory Peck Trust,[16] a charity that supports freelancers and their families, have led a concerted effort to ensure news organisations understand their duty of care to their freelance colleagues, with the Trust launching a fund through which freelancers can access a series of free therapy sessions.

There are those who are starting to take seriously the issue of mental health, who make the connection between the wellbeing of journalists and the wellbeing of journalism. But there are others who still don't. So, what will it take to put news leaders' feet to the fire, and make them see mental health as a priority? This chapter has referenced the moral and financial duty of care news organisations have towards their workers. However, this may not be motivation enough. It may be that journalism organisations are forced into action, rather than voluntarily opting to support their journalists because it is the right thing to do.

David Walmsley, Editor in Chief of the *Globe and Mail* newspaper in Canada, pointed out the external drivers that may begin to influence this sector:

The industry has done a better job in terms of physical training. People are sent off on security courses when they are going to conflict or the hot zones. And that's often because the insurance companies have demanded that. So, did newsrooms honestly get to that point [by themselves]? Or did insurance force it? Almost invariably, because insurance, at the end of the day, is like a bureaucracy, it will expand into mental wellbeing as well.[17]

In 2019, *The Age* newspaper in Australia was found legally responsible for the PTSD of one of its former journalists because it had failed to provide a safe workplace. The paper was ordered to pay $180,000 in damages, marking the first time a news organisation had been successfully sued. An earlier case against it by another journalist was rejected, and there have been other cases of journalists suing their news organisations, some of which settled outside of court. But this global first could have implications, forcing news organisations to consider the measures they need to take to protect the mental health and wellbeing of their journalists.

Yet it's arguable that it is in the legal departments that the biggest obstacles to advances in mental health provision in newsrooms lie. There seems to be a tendency to keep quiet, not to speak certain words, as though there's a fear that articulating anything to do with mental health could lead to a potential breach of duty of care. I know I am not the only person who feels saddened and frustrated by this, or who also believes that there are far fewer journalists who want to seek compensation than those who want compassion.

Dean Yates expanded on this: 'If anything's going to change in Australia, it's going to be the threat of legal action. It's not going to be because media organisations think it's the right thing to do. It's because there is finally a law that will compel them to actually make the changes.'[18]

With increasing discussion about the law, and the duty of care of employers, the more we learn about trauma, the more related injury is recognised as a foreseeable harm, according to Dave Seglins, the wellbeing champion for CBC in Canada. In his view, companies risk heading for trouble, if they:

> keep having reporters covering big trauma events without building in safeguards, without having training, without having downtime, without having proper debriefing, without making sure that [their] people are trained to know what the hell they're doing. We have the one case in Australia, where *The Age* newspaper was found negligent – I think that the law and compliance will drive some of this. But right now, there's inertia. [We need] to begin pushing to news organisations to say, 'Hey, what is your duty of care to your people?'[19]

Surely, after everything our industry has been through in recent years, we have sufficient tools at our disposal to recognise the ongoing crisis that threatens to injure our journalists and journalism. Ensuring we prioritise the mental health of our people is not only important from a financial and legal perspective, and for our profession's longevity and links to our audiences: it is also the right thing to do. Walmsley puts it like this: 'I think it would be much better if the industry got there first, rather than being forced into training for insurance reasons. I think that one of the things the editors-in-chief for news organisations have to do is set the tone.'

They need to show they are human and recognise that those around them are too.

Notes

1 Author interview with Professor Anthony Feinstein, July 2022
2 Author interview with Phil Chetwynd, March 2023

3 Stacy-Marie Ishmael's tweet has since been deleted, but various articles reference her decision, including the Poynter piece below
4 Jaden Edison (2021) 'Why Stacy-Marie Ishmael doesn't see leaving a job as a failure', Poynter, 5 August. Available at: https://www.poynter.org/business-work/2021/stacy-marie-ishmael-quit-every-job-shes-ever-had-including-at-the-texas-tribune-heres-why
5 @edyong209
6 Author interview with Tanmoy Goswami, August 2022
7 Author interview with Dean Yates, September 2022
8 Bron Maher (2023) 'UK and North American news media have cut 3,300+ jobs so far in 2023', Press Gazette, 13 April. Available at: https://pressgazette.co.uk/media_business/news-media-job-cuts-first-quarter-2023
9 Author interview with Professor Elana Newman, August 2022
10 Deloitte (2022) 'Mental health and employers: the case for investment – pandemic and beyond'. Available at: https://www2.deloitte.com/uk/en/pages/consulting/articles/mental-health-and-employers-the-case-for-investment.html
11 Author interview with Kiran Nazish, July 2022
12 Chetwynd, 2023
13 Author interview with Professor Elana Newman, June 2023
14 Author interview with Anna Blundy, July 2022
15 https://www.acosalliance.org/
16 https://rorypecktrust.org/
17 Author interview with David Walmsley, February 2023
18 Author interview with Dean Yates, September 2022
19 Author interview with Dave Seglins, January 2023

Reference list

Deloitte (2022) Mental health and employers: the case for investment – pandemic and beyond'. Available at: https://www2.deloitte.com/uk/en/pages/consulting/articles/mental-health-and-employers-the-case-for-investment.html

Edison, J. (2021) 'Why Stacy-Marie Ishmael doesn't see leaving a job as a failure' – Poynter, 5 August. Available at: https://www.poynter.org/business-work/2021/stacy-marie-ishmael-quit-every-job-shes-ever-had-including-at-the-texas-tribune-heres-why

Maher, B. (2023) 'UK and North American news media have cut 3,300+ jobs so far in 2023', 13 April. Available at: https://pressgazette.co.uk/media_business/news-media-job-cuts-first-quarter-2023

Their story – Santiago Lyon[20]

I spent ten years covering war and conflict around the world between 1989 and 1999. I think I covered eight full-on conflicts, and a whole host of other disasters, earthquakes, famines, all sorts of traumatic stuff during that period.

And fairly early on, I realised those experiences were having an adverse effect on my mental health. And my response was really just to push through and carry on.

I was taken prisoner by Saddam Hussein's army at the end of the first Gulf War and held for a week near Basra with a large group of journalists. And then in 1995 I was wounded in the leg by mortar fire in Sarajevo, continued to operate in the city and was ultimately evacuated by land to Croatia and onwards.

I think I was formally diagnosed with PTSD as early as 1992, following a particularly harrowing trip to Sarajevo, where a colleague, who was part of our small group of journalists, was killed, and another was severely wounded. And I came out of that, you know, not feeling great, obviously, and went to see a psychiatrist in London by the name of Martin Deahl. And he took a look at me and came to the conclusion that I was suffering from PTSD.

I didn't really do anything about it, I just sort of carried on. And then as the years went on, it was just one dramatic or frightening experience after another. And I came to the conclusion that if I were to carry on doing that line of work, that I was really facing two options: one, insanity, and the other, death. I've kind of lost count at this point – but at that time, I think I had lost 12 friends to violent death, some closer friends than others, and some very close friends. So, I was well aware, obviously, of that sort of outcome. And my mental health was not good. I would come back from assignments, and I would self-medicate, and be antisocial and have all the classic symptoms.

So, in 1999, after ten years of doing that [work], I just stopped cold turkey, which I thought was the easiest part of it. What I didn't really fully understand was that my identity had been become so wrapped up in photographing violent things around the world. That I was doing very successfully. I was winning multiple prizes. I was at the top of my game.

I was working for the AP [Associated Press] for most of that time. And I was part of a group of sort of 'go to' people for the AP. There were maybe half a dozen of us, or so, who would consistently volunteer for those kinds of assignments.

And those two years following my decision to stop doing that were probably the most difficult years of my life because I had a profound identity crisis. And I was trying to figure out what to do with myself and it was just pretty miserable. And then my first child was born and shortly after that, I was able to take a year off and do a Nieman fellowship at Harvard, which was great in terms of allowing me to refocus.

I also took advantage of that time to see Bessel van der Kolk [American psychiatrist, specialising in post-traumatic stress], in a professional capacity and was his patient for six months or so and took care of a lot of the mental laundry, or at least the most disturbing aspects of it.

And then the AP asked me to become their director of photography, overseeing the global photo staff. I think we had – between staff and regular freelancers – something like 1,000 photographers out in the field. So, one of the first things that I did there was, having received a sort of unsatisfactory response from the AP when I was in need, I made it my business to try and set up some mechanisms to help with the mental health of the people who I was now responsible for sending into harm's way.

And so, through Anthony Feinstein (I had participated in his 1999 survey) and Jack Saul, a psychologist here in New York, we set up a sort of informal network around the world, for AP journalists who were having difficulty processing their experiences, trying to come up with resources locally for people to be able to talk to people in their own native tongues and in their own geographies. And that was pretty useful for a lot of people. Although as an employer, of course, it's a fine line: you want to look after the wellbeing of your employees, and at the same time recognise that medical information is confidential. And mental health information is particularly sensitive, because of all the stigma associated with it and people's reluctance to admit that they have a problem and fear that if they do admit that they need some time to process their experiences that they'll somehow be seen as damaged goods and not be sent out into the field again, and all of those kinds of things.

So, I think we did what we could, we certainly improved on the situation that the AP had prior to that, which was with an employee assistance programme, working with an agency that was probably well suited to deal with substance abuse, people going through divorces or bereavement, or the typical kinds of things that you see in the corporate environment, but were in no way qualified to deal with trauma.

And so, once we determined that, that allowed us to set up this sort of alternative network. So, my interest in the topic runs deep from my own experiences in the field, and then subsequently, my experiences as a newsroom leader, trying to look out for the wellbeing of the people who are working for me.

Note

20 From author interview with Santiago Lyon, April 2023

4 Culture, coping and conditioning

> So, for the longest time, and still, I suppose to some degree, journalism has been a very male-dominated profession. And as a result, at least historically, there was a tendency for people to solve their problems at the bar – self-medication, alcohol, other drugs – in that sort of silly, macho way that a lot of men unfortunately have [for] dealing with problems. And as a result, mental health issues were seen as a sign of weakness, and the newsroom culture didn't do anything to change that. It was fine, even though it clearly wasn't.[1]
>
> —Santiago Lyon

Santiago's story was shared in the previous section, and his quote above shows how our industry conditioned many journalists to engage in a form of unhealthy coping, with admissions of vulnerability rarely encouraged.

Many news organisations have been led by journalists who cut their teeth on stories that impacted them. Lacking support for their own mental health and training in how to manage colleagues, they were often silenced by stigma and unable to process the cumulative traumas and stresses to which their journalism exposed them. Unable to have an open discussion about the potential toll of regularly covering traumatic stories often translated into a reliance on alcohol, increased risk-taking, anger, bullying or other maladaptive behaviours. And when these journalists became leaders, they carried these habits with them, perpetuating a toxic cycle in newsrooms. They may have not consciously realised the extent to which they were damaged, disassociated or potentially abusing their positions of power, nor that they were conditioned by stigma and shame.

Journalist Tanmoy Goswami, founder of the storytelling platform Sanity, said:

> I think one of the biggest challenges is the fact that most leadership roles in large media organisations are held by people of a certain vintage, who, purely because of the environment in which they grew up, have absolutely no access to the mental health conversation – like they are schooled in a style of leadership in journalism that is not even 'tough

DOI: 10.4324/9781003344179-4

love': just very mean, sometimes. I think the sort of battle-hardened, macho aura that newsroom leaders have cultivated over decades is still very much there. There must be exceptions, but by and large, leadership folks believe in this sort of weird combination of hustle culture and just being mean, and driving people very hard.[2]

Historically and globally, most newsrooms have been run by men, giving rise to a status quo dominated by privilege and macho behaviour, where those who do not see themselves reflected in leadership are even less likely to speak out. Of course, newsroom cultures are not uniform, but throughout my interviews, those I spoke with noted certain toxic tendencies associated with people who had run newsrooms.

When Gwen Lister, founding editor of a Namibian newspaper, began her career in 1976, there was no talk of mental health or physical safety. She was simply expected to get on with the job, even after a serious car crash the year after starting out.

> Back then, it was pretty unheard of for a woman, in particular, to be writing [about] politics as I did. Those were tough times, and I think when you are given that type of baptism of fire, you disregard [mental health] kinds of issues because you subvert everything and repress all those kinds of experiences that you have, particularly at the hands of misogynistic editors. As I said to someone way back, you almost try to act like a man. Any pain, any heartache – and those sort of things – you filed away neatly into little boxes somewhere and sort of said, 'Get on with the job, because if you don't, you're going to lose the job and you're not going to be able to do what you want.'[3]

I heard similar sentiments from Catherine Gicheru, who was the first female news editor at the Nation Media Group, the largest media group in East and Central Africa, and the founding editor of the *Star* newspaper in Kenya:

> We have these men who run these news organisations making decisions. And for them being tough is: you're not supposed to show any emotions; you're a man. An African man is not supposed to be vulnerable, to show any emotions that might be perceived as weak, and if you're operating in these spaces, you too cannot show any weaknesses. So, it's a kind of cultural, societal attitude change we need. Men who make these decisions must also accept that vulnerability is not a weakness if they want to change their organisations and introduce policies or guidelines or whatever in the newsroom. But first, it starts with them as individuals, then secondly, as the decision-makers in their organisations.[4]

Leona O'Neill began her career in the 1990s during the final years of the Troubles, Northern Ireland's four-decade-long sectarian conflict:

> You had reporters covering, perhaps, a murder every other day, then the funeral after that. It was a really trying time. A lot of the journalists, as soon as they finished work, went to the bar, got drunk, went home, slept, got up the next day and did it again. It was a hugely toxic, unhealthy kind of lifestyle, with bars outside some of the newspapers, across the road from a newspaper that I worked on. There were bars inside some of the media outlets as well, which was almost like feeding this toxic environment. Nobody talked about mental health. If someone struggled, had a mental breakdown, it was kind of hushed, or it was said, 'They've gone mad.' I thought it was very strange as a young reporter that you're going to cover all these terrible crimes and murders, and sometimes you're caught at a scene and there were bodies still lying on the ground. As a 19/20-year-old, I thought, this is really rough.[5]

Now head of the journalism school at the University of Ulster, O'Neill is passionate about the need to normalise mental health conversations, to show how journalists' work can impact them, and advocates for coping strategies that newsrooms and individuals can use to support healthy journalists and journalism. She faced resistance after publishing the book *Breaking: Trauma in the Newsroom*,[6] in which she shared stories of journalists who suffered after covering traumatic stories: 'There was still a huge pushback, even when we brought the book out. People were saying, 'You're going to create snowflakes in the newsroom, doing this.'

I've heard from several news leaders in different countries of their concerns that speaking about mental health will create a generation of journalists who cannot hack the job. This attitude worries me. At the same time, I hear colleagues recognise that younger people – particularly from Gen Z and younger millennials – tend to have greater literacy where their mental health is concerned than their forebears did, and they often cement this by establishing boundaries between their personal and professional lives, while being less inclined to accept environments where their wellbeing is overlooked.

News leaders might do well to learn from their younger colleagues about the need to prioritise wellbeing and boundaries. In tandem, those entering our profession do need to be supported to recognise the potential toll difficult work can take, and to develop and access strategies to cope. Kari Cobham, head of fellowships at The 19th News, an independent, not-for-profit newsroom in the United States, recognises the pressure on new journalists:

> We work in an industry where traditionally the attitude has been, you just kind of suck it up and move on. Nobody teaches you that the news, what you cover, is going to have an impact on you, especially when you're a new journalist. I think foundationally, this is where the industry

used to be, and some of that still exists. That's where I think the stigma comes out in the industry – journalists not wanting to be seen as weak, or not wanting to be discounted for certain stories or roles in the newsroom because of mental health challenges with the stories that we're dealing with.[7]

This stigma is fairly universal, although less severe in some places and often less debilitating for those in privileged positions or with more secure roles.

It can be a difficult decision for a leader, whether to share their own experiences, especially if they lead an international organisation, where views on mental health vary from country to country. Yet my conversations with news leaders from around the world, as well as clinicians, indicate that in organisations where leaders tend towards compassion, candour and self-care, there does seem to be more progress in tackling stigma and taboos, albeit that it may not be possible to please everyone all the time.

Advocating for mental health may require cultural change within an organisation, whereby leaders model effective and empathetic behaviour and where diversity and inclusion is central to creating newsrooms where people feel safer to share their experiences. Kiran Nazish began her career in Pakistan, and spent two decades as a journalist, covering conflict globally, mostly for Western media:

> I was raised in an environment where, for journalists, talking about mental health was seen as a sign of weakness. When I became a foreign correspondent, among my Western colleagues the culture was similar; it was seen as a disability to talk and directly impacted your career. I was very competitive and ambitious, as most journalists are, and like many other journalists I continued to hide my mental health issues as well.[8]

Now based in North America, Nazish is the founding director of New York-based Coalition For Women in Journalism, a global press freedom support and advocacy organisation for women and non-binary journalists. A huge focus of their mentorship and support work includes the mental health and wellbeing of journalists seeking assistance on press freedom issues.

Like Nazish, Catherine Gicheru's personal experience inspired her to support other women journalists – which she does through the Africa Women Journalism Project – and to advocate for more open conversations about mental health:

> I've had to live through it, and I don't want to see people going through the same kind of mess that I did. I think it's something we don't talk about. I remember when I was starting out in journalism, and you had to be this macho person. You're dealing with weird stuff, going into morgues, looking at dead bodies, and you're not supposed to show emotion. You're supposed to be this hardened person.

What affected Gicheru most was her sense of being two separate people when returning from covering difficult stories: the journalist, and the non-journalist:

> I had to create a time lag between the time I left the office, and the time I got home; I had to kind of unpack, to de-stress so that I didn't take it home. So that's now where the persona comes in, the home persona, the Catherine who is the mother, the sister, the daughter; and Catherine, the hardened journalist. You have to kind of create that gap. So I've always wanted to help, especially young women journalists, see how they can disconnect without necessarily switching off.

That hardened person Gicheru referred to is a familiar figure in newsrooms around the world, conditioned to not ask for help, because decades of journalism have created cultures where this is perceived as tantamount to an admission of failure. Even where leaders make it clear that conversations around mental health are confidential and there will be no negative repercussions, stigma can still persist. Overcoming this will take time as well as a concerted effort by leaders to create cultures that really are safe and inclusive.

Dave Seglins, a journalist and the wellbeing champion at CB in Canada, talked about his experience of this:

> I've had some of the most senior people at CBC and at other news organisations Canada confide that if I were to be open in my workplace, about my mental health struggles that relate either to work or my own personal life, it would be a career killer. I would no longer be on those big assignments; they would work around me and I would get sort of drummed out.[9]

At Headlines Network,[10] which I launched to promote more open conversations around mental health, we have published a series of podcasts. In them, we heard from well-known journalists about the stories they covered, those which impacted them, and how conversations around mental health had changed. One of our guests was Stuart Ramsay, Sky News' chief correspondent. He told us about the early years of his career:

> If you said to the company, 'I can't do this because I need a break and it's really affected me,' you'd sort of feel like, Stuart's lost it; he'll never go again, and that was something that I know I felt and I know many colleagues doing a similar job, particularly in the United States, felt: that they would basically be signing their unemployment papers.[11]

Ours is an industry that prides itself on existing outside of the normal. By definition, news is new and different. But sometimes this means we feel we're ill-equipped to deal with those diversions from daily life. We bury our heads in the sand, unable to accept there are healthier ways to process pain, trauma, stress, heartache, extremes and excesses than behaviours that sabotage our wellbeing and impact our industry. Of toxicity in newsrooms, Seglins said:

> I think that is a byproduct of us not being very good at understanding or talking about stress and trauma. We're like the frogs in the boiling pot, right? And so that's where toxicity comes from. It's not because the news industry has an inordinate number of assholes working together. It's just that stress turns people into assholes. There hasn't been a way or a space for these kinds of discussions [to take place]. It's really ironic that the news industry reports on the failings of all other industries: about mistreatment in the workplace, poor treatment of discrimination claims, #MeToo – we're very capable of making headlines out of the misdeeds of other industries and corporations – but who is looking critically at us? And so we don't report on ourselves very often. It can be career limiting.

The truth is, in our industry it is sometimes easier to keep on pretending we are immune to hurt, ignoring the fact we are not invincible, heading towards a destination that is self-destruction, since distress is too hard to admit. Because that would mean showing compassion to ourselves and our colleagues, accepting we have been hurt by what we have been exposed to. It would mean admitting vulnerability and recognising that those individuals who do not yet see vulnerability and empathy as forces for good have probably been told to put up and shut up by folks who have previously done the same for years.

But what if we could recognise that an admission of vulnerability was a sign of strength, evidence of our empathy, proof we were more connected with our world and with the stories and communities we serve. And what if we did that throughout our news ecosystem, right down from the leaders of organisations?

Then we might start to rewrite the stereotype that journalists are not impacted by their work and create a culture where people do not need to fear that sharing their stories will bring negative consequences. Then we might start to rebuild systems and cultures that condition us to be compassionate, to care, to connect, to create spaces where conversations lead us to better support each other and ourselves.

Notes

1 Author interview with Santiago Lyon, April 2023
2 Author interview with Tanmoy Goswami, August 2022
3 Author interview with Gwen Lister, August 2022
4 Author interview with Catherine Gicheru, May 2023
5 Author interview with Leona O'Neill, November 2022
6 Breaking: Trauma in the Newsroom, edited by Leona O'Neill and Chris Lindsay, Maverick House (2022)
7 Author interview with Kari Cobham, October 2022
8 Author interview with Kiran Nazish, July 2022
9 Author interview with Dave Seglins, January 2023

10 www.headlines-network.com
11 Headlines Network, (2022) *Behind the Headlines*, Episode 8: Stuart Ramsay [podcast]. Available at: https://audioboom.com/posts/8122796-stuart-ramsay

Reference list

O'Neill, L. and Lindsay, C., eds (2022) *Breaking: Trauma in the Newsroom* (Maverick House, London)

Headlines Network, (2022) *Behind the Headlines*, Episode 8: Stuart Ramsay, [podcast]. Available at: https://audioboom.com/posts/8122796-stuart-ramsay

Their story – Dr Khaled Nasser[12]

Dr Khaled Nasser is a Lebanese trauma and mental health consultant who works with journalists covering conflict in the Middle East and Africa. He completed a BA in filmmaking, as well as a master's in advertising, and worked in television stations before his clinical training. With a doctorate and post-doctorate work in trauma therapy, he has treated hundreds of journalists in the past decade.

> From an industry perspective, from a field perspective, being a journalist equals, 'no fear, man up, be strong' – stuff like that. So it is not just [that] stigma com[es] from their society; it also [comes] from the profession, and the requirements of the profession itself – how much it dictates the idea you should ignore your emotions, and just go into the field.

Dr Nasser finds many news managers believe they don't have time to consider mental health, as if prioritising it is at odds with a focus on productivity.

> They will tell you, 'Yes, of course, we do this and that', but it's still at a very theoretical level for them. Because they are not used to this. They are coming from a different generational culture, mental mindset. And they think, we need to be on the ground, and the pace of work is really fast. The whole system is constructed, just to kind of disregard mental health. They don't understand that, actually, [they're] sending this person to cover this story, but this story is toxic in itself. So, you have a sense of desensitisation. Over time, we get used to blood. So they don't have the empathy to consider or ask about their staff's mental health.
>   I tell them, 'On the surface, you're desensitised. But deep down, you're not. The lava is inside. And at any point, your volcano will explode. And this is why you have all those aspects of anger and emotional dysregulation. You have all those negative coping mechanisms in your life; those are indications of how much you're not okay. You can barely focus in any sense, and do not have a healthy attention span.'[13] So, I show them the areas where they're not okay, [and tell them], 'Don't treat it as okay just because you're not feeling. You're desensitised. You're numb. Numbing is basically for you a defence mechanism. But this is not a healthy mechanism.' And I also explain this from the perspective of how much they are in sync with their external world. I tell them: 'It's not just you're numb from the pain and the negativity around you. You're also numb from the happiness around you.'
>   I mean, the good thing is that I'm saying this in a workshop where I can channel [help] or [in] individual sessions, where I can start with this and then start [showing] them the mechanisms that they can apply

and use to get better. But at the same time, the community of journalists are typical – how shall I say – [they] are professionals in avoidance? Emotional avoidance. And this is our main challenge, because many of them refuse therapy. When you study how to do therapy, you're really studying it from a Western perspective that focuses heavily on the individual, focuses on the I, focuses on you taking care of yourself, disregarding the context around you, because there is this assumption [that] the context is really in order [stable].

And there's the assumption, I would say, that your pain happened. It's not happening *now*. Something happened. And I'm taking care of you now after it happened. And it's passed. Post-traumatic stress disorder. But I don't work from this concept. Of course, because there is no *post*. There is traumatic stress disorder.

I was working with a journalist in Idlib. He was doing this session in the bathroom, I think, because they were under bombings from the regime at that time. During the morning, he told me, he was walking, and he had to just run away and hide at the side of the street, because bombs were hitting this area.

So how can you do therapy, even post-traumatic stress disorder therapy, with this person who is actually going through trauma at the moment? And if you don't consider this, you're at the end of ten to 12 sessions, [and] he or she will not benefit. By just discussing what happened in the past or in the near past and [thinking that's been dealt with], what you'll end up with, in essence, will not be as effective.'

Dr Nasser has developed a therapeutic method comprising six areas, born from the socio-political context, assumptions around therapy in the Middle East and the limitations of the programmes within which he works, which include access to funding and unreliable internet. These six areas include building relationships, psychoeducation, developing self-appraisal, problem solving (which includes addressing environmental challenges), reprocessing memories and grounding the body.

In the face of constant danger and multiple traumas, my best offensive is to make [the journalists] trust themselves and believe in their ability to fight or, at least, to survive these dangers. Typically perfectionists, journalists often lack the confidence that they can find solutions. They go through phases of low self-esteem. So, we go over the multiple attacks and disappointments they have been through. I help them note how well they behaved in the face of trouble. Regardless of the problem, it will seem a little easier if you feel you can solve it. And I have to say here that journalists in the Middle East are unbelievably resilient. Whether they know it or not, they constantly rise from the deep end. They have a strong belief in their mission, and this helps, but my mission is to promote their belief in themselves and to build their sense of agency. As a frustrated man from the Middle East, I unfortunately cannot alleviate the problems of my region. But I can surely help myself and others take on these problems with more confidence and more courage.

Notes

12 Based on interview with Dr Khaled Nassr, October 2022
13 Author interview with Dr Khaled Nasser, October 2022

5 The journalist's brain

'When you are in a dangerous situation, your body is programmed to respond. It is actually quite amazing. If you see a bear in the woods, you have three options. You freeze, you run, or you fight. Those are the ways your body goes into emergency mode. As you're talking to me now, the front part of your brain is working. But when you go into an emergency mode, the back part of your brain takes over. You're just focused on what is the danger, how do I survive? You're not even thinking that your body's taking over.'[1]

—Professor Elana Newman

Professor Newman has spent decades working with journalists. The above is her explanation of the traditional PTSD model of fear processing, with the three most common responses of flight, fight, freeze. In some situations, when an individual is exposed to trauma, there may be additional responses, as outlined by psychotherapist Mark Brayne, also the founding director of Dart Centre Europe and a former Reuters and BBC journalist. Specifically, he calls these reactions 'the survival cascade':

> When we're overwhelmed, there's a succession of survival responses, burned into us by evolution: 200,000 years ago, on the plains of Africa, [faced with] sabre-toothed tigers and hyenas. And that, fundamentally, is who we are still. It's what I find useful to understand as a kind of survival cascade, going flight/fight/freeze/flop/friend, the five Fs.[2]

He described the 'cascade' as follows:

> The first, nervous system and evolution-driven response – if we see a threat to our physical survival or fundamental identity – is fear-driven flight: 'Whoa, I'm outta here.' The amygdala says, in effect, 'Oh shit, I can be eaten,' so we avoid; we don't want to be seen. If we can't flee, and if we are seen, the next response is fight, where the driving emotion is anger.

DOI: 10.4324/9781003344179-5

If that doesn't work – and the sabre-toothed tiger is, after all, way bigger and hungrier than you – then the next response, coming perhaps within milliseconds of the first two, is freeze: deer-in-the-headlights stuff. Stop! Don't move! Hope you are invisible. Feline predators are, after all, only drawn to prey that moves.

If that doesn't work, there's the flop response: the complete loss of body and muscle tone. It's perhaps a bit like playing dead. Think Bosnian men and boys in Srebrenica. The very few who did survive that dreadful massacre did so by playing dead. Not because they chose to, but because their nervous system switched automatically into that place, like a mouse that's been caught by a cat and goes limp. Freeze and flop are two sides of the same coin.

And if all that fails, with us human beings, what can happen is friending, or fawning. Think Stockholm syndrome or a rape victim colluding with their attacker to neutralise the threat of being killed – and it often works. These are things we can't choose, because we are creatures of survival.

When our body is in emergency mode, our heart rate and breathing increase. Our body effectively shuts down anything deemed unnecessary for survival, meaning our digestive system slows, sometimes expelling contents that would otherwise be drawing energy needed elsewhere. Our skin pales and blood is directed to where it is more important. We might tremble. Our pupils dilate.

When we experience trauma, a part of the brain called the amygdala sends an alarm signal to the hypothalamus, which Newman calls 'the communication system', from where a message goes to the pituitary to release hormones, the body's way of saying 'Help!'. She went on: 'And the kinds of things that it releases are that fight, flight, or freeze response, cortisol, this energy where moms can, like, lift up cars when their infants are in stress.'[3] In such a situation, Brayne said:

> You get natural opioids. Severely injured people in the immediate aftermath of being wounded often feel no pain – though that kicks in soon enough. And so, there's this hormonal flood that comes in to get someone out of immediate danger without collapsing.[4]

He explained that after witnessing or being exposed to something difficult, we may feel 'a whole kaleidoscope of emotions, from sadness and anger, or fear and shutdown. These are normal reactions to encountering extreme situations.'

Our amygdala, which is responsible for detecting threats, resets after trauma in a way that our subsequent danger cues can become more heightened. Because our bodies are programmed to respond to danger, we may remain in an 'alarm state' after the traumatic event has passed, according to Professor Newman:

Sometimes the alarm state doesn't shut off. Sometimes a journalist will be re-exposed, and the alarm will get bigger. If you've been attacked by a bee, and you have an allergic reaction, you're going to be more nervous when there's a bee. It's a danger cue to you now. You are going to respond to whatever happened at that time: whether it is the smell of a perpetrator, noise, the things that were around at the time. Your body is going to go into an alarm state when you're reminded, because it's trying to keep you safe, but you no longer need to be [kept] safe in that situation.[5]

Broadcaster, author and psychologist Dr Sian Williams has studied the impact that her news media colleagues' work has had on them, a subject she came to following her own experience of covering traumatic stories. She has shown that, while journalists are resilient, their exposure to traumatic situations can affect them in the longer term.

Alongside her broadcasting, Dr Williams now works in the UK's National Health Service with the emergency services, and she told me that police, fire, and ambulance personnel have similar responses to journalists, who also run towards danger or immerse themselves in it:

The nature of journalists' work means we often run towards danger and are potentially exposed to more trauma than the average person. This underscores why, as a population, we are more at risk of post-traumatic stress. Constantly being exposed to trauma, or to other people's trauma, so we're witnessing it, can be a real threat in the long run, because you've got no time to get back to normal again. And you could be working on a very highly elevated cortisol and adrenal response [. . .] and that's not good for your body.[6]

Ana Zellhuber is a Mexican psychologist and emergency psychology specialist, whose experience echoes that of Dr Williams:

Journalists behave exactly the same as first responders. It's amazing. Because, in a way, you're all first responders. And all of the first responders I've worked with, throughout my life – firefighters, police officers, in the medical sector, the rescuers in disasters, journalists – they all have this idea of, 'I am a hero, I have to be a hero. I have to be tough. Emotions cannot get me.' One of my patients once told me that she was taught at university that she couldn't feel while she was being a journalist – that she had to make the news, do her job without feeling. And I said, 'Okay, I understand they say that because you're not going to start crying in the middle of an interview. But then you come home, and then you become human again and then you have to process those emotions. If you don't, if you just put them aside, they're gonna eat you alive. Eventually, you're going to start presenting acute stress, even PTSD, vicarious trauma, and that's going to impact your work. Funnily enough, once you get there, you stop wanting to be a journalist. Because you're disappointed because you're exhausted, because you're drained emotionally.'[7]

It is important that journalists are educated to recognise how we might react in stressful situations, and when those reactions might be cause for concern. As Dr Williams said:

> I think we have to be really aware of where our behaviour is shifting or where our thoughts are going, what our moods are, and think about our coping strategies. Even though you think you're getting used to it, an elevated level of adrenaline, cortisol, your body feeling like it's in constant threat – [this] is not a good place to be. So perhaps before we go into an assignment, think about our emotional load: what else are we dealing with at the time? Think about our social support: who is helpful to us and why? And think about what kind of things get us through and help us on the other side; you need to practise those coping responses.

When journalists are sent into physically hostile environments, good practice dictates that newsrooms educate and prepare them for what they might encounter. This includes offering training, helping them recognise and mitigate risks, and putting in place a plan prior to any potentially dangerous assignment, which will ensure support is available before, during and after.

Where there is the possibility of physical harm, journalists should be deployed with safety equipment, for instance, a first aid kit and, depending on where they are working, body armour, such as a helmet and a flak jacket. If this is good practice from a physical perspective, it should be no different from a psychological one.

There's a rising awareness, championed by people like Dr Sian Williams, that journalists should have access to an 'emotional flak jacket', with newsrooms ensuring they are as educated and equipped psychologically as they are physically.

Dr Khaled Nasser works with journalists in the Middle East and Africa who live and work in environments where danger and trauma are common. He has found that explaining to them how their bodies and brains react is helpful: 'Many of their anxieties come from the feeling that they're the only one suffering. So, by giving them enough information to calm their anxiety, [they gain a] sense of control through information or through actions.'[8]

Many other colleagues have told me of their 'eureka' moments, when they came to understand the impact trauma had had on them and how connected the body and brain were. For me, a watershed moment arrived when I encountered the work of psychiatrist and researcher Bessel van der Kolk, who wrote *The Body Keeps the Score*,[9] in which he details how much trauma our physical bodies can carry. This helped me see how some of my physical symptoms were likely related to my psychological injuries.

Dave Seglins, from CBC, explained the moment he realised the connection:

> When I first sat in a seminar about stress and trauma – and how it affects the brain – it was a eureka moment for me as a journalist. To see an illustration of the brain and its fear centre (amygdala) reacting to extreme pressures [and flooding] the body and mind with adrenaline and stress hormones was to finally grasp the bio-physical responses too many of us have that turn us into anxiety cases and adrenaline junkies. I'd heard about 'fight, flight and freeze' responses to extreme distress. But I'd never fully applied it to myself or my job. It was eye-opening to learn how a brain under chronic stress can put us at risk of heart attack, stroke, mood disorders, PTSD, social isolation, for example.
>
> Instantly, I understood the mechanics behind years of high-stress work. It helped explain behaviours and newsroom cultures that we quietly tolerate – shouting, dark humour, heavy drinking and self-neglect. Our industry has for too long had an unspoken pact whereby we kind of accept occasional colleague meltdowns or outbursts in the shared understanding we are all just frogs simmering in the same pot of stress-soup.[10]

Kiran Nazish spent over a decade on the front lines of global conflict, as a foreign correspondent. She explained how, after leaving this line of work, her body effectively shut down. Her psychological and physical collapse was catalysed by her attendance at a Hostile Environment First Aid Training (HEFAT) course in New York. This then led her to enrol in neuroscience courses, because she was curious about what was happening in her brain:

> It was after the HEFAT training, I crashed. I ended up in hospital several times. Now that I've studied it, I know my body stopped functioning because my brain stopped functioning, and it had other effects on my body, for example, developing illness I did not experience before. I think that mental health is something I have ignored for the majority of my life – being raised in an industry where it was ignored. Then I finally confronted it, because it took over like a monster. It's not an exaggeration to say that I was on my deathbed, because not only could I not move – I [also felt I] couldn't breathe. I felt physically paralysed. And what made it even worse was to see that people around me did not necessarily understand it either. No one seemed to have answers to a question that is very, very real for too many journalists.[11]

As part of her recovery, Nazish connected with other women journalists, sharing some of their experiences and the obstacles they overcame. Her mental health crisis and the connections she made afterwards were instrumental in her motivation to establish the Coalition For Women In Journalism.

Only when we really take stock of our reactions, and how they are impacting our work, will we really be able to put in place measures to mitigate some of the risks we might face and identify what support structures are available to help us cope, either individually or through our newsrooms. Professor Newman highlights the importance of recognising these responses early on: 'Most people have a strong reaction to a strong experience. We all have stress, and knowing your symptoms and your signs can help you before things get worse and your body gets programmed to those kinds of things.' Although she began by studying PTSD in journalists, her work helps people deal with various levels of unhealthy coping that might impact on their mental health:

> Not everybody develops post-traumatic stress disorder, or depression or anxiety; [some] have lower levels of those things. They don't meet the [level of] clinical diagnosis, but they get in your way. They can affect your news choices. They can affect your happiness in life. I still study PTSD and journalists. But when I train, it's about helping people with those trauma reactions that get in their way, that maybe don't reach the clinical diagnosis and I think that's important because it reduces stigma. So, while I can't prevent PTSD, per se, we can prevent long-term maladaptive reactions. I think that is the way we'll get further in the industry as well, because [we can] help people who have PTSD, but [. . .] also help people who have lower levels of problems.

Sometimes the behaviours that we develop after trauma can benefit us, at least temporarily. In *The Madness*, the BBC correspondent Fergal Keane explained how childhood trauma made him hyper-vigilant, a characteristic that he employed throughout his journalism:

> The therapists call the skillsets I acquired in childhood 'maladaptive behaviours.' I relied on those skills when pulling up to a roadblock in the South African townships, or during the civil wars in Liberia and Sierra Leone, where jittery teenagers with guns held the power of life and death.
>
> Unconsciously I read their body language, facial expressions, tone of voice, and responded accordingly. I worked to de-escalate hostile situations, to make sure I presented no obvious threat. [12]

I have met numerous journalists who, having survived trauma, found themselves being able to apply similar skills. Professor Newman explained how they can help in certain situations:

> Particularly for people who go on assignment into dangerous situations, or who live in communities where it's dangerous, being hyper-vigilant is a good thing. Except when it gets in your way, and you can't go to fireworks on a holiday. So, it is when it gets in your way that it becomes a problem. I think it is better to deal with those kinds of things. And I also think when people come back from an assignment or have a hard assignment, they don't need to be shipped off to the shrink. What they need is social support, a little rest time.

I think we tend to rush. 'Oh, go check this person out. . .', when in fact, those reactions will go away. And most people's reactions go away within a month to three months if they're not re-exposed. And I always tell people who are not interested in treatment, there's natural healing that occurs, but if, after three months, they aren't feeling better, that's a good time to say, 'Hey, I think I need to check in with a professional.' A lot of natural healing occurs during those three months. It's unpleasant, but your body can readjust.

Avoidance is one of the most important things to keep an eye on, according to Professor Newman, and although she explained she didn't like giving lists, as that could be suggestive, she pointed out some potential signs:

Avoidance gets you in trouble over time: avoiding memories, avoiding places, avoiding things. If there's a real change in their work habits. If they find that they're dreading work, and they didn't used to dread it. If they're having actual flashbacks, or images popping into their head all the time that they can't control. If they're thinking about suicide, that needs immediate attention. If they're only seeing the negative in the world – more than they used to, because journalists are cynical, by nature, as they should be. They're sceptical, but they're becoming so sceptical that it becomes cynical, and that's different for them, only seeing the bad, nightmares, displaying more risky behaviour than usual. Though, again, some journalists are risk-takers.

The key thing to note here is a real *change* in behaviour, Newman points out: 'If you're doing things that just aren't like you, you're really feeling out of sorts, not just a bummed day, but feeling out of sorts for days, or just having weird experiences, that's the time to say, "Let me take a look at myself and what I need."'

It is important that journalists are not only attuned to their own responses but also sensitive to possible reactions in those they connect with through their work, who have been exposed to trauma, such as in interviewees. 'It's why, when people tell their stories, they can act goofy,' said Newman, for example, by way of their facial expressions or the words they choose. 'When you tell your story, your emotions may not fit the way that you felt at the time.'

When we are speaking with people who have been through traumatic experiences – as well as bearing in mind from our own perspectives, it is helpful to understand what trauma can do to memory. Newman explained the physiological aspect:

The hippocampus is your memory maker; it sort of gets your information and puts it in packets and stores it. And what happens sometimes in trauma is that your hippocampus, which basically organises, encodes and consolidates information, and the amygdala, which specialises in emotional memories – when all those hormones flood – they're [both] very sensitive to those fluctuations. So, the amygdala again detects the threat, all those hormones kick in, but your memory processing is affected by that, and memories get fragmented. You can get the information there, but it's not neatly arranged in the packets. That way, if I asked you what you had for breakfast, you could easily access [it]. But if I asked you what happened during your assault, you may not be able to tell it in a linear fashion.

While it is important to know the science behind such reactions, we should remember this is about people and not solely pathology, with Newman concerned that 'we're using terms loosely'.

Trauma exposure doesn't equal PTSD. Trauma exposure doesn't equal trauma reactions. You can be exposed to trauma, and it can affect the way you think about the world. It can change your life. But it doesn't necessarily mean that you have a psychological problem.

If the science helps us understand our reactions, this is great. Ultimately, we want to equip journalists with the tools and understanding to recognise how they might react in certain situations and how to manage those reactions to promote their wellbeing. We want to equip journalists with the knowledge that certain reactions are normal, and that by and large we are resilient, while also ensuring they know what to look out for, what helps and where to find that help.

Notes

1 Author interview with Professor Elana Newman, August 2022
2 Author interview with Mark Brayne, August 2023
3 Author interview with Professor Elana Newman, August 2022
4 Author interview with Mark Brayne, August 2023
5 Author interview with Professor Elana Newman, August 2022
6 Author interview with Dr Sian Williams, April 2023
7 Author interview with Ana Zellhuber, May 2023
8 Author interview with Dr Khaled Nasser, October 2022
9 Van der Kolk, Bessel (2015) *The Body Keeps the Score* (Penguin, London)
10 Author interview with Dave Seglins, January 2023
11 Author interview with Kiran Nazish, July 2022
12 Fergal Keane (2022) *The Madness* (William Collins, Glasgow), p. 79

Reference list

Fergal Keane (2022) *The Madness* (William Collins, Glasgow)
Van der Kolk, Bessel (2015) *The Body Keeps the Score* (Penguin, London)

Their story – Dave Seglins[13]

I got injured in 2010 working on a horrific court case involving a serial sexual killer. It flattened me. I got myself to a trauma counsellor, who told me that all of these feelings – that I was dying and unable to get out of bed, that I thought the world was ending and I was just freefalling – were normal, and a classic response to trauma. It was a post-traumatic stress response.

That was the first time I'd ever really heard that word or thought about trauma in relation to journalism. Because you don't like to think about it. Our job is to go in and cover these horrible things and there's the thrill of getting your story out, being the first people to do it.

I had never really thought, 'Oh, my God, I could be grossly affected by that.' But the counsellor was asking me what I did – what had I been through in the week or two previously? But then she also asked what I had been doing for the last ten years. I realised that the nature of the work: covering crime, violence, death, suffering, [meant] there was a cumulative effect. And that this one court case was not the single thing that had broken me.

What's more, through therapy, I came to understand that it's not only the trauma encountered on the job. I began to examine what I have lived through in my own personal life. And sure enough, you know, I have suffered loss. At a young age, I lost my father to suicide. I had a brother who died under difficult circumstances. And so with all of this grief and trauma and personal life melding with what I was doing for a living, I got diagnosed with complex PTSD.

That's the personal piece and the beginning. But what I marvelled at, at the time, is the total lack of discussion within my newsroom. There had been an understanding for any of the people covering this horrible court case, 'Oh, yes, we understand this is really difficult, so if you need to talk to a counsellor, we have an EAP [employee assistance programme]. Go ahead and do that.'

When I initially called the EAP, they were useless. I had to go through other means and a family doctor to get to a trauma specialist. But when I came back to work, feeling a bit better, there was no discussion and no acknowledgement. There was nobody who asked, 'Hey, we're gonna send you out on this next story. It's a similar crime, violent story, how do you feel about it?'

I was just right back into the flow of things. And it always bothered me that the newsroom didn't seem to have the capacity to talk about this stuff. And here, I was learning and struggling with my own injury, trying to figure out, why isn't this part of the job, so that we're not throwing people back into dangerous or risky or potentially harmful situations.

Fast-forward a decade, during the Covid pandemic – mental health was a thing for everybody, forget just journalism. And I was involved in our training department, and somebody asked me, 'What do you think we really need? Because I was thinking I was going to do training on investigative journalism, which has been my beat for 20 years,' and I said, 'You know what we really need? We need something on mental health and trauma.'

And they say, 'Great, why don't you teach a course?' And I said, 'Well, what the hell do I know about it?' And they said, 'Well, go take some courses, we'll support you.' So, I said, 'Well, I've got my personal history.' But anyway, they sent me off. I took a course through Harvard Medical School, on global mental health and trauma, to learn some of the brain science. I wound up on the Dart Center's fellowship this past summer, and calling around different newsrooms around the world to ask about their own best practices of what they do and working with CBC's own internal people.

I spent half a year developing a course that we are now rolling out – Well-being in Frontline Journalism, or Leading Well-being in Journalism for our supervisors and managers. We've had several hundred people through it so far, and we're rolling it out across the corporation. That's education. But in the work, I also said, 'You know what, there's so much more we could be doing, how about create a job?'

I pitched to them: I want to remain a journalist, because I think working in the newsroom from the shop floor is really helpful. So, it's not another management initiative, because there's a lot of scepticism and toxicity and concern among journalists about revealing their state of mind [and] their mental health. I said, 'Hire me as a journalist and wellbeing champion.'

Note

13 Taken from author interview with Dave Seglins, January 2023

6 Post-traumatic stress disorder (PTSD)

Post-traumatic stress disorder is a mental health condition that can develop after a person experiences or witnesses a traumatic event. It can be characterised by various symptoms. Among the most common are intrusive thoughts.

According to Professor Anthony Feinstein, who has studied the mental health of journalists for more than two decades, PTSD is 'a very significant mental illness and it can bring people down very hard [but] it's very treatable.'[1] His research – and that of others – shows that journalists are resilient, but the nature of our work, which often exposes us to traumatic events, means we are at greater risk than the general population of developing PTSD:

> I keep on saying that all the research I've done shows that the majority of journalists will never get PTSD. They will never develop a major depression. I think it's important to remind people [of] that, because otherwise you're saying the whole profession is traumatised, and it's not. But the percentage who do [develop it] is higher than you would expect in the general population. And that's not surprising because, given the nature of what you do when you put yourself in harm's way voluntarily, you're leaving yourself open to the kinds of events that do cause PTSD.[2]

The Dart Center for Journalism and Trauma[3] notes that 80 to 100% of journalists have been exposed to a work-related traumatic event. Its data suggests many experience repeat exposure, with nine out of ten having been exposed to at least four traumatic incidents. For journalists, the lifetime prevalence – the proportion of a population which will have PTSD at some point – ranges from 4 to 59%, depending on the study. By comparison, in the United States, the lifetime prevalence for the general population is 8%.

In clinical terms, PTSD symptoms must last at least a month, and be of significant severity. To meet these thresholds for diagnosis is relatively uncommon. Two people might experience the same trauma yet react differently, with one potentially developing PTSD and the other not. As with many mental health conditions, PTSD symptoms vary between people. However, they commonly include intrusive memories, as mentioned in Chapter 5, which can be in the form of nightmares, flashbacks, unwanted recollections or situations

DOI: 10.4324/9781003344179-6

where people feel physically or emotionally as if they are reliving the trauma. Avoidance is another common symptom, whereby individuals keep clear of reminders of their trauma and may suppress memories or thoughts related to their experience.

PTSD can lead to hyper-arousal and hyper-vigilance, which may affect sleep or concentration, make the person feel on edge or irritable, or lead to them practise risky behaviours. Individuals with PTSD may struggle to remember aspects of the traumatic event, blame themselves, feel isolated, have negative feelings about themselves and the world around them, and be unable to find pleasure in things. PTSD can also cause physical symptoms, such as digestive issues, insomnia, palpitations, increased sweating, headaches, body pains and fatigue.

This book reminds us that it is normal to react to trauma. We can expect some post-traumatic stress from difficult experiences. This might include feeling anger, sadness, or other emotions. Our sleep might be temporarily impacted, or other behaviours briefly affected. These reactions are a way of processing what has happened. Sometimes, the trauma might have a longer-lasting impact, in the form of maladaptive behaviours, albeit those that do not reach the level of severity required for a diagnosis of PTSD. Being aware of our reactions to trauma is important, because they can affect our health and our work.

'There needs to be an awareness of lower-level, persistent, repeated exposure to traumatic events,'[4] said Dr Sian Williams, broadcaster and clinical psychologist:

> So although a lot of focus has rightly been on post-traumatic stress disorder, and although we know that journalists do experience levels of PTSD higher than the general population – and I noticed this working in the National Health Service (NHS) during the pandemic – I think there will be quite a lot of people who will be experiencing stress responses or traumatic responses that wouldn't qualify for a clinical diagnosis, but which can still in the long run, if not adequately recognised and reflected on and treated, lead to difficulties.

As explained in Chapter 5, it helps to be attuned to maladaptive behaviours, and to recognise that trauma can leave its mark whether PTSD is diagnosed or not. However, we need to take care to avoid pathologising people's experiences incorrectly. There has been a tendency to ascribe PTSD in a way that underplays its severity as a mental health condition. Additionally, there is a growing field of thought that questions the value of a diagnosis that labels someone with a disorder. For some, the term PTSD can be problematic because it reinforces stigma and suggests blame, despite the fact that PTSD is not the fault of the individual who experienced the trauma.

Definitions of PTSD differ but have certain aspects in common, as follows: it is a condition some people develop after being exposed, directly or indirectly, to a traumatic, dangerous, or life-threatening event. The definition is broader than it used to be, because it is now accepted that PTSD can result from exposure to other people's trauma. Known as vicarious or secondary trauma, this is discussed in Chapter 7.

The American Psychiatric Association (APA) first created PTSD as a diagnosis in 1980. It had been known previously as 'shell shock' during the First World War, 'battle fatigue' and 'combat stress reaction' during the Second World War, and later still 'gross stress reaction'. Complex PTSD (or c-PTSD) is a newer diagnosis, recognised by the World Health Organization in 2019[5] in its 11th revision of the International Classification of Diseases. The APA does not separate it from PTSD in the latest edition of the *Diagnostic and Statistical Manual of Mental Disorders* (DSM V[6]). However, as the term 'complex' suggests, c-PTSD results from a series of traumatic events. There does not yet appear to be any research about c-PTSD in journalists, but in many of my conversations informing this chapter, individuals who had PTSD reminded me that journalists rarely experience only one incident of trauma.

PTSD symptoms may take a long time to develop, sometimes years. This may also pose a challenge in terms of diagnosis, as well as compound the shame felt by the individual. This speaks to the need for greater education around PTSD, so news organisations can ensure appropriate support mechanisms, normalise conversations and reduce stigma.

'For me, everything starts with education,' said Professor Feinstein. 'You just have to educate journalists about what's good emotional health, what to look out for, because I think educated people are informed people and they are more likely to react in the way that's healthy if you're educated.' He went on:

> The next thing that has to be in place is access to counselling that is easy and confidential. Those are two critical variables. You need to be able to find a therapist quickly, not going through multiple hoops, and it has to be completely confidential. Management should not know which journalist is receiving counselling. It's none of their business; your health care is private. We all take an oath as physicians that you will keep the confidentiality of your patients sacrosanct.

He expressed concern that some news organisations have given little thought to the quality of their employee assistance programmes:

> They have an EAP that doesn't understand journalists. And so, a journalist phones up, they've just had a horrendous experience, and they come face to face with a very junior person who hasn't got a clue as to what journalists do, what they go through. And then the process becomes destructive. The journalist becomes frustrated. They feel that this therapy is a load of nonsense – 'I'm wasting my time' – and chases them away.

There are many people with whom this will resonate. It does with me. On more than one occasion, I've contacted an EAP only to end up feeling worse than before, because they did not understand my work, experiences or motivations. Shame and guilt are common symptoms of PTSD, exacerbated by industry taboos. It can be difficult to seek help, meaning some people only do so when they hit rock bottom, and so it's really important that those providing the help have the relevant experience.

Anna Blundy is a former journalist, and founder of The Mind Field,[7] which provides therapy for journalists and humanitarian workers given by trained clinicians who really understand these professional fields. She told me how, initially, she found the idea that a therapist should share one's work background strange:

> But I now realise how important it is – the acceptance of the relentlessness of it all. It's very tempting to encourage people to stop, say, 'This sounds terrible. Why are you doing this to yourself? Stop.' But of course, they've gone into it. It is their job, they need to work, and it is very relentless. So you have to kind of meet them where they are. And I think that's quite difficult for therapists.
>
> They also often can't make sessions. I try to be really flexible and reschedule. I don't charge people for my session if they give me 24 hours' notice. I don't do all the really shrinky things that you're used to, because then they're just not going to be able to do it. If you put all those boundaries up, they'll have no therapy. So, better to have some flexible, not completely straight-down-the-line therapy than none at all, which is the alternative.[8]

Professor Feinstein first researched PTSD in war journalists at the turn of the millennium:

> We were able to show that their lifetime diagnosis, lifetime prevalence or diagnosis [is] very close to what you find in frontline veteran soldiers. This was a group that had spent on average 15 years in war zones. There is no other profession, I believe, that has such a lengthy exposure to war and trauma. Soldiers had a tour of duty, maybe two, and they came home. But who spends 15 years or more in the world's worst places? Journalists do, and in response to that, over the course of all the years, the rates of post-traumatic stress disorder were actually quite high.[9]

Several of Professor Feinstein's later studies focused on journalists working within their own communities, including Mexico, Kenya, Iran and Afghanistan, shifting some of the focus of conversations around PTSD. In these environments, he explored the coping mechanisms some journalists resorted to, often facing significant societal stigma, and with limited or no mental health support at work.

Over 23 years, Professor Feinstein analysed the responses of more than 1,100 individuals, identifying two key factors that made journalists more vulnerable to PTSD. Being a woman was one factor, most likely because of the greater risk of sexual assault. If we take PTSD resulting from sexual violence out of the equation, Feinstein believes there would be little difference in the PTSD rates between men and women. The other factor that makes journalists vulnerable is previous experience of mental health conditions.

In what has long been a macho and male-dominated industry, women journalists have often been regarded as a liability. They have been told to change their behaviours to mitigate risks, or have been sidelined because men are less vulnerable to sexual violence. This underscores the systemic sexism that has underpinned safety discussions. If journalism is macho, then media safety is even more so. This entire field needs to be more diverse, with women playing a greater part in the decision-making process.

In my interviews for this book, several individuals expressed their concern about sexual violence and harassment against journalists, and about how often this issue has been brushed under the carpet, despite it impacting upon journalists' mental health.

In 2012, I co-authored *No Woman's Land: On the Frontlines with Female Reporters*,[10] the first book that focused on the safety of women journalists. More than a decade on, it continues to be regarded as a key reference in safety conversations, and yet there is still not enough being done to ensure women journalists are safer at work.

News organisations must address identity and gendered violence, so that diverse journalists can feel safer doing their work, physically and psychologically. We have a long way to go to normalise these conversations and to put in place measures that ensure those marginalised by our industry do not feel like the weight of responsibility to stay safe is on their shoulders. The onus to change ought to be on the systems and processes that have sustained this inequity. It's easy to see how Feinstein's conclusion might be taken by some newsrooms as reinforcing the notion that women are the liability, rather than encouraging those organisations to create safer environments where those women can do their work, while recognising they also bring a different perspective, and often gain access to communities who themselves are less frequently heard.

Although we are seeing some movement in newsrooms towards an understanding that PTSD can affect people in different ways and that it is not just the preserve of men, it has historically been men who spoke about it. Chris Cramer, the former BBC and CNN International news executive who died in 2021, was one of the first high-profile news leaders to discuss his PTSD, which resulted from his experience of being held hostage during the Iranian Embassy siege in London in 1980. In an article[11] published in 2010, Cramer, then Reuters' global multimedia editor, was quoted as saying:

> I went through real anguish for a couple of years. I had flashbacks, I had extraordinary claustrophobia, which I'd never had before. For several years, I did not go to a cinema, I did not go into an elevator. If I ever

went into a restaurant, I positioned myself near the door for a fast exit. For many, many months after the incident I checked under my car every morning before driving it. I was a basket case, I was a mess.

Cramer later called his experience the 'single most terrifying thing of my entire life',[12] something that was remarked upon in an obituary for him, written in the *Wall Street Journal*, which described how he had been propelled to advocate for journalism safety, becoming the founding president of the International News Safety Institute and coining the phrase 'no story is worth a life'.

Catherine Philp was one of the first women in the news industry to speak about her PTSD, and her story is shared at the end of this chapter. The BBC journalist Stuart Hughes regards her as instrumental in advancing the mental health conversation in UK media. He has also spoken about his PTSD, after he lost his leg and suffered other serious injuries in a landmine explosion that killed his cameraman colleague, Kaveh Golestan. Hughes has spent many years highlighting the impact of PTSD on individuals and encouraging news organisations to take seriously their duty of care to the media workers who put themselves in harm's way for journalism. It was Hughes who helped me recognise my own PTSD, and he has been a great ally in my recovery. He told me:

> I think my mission is, as someone who has suffered physical and psychological injuries, [. . .] to talk from personal experience about what [PTSD] is, what it does to you, how it needs to be managed, how it needs to be treated, and particularly how you can – if not recover completely – manage it. That needs a hell of a lot of support, some of which is financial, but not exclusively. Recovering from trauma takes a village, to quote Hillary Clinton.

However, he warned, 'I think the phrase PTSD is now sadly overused in general discussion; it is a very specific clinical diagnosis.'[13] In his view, more needs to be done to tackle stigma and the perceptions held by many of those who experience mental health difficulties:

> We need a community at the micro level and a society at the macro level that is not scared about people who have had mental difficulties, not worried that they're going to turn into axe-wielding murderers, that is comfortable being around those people.

Despite his injuries, Hughes said he did not want to be labelled a victim, and he was a journalist first and foremost.

> I decided quite early on after my injury that I wanted to consider myself to be a journalist and landmine survivor, not a landmine survivor and

journalist. And I stressed the word survivor, not victim. The one thing that I pick people up on is I'm never a victim. But the word journalist comes first. The word landmine comes second. [Then] survivor, and also survivor of psychological injury brought about due to the work that I've been doing. So that's what I hope to achieve. I also hope I can speak truth to power in certain contexts when needed, and if I don't feel the industry as a whole is doing enough to ensure that the journalists are able to access the help and support that they need.

Although PTSD has been a part of newsroom conversations for some time, the number of people who specialise in supporting journalists with the condition is still small, in Hughes' opinion – though he noted things are improving:

The next generation of clinicians is starting to be trained, so that's absolutely massive. But I think we are not where we need to be. We have come so far. And I think it's only in the last three, four years, since just before the pandemic, when actual money, real money for real treatment, started to come on stream, but it's not enough.

Cramer, Philp and Hughes pioneered conversations around PTSD in the UK and US, overcoming their own health crises and the stigma often associated with it. In 2008, Catherine Philp wrote a landmark article[14] for *The Times*, entitled, 'Trauma, kidnap and death: all in a day's work for journalists in Iraq', in which she explained what prevented many from speaking about their mental health: 'Shame and a sense of inadequacy have stopped many journalists talking publicly of their inner battles. After all, when you have witnessed such suffering, your own anguish seems woefully small.'

Professor Feinstein explained how journalists often felt they ought not to compare their experiences with others, particularly those exposed to trauma who do not have the agency or ability to leave situations. He told me it is important we also recognise the impact our work can have on us and acknowledge the validity of our experiences. Doing so is protective for our mental health and a reminder of our purpose.

Two decades on from Feinstein's groundbreaking research into PTSD, the conversation has advanced, but not to the extent it might. We have a long way to go to understand how best to support those with PTSD, especially where it stems from identity violence. There have been developments in realising that cumulative exposure to trauma can affect people significantly, with one of the biggest shifts being the recognition that repeat exposure to violent and distressing material in one's work can lead to PTSD. This is discussed later in this book, and it does mean the conversation has broadened.

As people experience and respond to trauma differently, so different forms of support and treatment help different people. Dr Sian Williams has researched the idea of post-traumatic growth among journalists. I asked her about her research and to what extent trauma can have a positive impact on people:

> Our perceptions of life can be shattered by a traumatic event or a series of highly stressful experiences. Post-traumatic growth is about recognising that a traumatic experience has affected us in some way and [we are] trying to reconfigure things. So, trying to put things back together in a way that makes sense. And that might mean that our perspective on ourselves and our place in the world and what life means to us shifts in some way. So, post-traumatic growth is a way of recovering well, from something profoundly difficult. But built into that is a recognition of the fact that that profoundly difficult thing has affected you in some way. Sometimes we can be affected by something difficult, and our defences and protective mechanisms are built up over so many years, that we can just get on with the next thing and we don't really feel it, and then it can catch up with us much later down the line. And that's when we see, for example – in journalists – we might see them struggling many years after the original event, or when we might see journalists struggling because they've had accumulation of difficult experiences. Or we see journalists who are highly experienced who've done lots of different difficult things and have reported on lots of traumatic events, and then suddenly they think, 'Why am I not dealing with this any more?' It's because the very effective defences and protective mechanisms that we build up to cope are no longer working. That's when we need to go back to what it is that's affected us. How has it affected us? How are we carrying it? How are we feeling it? And what might we do to acknowledge it and reflect on it safely, so that we can go back into battle again?[15]

Dr Williams explained that this did not mean growth was inevitable after a traumatic event – or that there was meaning to suffering, because this could feel invalidating to someone experiencing trauma. However, she noted that, with the right support, it is possible to recover well from a traumatic injury and find meaning and learning from the process.

People have different experiences of mental health conditions, symptoms and recovery, and of what helps and hinders. The more stories we hear, the more conversations will be normalised, and we will recognise the diversity of those experiences. One constant in my conversations with people who have had PTSD is that their recovery is not linear. Stuart Hughes noted above that 'it takes a village to recover from trauma', and his BBC colleague Fergal Keane described himself as a 'work in progress'.[16] I am one too.

Nobody chooses to have PTSD. It is something that some people experience when their bodies and brains react to traumatic experiences. With hindsight, I know that more education and support would have helped me, which is one of the reasons I feel so motivated to channel my experiences in a positive way. It is a mission I hear shared by other journalists who have been to this dark place and have decided to channel their own experiences, and their storytelling abilities, to support others.

Notes

1 Anthony Feinstein (2020) 'I've studied journalists under pressure for 20 years. Here's what I've learned so far', Reuters Institute for the Study of Journalism, 5 June. Available at: https://reutersinstitute.politics.ox.ac.uk/news/ive-studied-journalists-under-pressure-20-years-heres-what-ive-learned-so-far
2 Author interview with Professor Feinstein, July 2022
3 River Smith et al (2015) 'Covering Trauma: Impact on Journalists', Dart Center, 1 July. Available at: https://dartcenter.org/content/covering-trauma-impact-on-journalists
4 Author interview with Dr Sian Williams, April 2023
5 WHO (2020) ICD-11. Available at: https://icd.who.int/en
6 APA (2013) *Diagnostic And Statistical Manual Of Mental Disorders*, Fifth Edition. Available at: https://dsm.psychiatryonline.org/doi/book/10.1176/appi.books.9780890425596
7 https://themindfield.world
8 Author interview with Anna Blundy, July 2022
9 Anthony Feinstein, John Owen and Nancy Blair (2002) 'A hazardous profession: War, journalists, and psychopathology', *The American Journal of Psychiatry*, 159(9), 1570–75. Available at: https://psycnet.apa.org/record/2002-04185-016
10 Hannah Storm and Helena Williams (2012). *No Woman's Land, On the Frontlines with Female Reporters* (International News Safety Institute, London)
11 Frederik Joelving (2010) 'When the news breaks the journalist: PTSD', Reuters Institute for the Study of Journalism, 17 December. Available at: https://www.reuters.com/article/us-ptsd-reporter-idUSTRE6BG3NG20101217/
12 James Hagarty (2021) 'News Executive Worked to Protect Journalists in Hot Spots', *Wall Street Journal*, 17 January. Available at: https://www.wsj.com/articles/news-executive-chris-cramer-worked-to-protect-journalists-in-hot-spots-11610916260
13 Author interview with Stuart Hughes, October 2022
14 Catherine Philp (2008) 'Trauma, kidnap and death: all in a day's work for journalists in Iraq', *The Times*, 20 March. Available at: https://www.thetimes.co.uk/article/trauma-kidnap-and-death-all-in-a-days-work-for-journalists-in-iraq-lw8fgxkxk59
15 Author interview with Dr Sian Williams, March 2023
16 *The Madness*, Fergal Keane, (William Collins, November 2022)

Reference list

American Psychiatric Association (2013) *Diagnostic and Statistical Manual of Mental Disorders*, Fifth Edition
Feinstein, A. (2020) 'I've studied journalists under pressure for 20 years. Here's what I've learned so far', Reuters Institute for the Study of Journalism, 5 June. Available at: https://reutersinstitute.politics.ox.ac.uk/news/ive-studied-journalists-under-pressure-20-years-heres-what-ive-learned-so-far,
Feinstein, A., Owen, J. and Blair, N. (2002) 'A hazardous profession: War, journalists, and psychopathology', *The American Journal of Psychiatry*, 159(9), 1570–75. Available at: https://psycnet.apa.org/record/2002-04185-016

Hagarty, J. (2021) 'News Executive Worked to Protect Journalists in Hot Spots', *Wall Street Journal*, 17 January. Available at: https://www.wsj.com/articles/news-executive-chris-cramer-worked-to-protect-journalists-in-hot-spots-11610916260

Joelving, F. (2010) 'When the news breaks the journalist: PTSD', Reuters Institute for the Study of Journalism, 17 December. Available at: https://www.reuters.com/article/us-ptsd-reporter-idUSTRE6BG3NG20101217/

Keane, F. (2022) *The Madness* (William Collins, Glasgow)

Philp, C. (2008) 'Trauma, kidnap and death: all in a day's work for journalists in Iraq', *The Times*, 20 March. Available at: https://www.thetimes.co.uk/article/trauma-kidnap-and-death-all-in-a-days-work-for-journalists-in-iraq-lw8fgxkxk59

Smith, R., Newman, E., Drevo, S. and Slaughter, A. (2015) 'Covering Trauma: Impact on Journalists', Dart Center, 1 July. Available at: https://dartcenter.org/content/covering-trauma-impact-on-journalists

Storm, H. and Williams, H. (2012). *No Woman's Land: On the Frontlines with Female Reporters* (International News Safety Institute, London)

World Health Organization (2020) *International Classification of Diseases*, 11th edition

Their story – Catherine Philp[17]

Catherine Philp is the diplomatic correspondent for *The Times* newspaper. In 2008, she wrote a pioneering article entitled 'Trauma, kidnap and death: all in a day's work for journalists in Iraq'.[18] The article was groundbreaking in its candour and for the fact it tackled stigmas that had not been articulated previously. As such, Catherine became one of the first women journalists to speak about the impact her work had on her mental health. In the piece, she describes some of the traumas she experienced, including the death in a suicide bomb of her best friend, a young woman for whom Catherine was also a parent figure. She reflects on her own diagnosis of PTSD, speaking about the dangers she and other colleagues faced in Iraq, and the toll it took. She also cites the experiences of two colleagues who experienced PTSD, both former Baghdad correspondents: the BBC's correspondent Caroline Hawley and NPR's Lulu Garcia-Navarro.

In her article, she described shame and the inclination to compare our own experiences proved barriers to many journalists talking publicly. 'After all, when you have witnessed such suffering, your own anguish seems woefully small. "I feel embarrassed to be talking about this when you set it against the monumental collective suffering of Iraqis," Hawley says. "I do feel guilty."'

The full impact of the trauma experienced by Catherine and her peers would take a long time to make itself clear. 'The psychological toll among journalists remains unknown; many who need help have not sought it and few will discuss it openly. The average time lapse for PTSD onset – seven years – harbingers troubles yet to come,' she wrote.

Of her own experiences, she explained: 'The phantom explosions began for me the night I left Baghdad, first in my airport hotel room in Dubai, then in Delhi the next night as I saw the whole window explode in on my living room. Back in London, I became withdrawn, jumpy and unable to sleep. A month later I was told I had post-traumatic stress disorder (PTSD).'

I was reminded of the pioneering role Catherine played in the mental health conversation by our mutual friend, the BBC producer, Stuart Hughes. Catherine agreed to speak with me after he introduced us.

Our interview took place 15 years after she wrote her article and almost exactly 20 years after the US-led invasion of Iraq. In that time, she believes our industry has improved in the way it addresses journalistic distress, though she says there's still a lot of shame. At the time of her 2008 article, though, Catherine saw no other option but to speak:

> I have been very open for a long time, because I felt there was a conspiracy of silence around this. People were unwilling to talk about it because they didn't want to be perceived as damaged, because they were scared that would mean they wouldn't work again. I had these fears too. But by the time I was treated, there was no other option. How do you

explain otherwise that you've been off work for six months? I thought if I had the confidence to speak, then other people who didn't could come and confide in me, and they did. I became the face of PTSD for a while.

Of her *Times* article, she said: 'It was really interesting that it was all women who 'fessed up. We were working in a macho environment already. If we admitted it, we were proving what they thought all along.'

During our interview, several themes recurred. One is the issue of complex trauma. Catherine and I share the belief that journalists often experience multiple traumatic incidents, and the cumulative effect of them can impact their mental health. She also talked extensively about her relationship with her news desk and colleagues back in London. Despite the risks she often faced, she recalls feeling as if they 'didn't understand the situation'.

At one stage, there was a rise in the kidnapping of foreigners, forcing some expats to leave Iraq. She was asked by one of her London colleagues to interview and send photos of people who had chosen to stay. '"You're asking me to sign their death warrants," I told them. I was so mad at this point. They asked me to go to this place where this Brit had been kidnapped, and I told them they would be watching me. So, they said, "Can't you send one of the Iraqi staff?" I refused.'

We discussed how having strong relationships with colleagues can be protective to our mental health and I asked how she fared given the frictions she often felt. 'I stood up for myself,' she replied, even when she was asked to do things that were ethically compromising, and this spared her from experiencing moral injury. She described a period shortly after the death of her friend, in which 'it just felt as though there was a bomb around every corner' as she travelled from Baghdad to Bali, Delhi to Jordan, narrowly avoiding getting physically hurt by several explosions. 'The one in Baghdad: I was asleep in bed, the windows came in, half the ceiling came down, I rolled under the bed, because you always knew there would be another.' If relationships with those in the newsrooms left a lot to be desired, those shared with colleagues on the ground brought comfort, camaraderie and sometimes comedy:

> I was in this windowless shell of an apartment. It was November 2005, and I had this photographer living with me, an old friend who'd moved into this apartment. We're [. . .] reading this stuff online and it was like doing a quiz out of *Cosmo[politan* magazine]. And it says PTSD symptoms last longer than four weeks, so we both decided that when the bomb went off was the moment. I was really empirical about it and walked away, thinking, 'I have got four weeks.' I had no concept that you can intervene before PTSD.

After being diagnosed, she was off work for several months, and had extended treatment, including Eye Movement Desensitisation and Reprocessing (EMDR). 'I went on the recommendation of a friend. The medical doctor

I saw in 2005 said, "In a way, you're lucky. We have seen too many of these cases. We can't have someone of your age essentially invalided off work." So I got treated and went back.'

On her return to work, there were new traumas. In 2008, her colleague Richard Mills took his life while they were in Zimbabwe. Catherine found his body and described how much more complicated and traumatic the process was because they were working undercover.

Our interview immediately preceded her return to cover the conflict in Ukraine. I asked her – given the extent of her exposure to trauma – what helped her mental health. She explained she felt she'd gained in confidence as she became more experienced, which helped her if she felt poorly treated by her managers. But she expressed concern that others don't have that privilege:

> I still don't think there is enough outreach. If I was 27 and hoping to make it big, I still don't think I would know what to do. I still don't think it's signposted. I was filling out a risk assessment the other day and it was asking about the potential for psychological trauma, and there was no box to tick [for] my own resilience. I think it is very difficult to prepare people for how they will react, for what you're going to experience. I do know there are danger signals, preconditions, and that these include poor support and not having a strong team, not having people who have your back.

We ended our conversation speaking about empathy, the idea that the soft skills that make us good journalists, that help us connect with those whose stories we share, are skills we can use to help promote the wellbeing of those around us:

> They do say you can't teach empathy. If I had no empathy, I wouldn't be any good at my job. The best journalists are empathetic; they are also the best team members. Are they vulnerable to psychological damage? Yes, that's what makes them human, but they are also able to do the emotional work to recover. I would not want to have done my job without empathy. It would have been grim. I can think of no greater glory than helping your friends when something shit happens.

Notes

17 Based on author interview with Catherine Philp, April 2023, and her article below
18 Catherine Philp (2008) 'Trauma, kidnap and death: all in a day's work for journalists in Iraq', *The Times*, 20 March. Available at: https://www.thetimes.co.uk/article/trauma-kidnap-and-death-all-in-a-days-work-for-journalists-in-iraq-lw8fgxkxk59

7 Vicarious trauma

The word 'trauma' stems from the Greek for 'wound' or 'piercing'. 'Vicarious' has its roots in the Latin, meaning 'taking the place of another'. Vicarious trauma is exposure to someone else's trauma and is sometimes also called secondary trauma. It can have a significant impact on journalists' mental health and, if left untreated, vicarious trauma can lead to post-traumatic stress disorder (PTSD), as discussed in the previous chapter. Experts have described it as having a 'drip, drip effect', or being like 'toxic radiation'. We may not realise at the time that we are being harmed.

Research shows there is a real risk that people working in our industry can be seriously impacted by frequent or repeated exposure to distressing or traumatic material or by witnessing the suffering of others. Unfortunately, vicarious trauma is still overlooked by some journalists and managers, who incorrectly consider it less valid than other forms of trauma that might impact journalists directly. This speaks to the need for more awareness of what vicarious trauma is and how it affects people, as well as what organisations, individuals and the industry can do to mitigate and recognise it, and support those who experience it.

The Dart Center defines vicarious trauma as 'psychological changes resulting from cumulative, empathetic engagement with trauma survivors in a professional context'.[1] It explains that the term was 'originally coined to reflect both the positive and negative experience of therapists working with trauma survivors but has been expanded to others such as social workers, humanitarian workers and journalists'. It offers a reminder that negative vicarious traumatisation can lead to psychological injury.

Journalists can experience vicarious trauma through interaction with distressing material in various forms of media. This might include interviewing survivors of trauma, hearing and reading court reports, and researching crimes, disasters and other traumatic incidents. It might include editing images and videos, verifying content or being exposed to misinformation and disinformation, as well as working on graphics. This list is not exhaustive but shows that people can be exposed in different ways. What is more, individuals have different trauma triggers. In any of these cases, doing this work repeatedly can put us at risk if protective measures are not in place. Given the risk and reality of vicarious

DOI: 10.4324/9781003344179-7

trauma, newsrooms should consider putting in place support for those exposed, from preparatory tools and training to resources such as peer networks and professional therapists. There should also be buy-in from leaders who normalise these conversations and recognise that some stories take their toll.

As mentioned, it is normal for people to react in certain ways to distressing material, perhaps feeling sadness, anger and frustration.[2] We need to be aware of when our responses do not feel normal to us. It is also important to take note, should we *not* react, as becoming desensitised or disassociated may mean our mental health has been impacted. Symptoms take on clinical significance when they interfere with work, disrupt relationships, cause distress or create combinations of these, according to the research by Professor Anthony Feinstein.[3]

Sam Dubberley, head of digital investigations at Human Rights Watch, was an author of a pioneering report into vicarious trauma by First Draft News and used the phrase 'digital frontline' to show how those working in newsrooms could be impacted. He contributed to a resource created by Headlines Network and explained how this 'can manifest [. . .] through general burnout, loss of faith in the world [. . .] or kind of a general questioning, why am I doing this? What am I doing this for?'[4]

Dhruti Shah, a freelance journalist who has experienced vicarious trauma herself, said different people have different reactions, and gave this example for the Headlines Network resource: 'Perhaps there's more risky behaviour, relating to drugs, relating to things you perhaps wouldn't usually do.'[5]

As well as being able to notice our own reactions, it is also helpful for us to be aware of when others might be impacted. Dr Sian Williams, who has researched the impact of vicarious trauma on journalists, explained:

> I would start worrying about a colleague if they were avoiding work, withdrawing from social activities, or perhaps plunging themselves back into it and not perhaps processing it, not standing back, and reflecting on what had happened [and not] being aware of what else is going on in their life.[6]

Since the earliest conversations around journalism and trauma, it's been accepted that journalists can experience trauma through their reporting in the field. However, the idea of being affected by exposure to someone else's trauma while still working in the newsroom environment is a relatively new concept. It really started to be considered during the Arab uprisings, when the growth of social media allowed for a huge increase in user-generated content from revolutions and conflicts in the Middle East.

'We were seeing the Arab uprisings and the first beheading videos,' said Mark Little, a journalist who founded the news verification agency Storyful. 'I remember realising that our journalists working on laptops in Dublin were witnessing more horrific and gruesome imagery than I had ever seen in war zones.'[7]

At around the same time, militant groups like the Islamic State started to weaponise social media platforms for their own propaganda. Videos that showed the worst of what humans could do to each other did not come with warning signs.

The first study into the impact on journalists of exposure to uncensored graphic images was published in August 2014,[8] when Professor Feinstein, Blair Audet and Elizabeth Waknine studied the responses of journalists from three international newsrooms. They discovered that the frequency of the exposure was more consequential than its duration, and that frequent exposure to violent video and other media put journalists at risk of psychological injury, such as depression, anxiety and post-traumatic stress disorder. The research found that many of those impacted had little experience they could draw on to prepare them for the kind of content to which they were exposed. Nor were they supported to recognise the purpose of their work. At the time, Bruce Shapiro, the head of the Dart Center for Journalism and Trauma, was quoted in Journalism.co.uk as saying that 'trauma is a violation of the social contract'.[9] This study was groundbreaking. Speaking about its impact to me in July 2022,[10] Feinstein explained:

> We showed that while journalists were not experiencing danger – they were not in any personal risk or danger – looking at horrible visual material for six, seven hours a day, for some people was very traumatic. What happened at the same time, and I think our research might have influenced this, is that the American Psychiatric Association changed the criteria for PTSD. They tweaked the criterion, and [. . .] There in the small print was this thing that basically acknowledged what journalists were going through: if, in your line of work, you are exposed to a relentless flow of traumatic images, that can be considered sufficient stress for PTSD. Now, we're very clear in stating that this doesn't apply to the general population [who] watch the nightly news. This was something for a profession whose job entailed looking at trauma.[11]

In early 2015, another landmark publication by First Draft News[12] built upon Feinstein's study by surveying and interviewing staff working for news, human rights and humanitarian organisations. It found that 'PTSD is now a real and serious issue for office-bound staff'. Fortunately, at the same time, it noted that 'vicarious trauma is now being recognised more widely as a real and serious issue'. It is accepted as a real and serious issue across many parts of the industry. However, this has not yet permeated all newsrooms.

Vicarious trauma came up frequently in conversations for this book. Many interviewees recognised it as a major challenge facing newsrooms, and one that was still not afforded the necessary resources because news leaders frequently regard it as being less significant than trauma encountered when journalists are reporting in person. This in turn may exacerbate the stigma and shame felt by those who experience vicarious traumatisation.

Some of those I spoke with did not distinguish, or scarcely differentiated, between primary and secondary trauma. This is an interesting point for news leaders to consider. Exposure to trauma can leave our brains unable to recognise whether we are experiencing it in situ or remotely. If we acknowledge this, it may help reduce some of the stigma and guilt that often accompanies vicarious trauma, and the notion that secondary trauma is somehow less important than its primary cousin.

Cait McMahon is the former head of Dart Asia Pacific, and she explained her reservations around distinguishing between different types of trauma:

> As a psychologist, I really struggle a bit with the concept of vicarious trauma. Because, yes, you're not there. And it's not your trauma, but you're bloody exposed, I often wonder if it's just primary trauma, frankly. So I tend not to talk about vicarious trauma so much these days, because I think it's almost, like, trauma is trauma, whether you're there or not, or you're hearing about it, or you're [. . .] interviewing someone, and they're talking about really graphic details of their child being murdered in front of them, you know?[13]

In early 2022, a few weeks after Russia invaded Ukraine, I received a WhatsApp from a senior journalist at a British news organisation, asking for help. They were worried about colleagues covering the conflict from London, one of whom had confided in them, saying they were on the verge of a breakdown. When my colleague rang their editor to express concern, they were told: 'Isn't this a bit indulgent? There are people dying.'

Not only is this attitude incorrect, but it is also dangerous. It advances the myth that journalists need to be iron-clad, that they must not admit any weakness. Recognising the trauma experienced by someone whose story we share through our work should not invalidate our own experiences as journalists. Sadly, people in conflict and disaster do suffer and die. Journalists covering distressing and dangerous stories are at risk of being impacted in the field and the office. It is not indulgent to want to help those impacted by their work. It is indulgent to live in such an ivory tower that you fail to support your colleagues. This attitude risks entrenching stigma and cultures where people cannot speak openly and their mental health is compromised further, leading to a point where it will affect their ability to work, and their journalism.

We need these conversations to be normalised, with news leaders raising awareness that stories can affect people, and showing empathy with those impacted. Dr Sian Williams, the broadcaster and counselling psychologist, has researched the impact of vicarious trauma on journalist colleagues:

> One of my participants had never left the office but was screening footage from the attacks in Syria [. . .] and she was seeing a lot of really difficult stuff with children who had been burned by chemical attacks in Syria, and she was seeing it repeatedly, over and over and over again.[14]

The journalist found it difficult to get away from the images and experienced nightmares and flashbacks. Dr Williams said the woman felt very alone doing her work, 'because it was just her and the images':

> The words that she used with me were: 'I feel like an emotional vampire.' You know, the need for the material was huge. And her bosses wanted her to keep going through it to get the most awful images. And she felt really guilty, that she was seeing people dying, children dying, in order to put it out on the news when she was unable to do anything about it.

In our conversations around mental health, Dr Williams often brought up the value of recognising that we are bearing witness, and how this can remind us of our sense of purpose and be protective for our mental health:

> We know that if she were to go back to why she was a journalist in the first place, and what was really important for her, it was to bring attention to a ghastly story and to see the atrocities, and for people to know what was really going on. But, in the course of that, she felt she was unable to cope. And that was really difficult.

For Dean Yates, the former journalist wellbeing and mental health advocate for Reuters, it's important to recognise that it is not always the people in the obvious roles in newsrooms who are affected; nor does the phenomenon always coincide with major conflicts and crises:

> Vicarious trauma is obviously a significant problem, but it was not something that I thought about until I actually got into this Reuters role. What was really striking to me was [when] I started in 2017, there were no big wars going on at the time. I don't think there were any major humanitarian disasters at the time. But what struck me very quickly was the number of people that were talking about vicarious trauma. And I hadn't really encountered this before.
> And it wasn't just the video editors and the pictures editors. I remember a graphics journalist talking to me one time about what it was like doing graphic after graphic of school shootings in the US. And it sort of made sense, right? These things were happening all the time in the States, and this woman was having to do these very detailed graphics, of where the shooter went. And so, for that, she would have to review video, photographs, this sort of stuff, to be able to produce a graphic.
> And so it quickly became apparent to me that, at Reuters anyway, vicarious trauma was actually a bigger threat to the staff than the old-fashioned trauma of going to war or going to an earthquake or a tsunami. And not only that, but the people who were exposed to this were really not trained or prepared. Some of them hadn't even done a hostile environment course, for example, because they're sitting in an office

somewhere in New York or London or Mexico City, monitoring social media, often 25 years old.[15]

Yates, like Williams, said shame was a big barrier for people getting support: They're too ashamed to seek help. I get these young journalists who say, 'I'd never compare my trauma to yours.' And I say, 'I just have to stop you there. You can't compare. The brain doesn't distinguish between whether you're in Baghdad or New York, right?' It's like, when the Christchurch massacre occurred in the Sydney newsroom, they're all crowded around the video, watching it over and over again, with the sound turned up because they're trying to verify if it's real. That's one day.

Yates would like to see the media industry undergo a major awareness campaign along the lines of the safety campaign that took place in the late 1990s and the turn of the century. 'I think vicarious trauma is that damaging that – I get a lot of young journalists talk to me about this sort of stuff – it is also driving journalists out of the profession; a lot of them don't know how to seek help.'

Joyce Adeluwoye-Adams MBE is head of diversity, editorial at Reuters. She joined after the period that Yates referenced but noted that many within the global newsroom were affected by vicarious trauma at that time:

> I think the world has become more stressful for journalists, with UGC [user-generated content] and vicarious trauma. And, when we used to think about PTSD, we thought about it through the lens of conflict zones, but, actually, I found in the newsroom that the people who are suffering from vicarious trauma or PTSD are the ones who are working on a really distressing story or dealing with distressing images. These are not things that we necessarily spoke about a few years ago.[16]

The pandemic changed the working conditions for journalists, and this brought additional pressures to those at risk of vicarious trauma. It is particularly important that the journalism industry starts to recognise the toll it can take. With an increase in remote working, more individuals are exposed to distressing material on digital devices and in settings that might also be used for leisure activities. Journalists might view graphic content in their bedroom or living rooms, or on devices they use to communicate with friends or family. This blurring of boundaries between work and personal lives can be problematic. Working remotely, journalists can't turn immediately to colleagues and explain they have just witnessed something awful. The sense of isolation is compounded when people feel disconnected from colleagues who could provide a listening ear, a shared language or spontaneous support. It is particularly important that leaders recognise the risks arising from this, particularly for more junior colleagues, who might have joined during the pandemic, who might never have been given the tools to deal with distressing material.

It is also worth noting the stressors that journalists might face if working remotely when they have carer responsibilities, or share their living and working spaces with others, such as young children, who they would want to protect from such material. These are just some of the added complications brought about by the pandemic, which also exposed many journalists to unprecedented levels of distressing material.

So what are some of the practical things that can be done to mitigate the risk of vicarious trauma, to recognise it and to respond when people are affected? To answer this, it is helpful to break it down into three areas: people, processes and purpose.

In the first instance, news leaders need to normalise conversations. Sam Dubberley said it is not always easy to create that culture, but it is necessary and a much better option than having people suffer:

> It's important that if you lead a team, you create a culture where it's okay to talk about the challenges of reporting remotely. If you're not creating that culture in a team, you're setting yourself up for problems down the road. Setting up that culture, however, is hard. It feels very contrived – because it often is. You have to work through that first bit of pain of saying: 'Hey, we're going to talk about feelings. We're going to talk about how everyone's doing.'[17]

Dhruti Shah explained that a person's identity or history can make them more vulnerable to trauma, and it's really important that news managers are attuned to this, that they make time for their colleagues to understand how they really are and to recognise that sometimes people may not feel able to cover certain stories because of their individual experiences. People's emotional loads vary, so this may also impact how vulnerable they are to vicarious trauma. Again, if managers are aware of this, it will help mitigate the risk.

In addition, rotating people between stressful and less stressful jobs offers them time to decompress. It is good practice, after individuals cover hostile environments, and when people are exposed remotely to trauma, to give them time to rest and recover. In these cases, managers should ensure they do not make the person feel as if they are being punished by being taken off a job temporarily.

Dr Williams' advice to managers is: 'Find time to have conversations. You know news is busy, journalists are busy. It's almost more important in a heightened traumatic news event or environment to [have these conversations].'[18]

Checking in needn't take long. When journalists know managers care, this can significantly bolster their mental health and reduce their risk of vicarious trauma. Regular conversations are extremely important when people work remotely. If individuals are impacted, they need to feel there is someone they can trust and speak to without fear of judgement or retribution. This person may not always be their manager. For journalists to really feel supported, conversations should take place on a regular basis, because trust needs to be built and maintained. Managers need to appreciate that there might be occasions when journalists do not feel comfortable covering certain stories, and the journalists need to know they can report their concerns without repercussions.

But if you work alone, rarely see colleagues or are freelance, this might be more difficult. In this case, Dubberley suggested creating a network of support wherever that can be found: 'Hopefully in organisations, it's a lot more easily found, but for those freelancers and consultants out there, I think it can also be found through colleagues who are doing similar work.'

Aside from creating a culture that acknowledges the impact of dealing with graphic content, there are specific practical steps that might help people mitigate some of the risks of covering trauma remotely. These will differ between individuals, but the following suggestions might provide a layer of armour for those exposed.

- Repeated exposure increases the likelihood of vicarious trauma, so it is important to limit time with the material. Actively scheduling breaks and ensuring we set reminders to take them can help us step away. The nature of the news business might seem at odds with this, but Shah advised: 'Just because you're in a professional team doesn't mean that having a break is an unprofessional thing to do.'
- It is also helpful to have clear boundaries between our personal and professional lives. This is not always easy, especially with remote work. Drew Berrie from Mind, the mental health charity in England and Wales, suggests a 'ceremony',[19] to mark the transition at the beginning of the working day and the end. This might be opening or closing one's laptop, going on a walk, changing rooms, lighting a candle, or something else. His advice and that of other colleagues cited throughout this chapter was originally used in a practical resource created by Headlines Network.
- Self-care is often something we overlook, but – as well as ensuring breaks – we should remember the value to our wellbeing of eating properly, getting sufficient sleep and exercise, and physically stepping away from our devices. There is more on self-care in Chapter 12, but when dealing with distressing material, it's vital we make time to see people whose company we enjoy, or practise activities that bring us joy too.
- Exposure can be limited in technical ways too. Graphic videos should be watched without sound initially, with the screen minimised, with auto-play off and, where possible, with specific images blurred. There might be a tendency to watch things repeatedly, or to expose multiple people to the same graphic material, so taking practical steps to consider workflows can mitigate this. 'Spreadsheets can actually be your friend,' said Shah. 'You can put down what you've already seen or heard so someone on your team doesn't need to necessarily see or hear the same thing.'[20]
- When working with colleagues, include warnings on the material so they are more prepared. In addition to precautions, an important way of protecting our mental health is to remind ourselves of the purpose of our work, that we are 'bearing witness'.

Gina Chua is now executive editor of Semafor, formerly at Reuters. She was a guest on one of Headlines Network's podcasts, and spoke about mitigation techniques, as well as the importance of recognising that exposure to graphic content is often an unavoidable part of journalists' jobs:

> You click on a link, you open something, there's a visual you need to look at or there's an account you need to read or a testimony you need to hear, and it can affect you, and the only way you can deal with that is to, I think at this point, reduce the amount of exposure, to take breaks, to share it around people. But at the end of the day, if there's ten videos that have to be watched, [there's] ten videos that have to be watched. You can spread them over ten people, so it's not one person; you can spread them over 20 people; you can spread them over ten days – but they're still being watched by somebody at the end of it all.[21]

Phil Chetwynd, the Global News Director at Agence France-Presse, is extremely concerned about the way in which his colleagues are often exposed to difficult material:

> You can't do enough training on vicarious trauma and difficult images. So we've done a lot of that [for] anybody who uses a smartphone, let alone anyone who sits at an editing desk and deals with difficult images. That sort of proactive, practical help, I think, generally goes a long way. And there's also again, the same effect, when somebody calls you up: the fact that the company shows you that this is important to your domain, that these are issues that are on the table, and we insist that you will be trained on this.
>
> I think that helps in creating this whole culture of a caring company, and that allows people to speak about it. As soon as you do a training course on this, people will then start speaking openly about it and say, 'Well, actually, yeah, I had a terrible time last year, with this or that.' So, the more support you can give, I think the more people feel comforted in coming forward.[22]

Notes

1 Isobel Thompson (2021) 'Dart Center Style Guide for Trauma-Informed Journalism', 22 June. Available at: https://dartcenter.org/resources/dart-center-style-guide
2 Headlines Network (2022) *Vicarious Trauma Guidelines*. Available at: https://img1.wsimg.com/blobby/go/6ca5410e-ac1d-4642-b85f-b717e6a71453/downloads/Vicarious%20Trauma%20Guidelines%202022.pdf?ver=1676045989580
3 Author Interview with Professor Anthony Feinstein, July 2022
4 Headlines Network video resource on vicarious trauma, Part 2. Available at: https://www.youtube.com/watch?v=bLLPyq4mbaY
5 See video, fn 4
6 See video, fn 4
7 Headlines Network, (2022) *Behind the Headlines*, Episode 7: Mark Little, [podcast]. Available at: https://audioboom.com/posts/8111138-mark-little

Vicarious trauma

8. Anthony Feinstein, Blair Audet and Elizabeth Waknine (2014) 'Witnessing images of extreme violence: a psychological study of journalists in the newsroom', JRSM Open. 2014;5(8). Available at: https://journals.sagepub.com/doi/10.1177/2054270414533323
9. Alastair Reid (2014) 'How are journalists at risk of vicarious trauma from UGC?' journalism.co.uk, 13 October. Available at: https://www.journalism.co.uk/news/how-are-journalists-at-risk-of-vicarious-trauma-from-ugc-/s2/a562758/
10. Professor Anthony Feinstein, July 2022
11. Author interview with Professor Anthony Feinstein, July 2022
12. Sam Dubberley, Elizabeth Griffin and Haluk Mert Bal (2015) 'Making Secondary Trauma a Primary Issue: A Study of Eyewitness Media and Vicarious Trauma on the Digital Frontline' First Draft News, 11 January. Available at: https://firstdraftnews.org/articles/making-secondary-trauma-primary-issue-study-eyewitness-media-vicarious-trauma-digital-frontline
13. Author interview with Dr Cait McMahon, August 2022
14. Author interview with Dr Sian Williams, April 2023
15. Author interview with Dean Yates, September 2022
16. Author interview with Joyce Adeluwoye-Adams, January 2023
17. Headlines Network (2022) *Vicarious Trauma Guidelines*. Available at: https://img1.wsimg.com/blobby/go/6ca5410e-ac1d-4642-b85f-b717e6a71453/downloads/Vicarious%20Trauma%20Guidelines%202022.pdf?ver=1676045989580
18. See video, fn 4
19. Conversation for Headlines Network in June 2023
20. See video, fn 4
21. Headlines Network, (2022) *Behind the Headlines*, Episode 6: Gina Chua, [podcast]. Available at: https://audioboom.com/posts/8096662-gina-chua
22. Author interview with Phil Chetwynd, May 2023

Reference list

Dubberley, S., Griffin E. and Bal, H.M. (2015) 'Making Secondary Trauma a Primary Issue: A Study of Eyewitness Media and Vicarious Trauma on the Digital Frontline' First Draft News, 11 January. Available at: https://firstdraftnews.org/articles/making-secondary-trauma-primary-issue-study-eyewitness-media-vicarious-trauma-digital-frontline

Feinstein, A., Audet, B. and Waknine, E. (2014) 'Witnessing images of extreme violence: a psychological study of journalists in the newsroom', JRSM Open. 2014;5(8). Available at: https://journals.sagepub.com/doi/10.1177/2054270414533323

Headlines Network (2022) *Vicarious Trauma Guidelines*. Available at: https://img1.wsimg.com/blobby/go/6ca5410e-ac1d-4642-b85f-b717e6a71453/downloads/Vicarious%20Trauma%20Guidelines%202022.pdf?ver=1676045989580

Headlines Network (2022) *Vicarious Trauma Guidelines*. Available at: https://img1.wsimg.com/blobby/go/6ca5410e-ac1d-4642-b85f-b717e6a71453/downloads/Vicarious%20Trauma%20Guidelines%202022.pdf?ver=1676045989580

Headlines Network video resource on vicarious trauma, Part 2. Available at: https://www.youtube.com/watch?v=bLLPyq4mbaY

Headlines Network, (2022) *Behind the Headlines*, Episode 6: Gina Chua, [podcast]. Available at: https://audioboom.com/posts/8096662-gina-chua

Reid, A. (2014) 'How are journalists at risk of vicarious trauma from UGC?' journalism.co.uk, 13 October. Available at: https://www.journalism.co.uk/news/how-are-journalists-at-risk-of-vicarious-trauma-from-ugc-/s2/a562758/

Thompson, I. (2021) 'Dart Center Style Guide for Trauma-Informed Journalism', 22 June. Available at: https://dartcenter.org/resources/dart-center-style-guide

Their story – Amantha Perera[23]

Amantha Perera is a Sri Lankan journalist who lives in Australia, where he is a PhD researcher in the School of Education and the Arts at Central Queensland University and project lead, Dart Asia Pacific. He began his career during 'the most brutal period of the Civil War' in Sri Lanka, working for the pro-opposition *Sunday Leader* newspaper, which he describes as being 'run on a shoestring budget':

> I got all kinds of opportunities to do things that I wanted to do. And one of them was reporting on the war. That was how I cut my teeth. I covered the war, going through some of the most brutal things that you could witness, including suicide bombings, including massacres of children, civilians, all that, but I never kind of realised the impact the story was having on me.

After spending a year at a journalism school in the United States, he returned to cover the Indian Ocean tsunami, still not recognising the toll of being exposed to extensive trauma. In 2009, his editor and mentor, Lasantha Wickremtunge, was assassinated on the streets of the capital, Colombo:

> The moment I heard that something had happened to Lasantha, I instinctively grabbed a camera [. . .] I'm not a photographer, I used to take pictures, because it was easy for me and it was also a way that I could market myself as a freelance, so they would get the full package. But I just grabbed the camera, and I went, and I started clicking images. Years later, when I looked at the images that I had taken, I had hundreds of images of the murder site, of the funeral, and, looking back, I kind of realised that the camera was like a flak jacket for me that I had instinctively put on to cover myself from the impact of the tragedy.
>
> I covered Lasantha's murder for quite some time without even realising this, but then somewhere towards 2010-ish, I started getting angry at this story. And because this was such a huge story, and because [President Mhainda] Rajapaksa was in power, the war had ended, every anniversary of the murder, it became big news. And all these international outlets wanted the story. But I kind of realised that every time I had to report on this murder, I became really angry. I became angry at Lasantha for letting himself get into this. I became angry at his family, his friends, for allowing him to put himself in such a dangerous situation. And also, I became angry at myself, probably for the same reasons. And the anger was kind of eating me from inside. It was making me really uncomfortable. And I knew that even though I hadn't really taken any concrete interventions, my journalism, when it came to reporting on that murder, and the murder's aftermath, was suffering, because I was kind of having this emotional weight on me.

It was at this stage that a colleague of Amantha's told him about the Dart Center for Journalism and Trauma. He applied and received a fellowship in 2011.

> That's where I started kind of looking seriously into the impact of trauma on my journalism. And soon after my fellowship, I came back and I looked at the stories that I had written, then I started realising [that] this is why I was having this kind of reaction to this story. Years later, I also realised that there was accumulated trauma of reporting on the war, reporting on the tsunami, and also reporting in a really repressive media environment where I had seen my colleagues killed, and flee the country.
>
> I had also tried to keep that impact bottled in because I had kind of come through in journalism, in this culture, in this set-up, which is steeped in the bulletproof journalism culture. You don't acknowledge any of these things. You just go through this. You know, you're a journalist, you're supposed to suck it up and go through this. When I look back at the coverage of the war, I understand that because I was talking [about] and reporting [on] this brutal war, that was happening in my own community; it had an impact on me.
>
> I remember [that] the foreign correspondents and the wire service reporters, who used to be based in Colombia, would always say, 'You have to have this kind of objective approach to the war.' I mean, it's easy when you don't live in that community. It's very difficult when you report the war, when you go back home and the war is the subject of your dinner table, the war is the subject [the] next day when you're thinking, 'Can I send my kids to school?'
>
> But we never acknowledge that. So, I think it's been a journey which has been difficult, but it's also been a journey, in some ways, that has been really fulfilling. Because now when I go back and talk to colleagues from Asia, and from parts of the world where I come from, I kind of understand the value that this kind of work can give them. When I first had this conversation, on trauma and the impact on me, and went back home, it was impossible to even to get a word in sideways on this. The whole journalism community, the culture, was still in that bulletproof mentality: you go out, you report, you come back, and we are these kickass kind of personas who do this.
>
> And this was across the board – there was no difference between male and female. It was very, very difficult to even have this conversation with very senior figures, and because there was no buy-in from the senior colleagues; the newcomers and juniors – even though they wanted to talk about it – didn't have the opportunity.
>
> One thing that kind of worked in my favour was that nobody could deny the fact that I walked the walk, that I had reported on the war, gone to these regions; I had experienced what war was like, but even

then, it was very difficult. I think what has changed is that, gradually, people have come to realise that we are strong, or we have a community that reports on these very traumatic events, and yet that doesn't mean we don't get affected.

In 2022, Sri Lanka went through seismic social changes when almost the entire country rose up to oust the once powerful Gotabaya Rajapaksa and the Rajapaksa clan from power. I went back to Sri Lanka to work with journalists on psychosocial safety after the protest wave. What I saw was not only the impact of the social unrest and an unprecedented economic meltdown, but also years of accumulated trauma, years of continuous community trauma. But the difference from a decade back is that journalists, especially from Asian backgrounds like in Sri Lanka, are now willing to talk about vulnerability. This is a big change from the bulletproof era.

Note

23 Taken from author interview with Amantha Perera, November 2022

8 Moral injury

> You talk to any journalists about the moral dimension of their trauma. It's like a light bulb goes off. It's not just the trauma that they have witnessed or experienced; it's also the betrayal in the newsroom that they've experienced in multiple ways.[1]
>
> —Dean Yates

Moral injury is a concept that has only been studied in relation to journalists since 2016, with a much longer history of research in the military. Although, anecdotally, it has long been an issue affecting some of our colleagues, the term itself is still relatively unfamiliar in our industry. It is something that Professor Anthony Feinstein, with whom I co-authored the first study into moral injury in the media, believes poses a real challenge for our industry.

Moral injury is defined as 'the injury done to a person's conscience or moral compass when that person perpetrates, witnesses or fails to prevent acts that transgress their own moral and ethical values or codes of conduct'.[2] In simpler terms, moral injury has been described as 'a bruise to the soul',[3] and is often linked to emotions such as guilt, anger or shame. Unlike post-traumatic stress disorder, it is not a mental health diagnosis. If left unaddressed, it can lead to a sense of disillusionment, bringing with it the risk that journalists might distance themselves from their work, as well as ultimately being a significant risk to our mental health.

It comes as no surprise to journalists that some of the ethical and moral choices we make in our work impact us, affecting our emotions and behaviours, even if we did not have a term to describe it. We have also long been aware that our work can put us in situations where we feel our core belief system is compromised. Journalists are often among the first responders to a scene, sometimes there even before paramedics, police or firefighters. Though our role is to report on news events, at times we are required to step outside of that role. In such situations, boundaries can become blurred, and we may find ourselves forced to choose between stepping in to help those around us and covering the events as a journalist.

The term 'moral injury' was coined by US psychiatrist Jonathan Shay, based on his studies with military patients, as well as his readings of Homer's

DOI: 10.4324/9781003344179-8

Iliad – demonstrating just how long humans have been affected by it. In a 2014 essay for the American Psychological Association (APA), Shay reflected on his work on the issue and offered his explanation of moral injury,[4] writing:

> Moral injury is present when there has been (a) a betrayal of 'what's right'; (b) either by a person in legitimate authority (my definition), or by one's self – 'I did it' (Litz, Maguen, Nash, et al.); (c) in a high stakes situation. Both forms of moral injury impair the capacity for trust and elevate despair, suicidality, and interpersonal violence. They deteriorate character.

He noted that, from his perspective, moral injury is something 'we can do something about. It is, to a degree, within our control.'

Journalist Matthew Green, a former colleague of mine from Reuters, wrote a book called *Aftershock* about the experiences of British military veterans who suffered psychological injury and, in his words, 'how the system essentially fails them and what might be a viable alternative'.[5] Green was motivated to write the book in part because he had experienced depression while serving as a correspondent in Pakistan and Afghanistan and he wanted to better understand trauma and recovery.

> Although the book was about the military, it struck me as an opportunity to actually dive deep into the question of how does anyone transmute trauma and suffering into, shall we say, wisdom and inner peace? So, I don't write about my own experience, particularly in the book, but I was using the soldiers' stories as a vehicle to explore that bigger question. And it was a great opportunity, because it dramatically opened my own perspective on trauma and how it impacts people, and what the mental health system does or doesn't do, but what could be done that would be much more effective. And that's definitely informed my subsequent conversations about mental health in the media. A lot of the issues are similar. Stigma is a huge issue in both systems. The other big theme in any institution is feeling betrayed or let down by the chain of command – whether that's literally the chain of command in the military, or the management of media organisations: that moral injury is very common in both contexts.[6]

My own interest in moral injury has a personal motivation, connected to my repeat exposure to situations in which I saw and felt a sense of betrayal of what I deemed ethical by people in authority, leading me to question my role as a journalist. I only really became aware of how I was impacted after co-authoring the first paper that considered moral injury in the media, with Professor Feinstein.

In 2015, unprecedented numbers of refugees were fleeing to Europe, in what became one of the biggest stories of human migration in living memory.

At the time, I was director of the International News Safety Institute, a journalists' safety organisation,[7] where – as part of my work – I coordinated safety discussions between some of the world's leading news organisations. While the refugee crisis was unprecedented in scale, it was not a story where the physical safety of journalists was a major issue. And yet, during a meeting at the headquarters of Agence France-Presse to share logistical and safety information about coverage, it became clear that many colleagues were being affected by their work.

With the support of AFP and several other major news organisations, Professor Feinstein and I researched the emotional impact of the refugee crisis on journalists who were covering it.[8] Our work was published by the Reuters Institute for the Study of Journalism (RISJ)[9] and, although we did not consider the issue of moral injury as we began our research, it emerged as the 'single biggest psychological challenge facing journalists covering the refugee crisis'.

As discussed throughout this book, everyone is different and has different experiences of mental health. But because of the degree to which our colleagues were reporting symptoms of moral injury, we wanted to try and determine what might make certain individuals more susceptible to it, so we considered the demographic, work-related and clinical factors associated with it. We found that:

> journalists with children recorded more moral injury-related distress, as did those with a higher workload within the past year. Journalists working alone rather than with colleagues reported that they were more likely to have acted in ways that violated their own moral code [. . .]. Those who had not covered war previously were more likely to record violating their own moral code by failing to do something they felt they should have done. Those who said they had not received the necessary support from their organisation were more likely to admit seeing things they perceived as morally wrong. Less control over resources required to report on the refugee crisis correlated significantly with moral injury and depression.

One other important group that was considered at risk of moral injury were journalists who were covering the story closer to home: 'Moral injury scores correlated significantly with guilt. Greater guilt, in turn, was noted by journalists covering the story close to home and by those who had assisted the refugees.'

We also showed that moral injury can cause 'considerable emotional upset', and create a 'significant stumbling block' for journalists reintegrating back into society. And we noted that journalists can and do experience moral injury at the same time as PTSD and depression.

As part of our RISJ report, I interviewed several journalists at length. Two of these, Yannis Behrakis[10] from Reuters and the AFP's Will Vassilopoulos, were Greek journalists who spent significant periods on the island of Lesbos, a focal point for the refugee crisis, because of its proximity to Turkey, from where many of the refugees left by boat. Both Behrakis and Vassilopoulos won industry awards for their work covering the refugee crisis. They explained the impact that working in their own country had on them, the challenges they experienced when returning home to their families, and how they dealt with the industry recognition, which they perceived as coming on the back of other people's suffering. When interviewed, Behrakis told us:

> A lot of times you are not sure what to do: leave the camera and actively help people come out of the sea or do practical things for them, drive them up the road, or give them clothes, or take their pictures. Of course, I always think this is the way I help and this is my job, to make sure that everybody around the world knows what is happening and that is my mission.

Even though his mission was clear, his work had an emotional toll:

> I have refugee blood: my grandmother told me stories about escaping Asia Minor, basically making the same trip as the refugees from the Turkish coast to the Greek islands. So, for me it became even more of a personal story. Plus, it was the Greek factor, so I was worried that the global community might say 'the Greeks didn't do as much as they could, and they weren't good people.' [. . .] I was really worried about a lot of things.

This impact grew over time, until – experiencing nightmares – he realised he needed to take time off. It was a decision born of decades covering conflict and crises.

Vassilopoulos was one of the first journalists to Lesbos in April 2015, as the crisis was unfolding:

> Back in those days, there was very little media coverage, and few authorities and NGOs. So few, that in the early days of April, May 2015 you could find yourself alone on a beach with a dinghy landing in front of you and you had to make that choice to help. For sure, you're keeping your journalistic integrity, you're not changing history [but] the problem is there is so much grey.

Vassilopoulos recognised there were times when that grey threatened to become overwhelming, but experience helped him. Between April 2015 and April 2016, he travelled to Lesbos 13 times. 'Every time I would gain a thicker skin, then the more easily I could speak with the refugees,' he said. 'The feeling of guilt was very strong,' however, when he told the refugees that, despite their joy at arriving on Greek shores, they still had 60 kilometres to go to the town where they could be registered.

I spoke with Vassilopoulos again in March 2017, shortly before the RISJ report was finalised. He was just about to travel to Lesbos for work for the 21st time and said he had become 'comfortable with feeling uncomfortable'. But he wasn't entirely comfortable that his work had been recognised with the Rory Peck Award for News: 'There is a percentage of me that still feels that this was won on the back of human suffering, but whenever I get that feeling, it is something I am uncomfortable with, but the positive aspects outweigh that.'

In early 2017, a cross-industry group convened to confidentially discuss the findings of our research before publication. At the heart of this meeting lay the seemingly intractable issue that recurs regularly in journalism conversations the world over: the idea that ours is an industry where many are concerned that 'any admission of distress may be perceived as weakness and affect future assignment prospects'. This meeting was important in attempting to normalise some of the conversations around mental health and wellbeing, but by 2023 there was still more work to be done.

Our research and subsequent conversations helped form a set of considerations for newsrooms. Following patterns for good practice in journalism safety, we looked at how to best support journalists before, during and after their deployments to mitigate the risk of moral injury – to recognise it and respond when people have experienced it.

One of the most effective means of mitigating it is by ensuring robust relationships in newsrooms between those in leadership positions and those covering stories. Journalists need to know their stories are going to be fully resourced, that they have the support of their managers and that they will not be let down by them. This links back to Green's and Shay's findings too.

In the experience of Dean Yates, a journalist and mental health workplace trainer, this can be the difference between developing moral injury after a distressing assignment and not developing it:

> It's not just the trauma that they have witnessed or experienced; it's also the betrayal in the newsroom that they've also experienced in multiple ways, as you and Anthony wrote about in your report: like the unwillingness of news organisations to throw the kitchen sink at a story. Like in the refugee crisis, some journalists maybe felt that they weren't getting enough, they weren't able to cover that story as well as they felt they should have. And I can see the sort of decisions that might have been made.

Yates, who covered the Indian Ocean tsunami for Reuters in 2004, described how despite being exposed to horrific experiences, he felt supported by his company, which was protective for his mental health.

> I spent nearly a month up there in Aceh after the Boxing Day tsunami, saw thousands of dead bodies. I mean, it was just indescribable: the death

and destruction. I went back six months later, went back a year later. I had flashbacks, nightmares where there is a connection to flooding, water. But I never had to have a single dedicated session of therapy because I felt within myself that I gave absolutely everything to that story, every ounce of energy in my bones I gave to that story. And so did Reuters, we threw the kitchen sink [at it]. Everything we had, we threw at it.

For Yates, recognising the purpose of his work helped, and the way he carried it out:

And my way of looking at trauma in some respects is that, depending on the circumstances, how you evaluate, how you assess yourself, is really important, and how you acted in those traumatic moments, days, weeks is really critical. And I'm very proud of the work I did in Aceh. So, while it was one of the worst disasters in modern history, I was never overly traumatised by it. Because I was proud of the work I did bearing witness. I was proud to be a Reuters journalist there. No moral injury. None.

If moral injury often comes with a sense of betrayal that can be mitigated to an extent by newsrooms effectively resourcing stories, it also underscores the importance of relationships of trust and open communication. News managers should lead by example, ensure effective communication that validates the work done by their colleagues, and work to establish robust relationships with their journalists.

Journalists need to feel supported, not undermined, when they face ethical dilemmas, and they need to know that their leaders too are making decisions for the right reasons. In order for this to happen, it's important that they have not only sufficient resources but also the information and training to make decisions in difficult settings. When we wrote our report, we suspected that journalists could also suffer moral injury as a result of stories such as terrorist attacks or disasters, or other major stories. This was before the global pandemic, which many believe has also been morally injurious for journalists. One of these is Andre Picard, who wrote an opinion piece[11] for the Canadian newspaper *The Globe and Mail* in June 2021, entitled, 'The invisible wounds inflicted by pandemic journalism'. In it, he explained:

When you *just* write about the suffering of others, or watch endless video reels of horrific events, your own feelings somehow seem unworthy of mention. Bearing witness is essential. But sometimes what reporters witness can leave scars, and deep psychic wounds. 'Moral injury' is the term academics use.

David Walmsley is the Editor in Chief of *The Globe and Mail* and has collaborated with Professor Feinstein on his work around moral injury. He told me the changing nature of the social contract between journalists and their audience was taking its toll on people:

> I think the pandemic has been morally injurious. Because one knows that the only weapons you've got in the arsenal of journalism is to provide the facts. And if the facts are chosen not to be believed, then you're impotent. I think there's a big challenge when people basically conclude that the currency you have used since time immemorial is not enough. That's existential. And I think for those who care about the industry from within the industry, and for those who care about the industry, outside the industry, there's a big impact that hasn't yet been resolved.[12]

He's right. It hasn't been resolved. It is clear that moral injury is an issue and yet, as well as not being resolved, it's still not recognised to the extent it needs to be. In May 2022, the Taking Care survey[13] into the mental health, wellbeing and trauma of journalists in Canada found that less than 18% of respondents knew what moral injury was. More work needs to be done to understand this issue and how it impacts journalists. Previously, one of the barriers to awareness was the lack of a tool to detect moral injury in journalists, though there had been one for the military. However, in late 2022, the first peer-reviewed scale was published in the APA,[14] consisting of nine items to enable the better detection and understanding of moral injury. The scale is free to newsrooms, and its existence means it will be easier to quantify the prevalence of moral injury in the media, and to ascertain who is most at risk, while helping the industry develop preventative measures and methods of support for those affected.

The tool was spearheaded by Professor Feinstein, who hopes it will serve to help educate and inform newsrooms and act as a catalyst for leaders to take appropriate steps. It comes at a critical time, when Professor Feinstein sees moral injury as a major challenge, and one he believes is 'bigger than PTSD':[15]

> I think PTSD is there. And I think it brings people down very hard, undoubtedly. But I think in terms of what's challenging people now, it's moral injury, a sense of having lost our rudder, somehow; we're morally adrift. There are so many morally egregious things that are going on, and because journalists are on the front lines of it, they're confronting it in much more visceral ways than members of the other professions. You see it in medicine, you know: people are now more angry, more irritable, but they don't take it out on physicians, because they see doctors as being there to help them. They're more demanding, but they're not nasty to doctors. They need [them]. They kind of thank [them], but it's not like that with journalists.
>
> I wrote an op-ed piece for *The Globe and Mail* on the challenges of the pandemic for journalists. And the responses from the general

population stunned me because people wrote back with hostility, [saying], 'Poor journalists, why should we feel sorry for you?' It wasn't like, 'Cor, you know, you guys are doing a great job.' Some people said that. There was a lot of hostility out there, to which I thought, 'Why?' And so that's a challenge.

Not everyone agrees that moral injury is more of a challenge than PTSD, and some believe a degree of moral distress can be a motivator for change in journalism. 'I think that to an extent, we need to have these reactions to journalism, to the kind of worlds in which we exist, in order to motivate us to do better,'[16] said Professor Elana Newman of the Dart Center, adding that she thought there was an over-emphasis on moral injury:

A few years ago, everyone was like, 'Oh, my God, that's just giving me PTSD.' People using that kind of language, right. But now people are kind of like, 'Oh, my God, I've got moral injury from that.' It's because moral injury for me is so complicated to even define, right? And if I can't define it, and I've been working in it for five, six years [. . .]. Plus, it's been conflated with other things like vicarious trauma; it's been conflated with people's legitimate reactions to things as well.

Newman noted that in the military most of the treatments that are being developed for moral injury pertain to actions carried out by members of the military such as 'killing other people'.

What we see in journalists, at least in my data, is that it's about witnessing; it's not about acts. I mean, there are a few where there are acts, but it's not the same when you make an ethical mistake that ends in someone's death, as opposed to when you actually rape villagers. It's still a problem. But it's a conceptually different kind of thing. And many of the treatments that are being developed for what the military is calling moral injury just don't translate for journalists, because it's about other things. I like the idea that it's not a mental health disorder, but an ethical or spiritual one. I think that framing it as an ethical issue means that we can address these things in ethics courses; I see real advantages [in that].

Her Dart colleague Bruce Shapiro referred to Feinstein's point about moral injury being a greater challenge than PTSD, telling me:

I don't think the science bears that out, number one. But, number two, within trauma science, there is still such huge debate about what moral injury is and means, so it's a confusing, complicated discussion. Journalists are raising it in almost every conversation I have but they are raising it as a kind of comprehensive way of covering a lot of guilt, distress, shame, outrage. There's a lot packed into there that needs to be unpacked. And actually, I think that in the history of journalism, moral pain, moral distress, moral outrage have sometimes spurred journalists to do really great, important work, make huge innovations, change. Like, the moral pain of journalists covering the American Civil Rights Movement, or Vietnam, for example, led to radical change in how journalism was done, and in whose stories get told, and why.[17]

Shapiro said he believed the conversation around moral injury was still important:

But it's not only or even primarily about mental health. It overlaps into the mental health realm, but it's about a lot of other things. And I'm a little concerned about whether we're all making this messier than we should, or whether we're conflating areas. You know, there's nothing wrong with distress and outrage at covering something like migrants and refugees. We *should* be in pain about this and should feel as if our toolkit is not adequate [for] it. The question is, are we able to take action or does it become gasoline on the flames of other mental health issues?

Whatever people make of the issue of moral injury, the idea that journalists can feel morally wounded by their work is clearly not going away. In February 2023, in the aftermath of that month's earthquake in Turkey and Syria, I wrote a piece for Journalism.co.uk,[18] expressing my concern that journalists covering the disaster were at risk of moral injury, particularly local journalists. I wrote:

There may be an added sense of guilt about the responsibility they feel they carry to cover stories impacting their communities. Local journalists are often most at risk physically and psychologically [. . .] Many journalists who are currently covering the aftermath of the earthquake in Turkey and Syria may face additional challenges which could expose them to moral injury. The nature of news tells us that there will come a time when the wider world moves on and when the story drops from the headlines, even though people are still suffering terribly. That can bring a great deal of frustration, and in turn, moral injury.

Colleagues of Shapiro and Newman at the Dart Centre Asia Pacific asked me to contribute to a piece on the same subject. In it, I highlighted the importance of reminding ourselves of our work's purpose, recognising what support we have, and understanding the necessity of giving ourselves permission to take breaks:

We know that speaking with peers helps, as does having an opportunity to take breaks both during – and after – the coverage of traumatic stories. We also know how hard it can be to take ourselves away from a story that has become so important to us, so it's important for managers to ensure journalists know they are supported and valued and that taking time to rest and recover, and perhaps cover another type of story, is not a sign of weakness.[19]

In this same piece, Amantha Perera, whose story is shared in the previous section (or after the previous chapter) offered his insights. He described the toll that more than a decade of covering conflict in Sri Lanka took on him, how he thought he was 'bulletproof', but how the death of his colleague changed his perceptions. 'That's when I realised my moral boundary had been breached. The journey back from that vulnerability to psychological safety was hard; it took me nearly ten years. Understanding moral injury can help us avoid this,' he wrote.

Since the publication of the RISJ report, we've seen the concept of moral injury more widely discussed, with the conflict that resulted from Russia's invasion of Ukraine in 2022 among a raft of news stories that are morally injurious. As the BBC's Fergal Keane explained in his 2022 book, *The Madness*, this issue remains a significant threat to him. He's not alone.

> If there is likely to be a threat to my emotional stability in Ukraine now, it will not come from imminent physical danger but from 'moral injury', the hardest wound to heal because the war being what it is, the injustices keep multiplying, the ones we see and report, and the countless others we do not.[20]

Notes

1. Author interview with Dean Yates, September 2022
2. Syracuse University: The Moral Injury Project. Available at: https://moralinjuryproject.syr.edu/
3. NPR (2014) 'Moral injury Is The "signature wound" of today's veterans', NPR, 11 November. Available at: https://www.npr.org/2014/11/11/363288341/moral-injury-is-the-signature-wound-of-today-s-veterans?t=1659692760429
4. Jonathan Shay (2014) 'Moral Injury', *Psychoanalytic Psychology* 31(2), 182–91
5. Matthew Green (2015) *Aftershock* (Portobello Books, London)
6. Author interview with Matthew Green, September 2022
7. https://newssafety.org/
8. Anthony Feinstein and Hannah Storm (2017) 'The emotional toll on journalists covering the refugee crisis', Reuters Institute for the Study of Journalism. Available at: https://newssafety.org
9. https://reutersinstitute.politics.ox.ac.uk/
10. Behrakis passed away in March 2019 from cancer
11. André Picard (2021) 'Opinion: The invisible wounds inflicted by pandemic journalism', *The Globe and Mail*, 7 June. Available at: https://www.theglobeandmail.com/opinion/article-the-invisible-wounds-inflicted-by-pandemic-journalism/
12. Author interview with David Walmsley, February 2021
13. Matthew Pearson and Dave Seglins (2022) *Taking Care: A report on mental health, well-being & trauma among Canadian media workers*, Canadian Journalism Forum on Violence and Trauma. Available at: https://static1.squarespace.com/static/60a28b563f87204622eb0cd6/t/628556ab6053c80a9e1d668d/1652905646075/TakingCare_EN.pdf

14 Osmann, J. et al A. (2022). 'Validation of the Toronto Moral Injury Scale for Journalists', *Traumatology*. Available at: https://psycnet.apa.org/record/2022-93448-001
15 Interview with Professor Anthony Feinstein, July 2022
16 Interview with Professor Elana Newman, August 2022
17 Author interview with Bruce Shapiro, August 2022
18 Hannah Storm (2023) 'Journalists at risk of moral injury covering Turkey-Syria earthquake', Journalism.co.uk, 16 February. Available at: https://www.journalism.co.uk/news-commentary/journalists-at-risk-of-moral-injury-covering-turkey-syria-earthquake/s6/a1009868
19 Erin Smith et al (2023) Journalists covering the Türkiye-Syria earthquake may face moral injury', Dart Center for Journalism and Trauma, 20 February. Available at: https://dartcenter.org/resources/journalists-covering-t%C3%BCrkiye-syria-earthquake-may-face-moral-injury
20 Fergal Keane (2022) *The Madness* (William Collins, Glasgow)

Reference list

Green, M. (2015) *Aftershock* (Portobello Books, London)

Keane, F. *The Madness* (William Collins, Glasgow)

Picard, A. (2021) 'Opinion: The invisible wounds inflicted by pandemic journalism', *The Globe and Mail*, 7 June. Available at: https://www.theglobeandmail.com/opinion/article-the-invisible-wounds-inflicted-by-pandemic-journalism

Pearson, M. and Seglins, D. (2022) *Taking Care: A report on mental health, wellbeing & trauma among Canadian media workers*, Canadian Journalism Forum on Violence and Trauma. Available at: https://static1.squarespace.com/static/60a28b563f87204622eb0cd6/t/628556ab6053c80a9e1d668d/1652905646075/TakingCare_EN.pdf

NPR (2014) 'Moral injury is the "signature wound" of today's veterans', 11 November. Available at: https://www.npr.org/2014/11/11/363288341/moral-injury-is-the-signature-wound-of-today-s-veterans?t=1659692760429

Osmann, J., Page-Gould, E., Inbar, Y., Dvorkin, J., Walmsley, D., & Feinstein, A. (2022) 'Validation of the Toronto Moral Injury Scale for Journalists'. *Traumatology*. Available at: https://psycnet.apa.org/record/2022-93448-001

Shay, J. (2014) 'Moral Injury', *Psychoanalytic Psychology* 31(2), 182–191

Smith, E., Wake, A. and Ricketson, M. (2023) Journalists covering the Türkiye-Syria earthquake may face moral injury' Dart Center for Journalism and Trauma, 20 February. Available at: https://dartcenter.org/resources/journalists-covering-t%C3%BCrkiye-syria-earthquake-may-face-moral-injury

Storm, H. (2023) 'Journalists at risk of moral injury covering Turkey-Syria earthquake', Journalism.co.uk, 16 February. Available at: https://www.journalism.co.uk/news-commentary/journalists-at-risk-of-moral-injury-covering-turkey-syria-earthquake/s6/a1009868

Their story – Dean Yates[21]

Dean Yates is a mental health campaigner, trainer, journalist and survivor of PTSD, who lives in Tasmania. He became involved in the conversation around mental health and journalism after being hospitalised when he was suicidal.

> I looked around me in the psych ward. And I saw these coppers, these veterans, and I saw how broken they were, and they couldn't advocate for themselves. They could not articulate what had happened to them, how they had been abandoned by their employers, by their organisations, how they lost their identity. They couldn't tell their stories of trauma, of PTSD, [of] being tossed on the scrap heap by their organisations. And within days of my first psych ward admission, I just felt this. It was almost like a revelation that this was going to be my path in life, to become an advocate for greater awareness of PTSD, mental illness in general, for anyone.
>
> Within days of going into the psych ward – ward 17 – I could see that I was going to rediscover meaning in life by telling my story of mental illness, and by extension telling theirs. The way that first unfolded was by persuading Reuters to create this mental health role for me a few months later, which enabled me to try to change the culture at Reuters, and to be able to really make Reuters a safe place for people, for journalists around the world to seek the sort of help they need.
>
> I had big ambitions for this role. I really wanted to change the culture. I wanted to institutionalise a whole mental health approach that made the mental health of Reuters journalists as important as their physical safety in a war zone. That was the approach I took. Unfortunately, I came across severe resistance, from management, from legal, from HR, and even from some senior colleagues who felt that I was encroaching on their turf. And after three years of trying to change that culture, I had to leave because it was actually making my own mental health worse.

Dean doesn't think that conversations around mental health in journalism are anywhere near where they should be: 'There's been a couple of cases in Australia; news organisations have had quite public incidents where their journalists have been diagnosed with PTSD and so on, and I don't think it's really resulted in any significant changes in culture.' However, he points to a 2022 ruling by the High Court in Australia, as something that might change things:

> On this occasion, there was a legal case involving a solicitor for Victoria's child protection unit who developed PTSD as a result of her work. The High Court ruling was that an employer in Australia is on notice from the moment someone starts in a profession where there is a known mental health risk. If anything's going to change in Australia, it's going to be

the threat of legal action. It's not going to be because media organisations think it's the right thing to do [but] because there is finally now a law that will compel them to actually make the changes.

In the meantime, he said one way in which organisations move forward is when people in positions of seniority are motivated to share their own stories:

> I think story sharing is massively important. And so, I just love it when I hear people, journalists, share their stories of dealing with their mental health issues. And from all parts of the world, the more we can have that happen, I think that is going to bring about as much change as anything. When I look back at what was most successful at Reuters in my mental health role, [it] was a series of blogs that we did. I just started doing a couple of blogs about my own PTSD, and then a couple of my colleagues of my generation did one, Emma Thomassen and Andy Cawthorne. It was incredible and the impact those blogs had – oh my gosh. I remember Andy and Emma were gobsmacked at the reaction. They got inundated by messages of support and people saying, 'Thank you for putting into words how we've felt for so long.' Emma, being a woman managing a massively stressful bureau, talking about depression, having kids, and Andy talking about how, for him, the worst thing was the daily grind, not covering the Haiti earthquake, but the daily grind – these things were huge. And then, we ended up running about 30 blogs by the time I left Reuters; they were a sledgehammer against shame and stigma. And it didn't cost the company a cent. I think this is where there is a powerful force for change: in the power of storytelling. And, I think, journalists – it just has to happen organically – just do it. Journalists just need to tell their stories.

Note

21 Based on author interview with Dean Yates, November 2022

9 The mental health impact of online harm

Online harassment has become one of the biggest threats to many journalists' ability to do their jobs. In recent years, the scale of digital threats and attacks has grown, with a significant increase during the pandemic. The internet has introduced violence directly into the lives of journalists, and in a world where most of us are almost constantly connected to social media, it has exposed greater numbers of our colleagues to a hostile environment and brought the violence closer to home.

Journalists no longer need to leave the office to be faced with danger. The idea of media safety – once more likely to be associated with physical front lines and fault lines – is changing and online is now a new danger zone, in addition to places of civil unrest, conflict and disaster. From research and industry conversations in newsrooms, we know women journalists are more at risk from online harassment than their male counterparts. Studies and anecdotal stories indicate that people of colour and LGBTQI+ journalists are also more likely to be targeted – all people who have historically been marginalised by the news media.

Online harassment takes many forms and differs in scale, but the aims of perpetrators are usually the same: to intimidate a person, undermine their journalism and reputation, and silence them. This might be through doxxing, where an individual's personal details are shared online, pile-ons, where multiple people threaten and harass an individual at the same time, or fake accounts and images in someone else's likeness. Online threats might include graphic and sexualised threats, such as murder and rape, which can also extend to family members, including children.

Award-winning Irish journalist Patricia Devlin has received many online threats, including one to rape her baby son. I spoke with her in June 2023, and she told me she was still on a waiting list for therapy, despite her situation being deemed as urgent, and despite suspected PTSD. 'It's crazy that our jobs have given us serious mental health issues. It certainly was not something I expected when I went into journalism,'[1] she told me. Leona O'Neill, whose story is shared later in this book, found her family threatened too, which had a devastating impact on her wellbeing. Both Patricia and Leona feared for their physical safety and that of their loved ones.

DOI: 10.4324/9781003344179-9

Though it originates from the virtual sphere, online harassment has a significant correlation with physical violence. In recent years, there have been two high-profile cases in which two women journalists – Daphne Caruana Galizia in Malta, and Gauri Lankesh in India – were murdered after receiving online abuse. Rana Ayuub, whose story is shared at the end of this chapter, and Leona O'Neill have both experienced horrific online violence, which has spilled into physical threats and intimidation.

Abeer Saady is an Egyptian journalist and safety trainer. Online harassment is one of the biggest issues faced by the women she works with. In cultures where there are significant barriers to women journalists, the job can bring a psychological and physical threat, particularly where women are blackmailed with falsified sexualised images, and rumours spread about them, she told me:

> People threaten to expose them to their family, and if they don't have their family's support, this is a problem in these countries. So, the women journalists have two choices: confront the issue, expose themselves and maybe get killed by their family, because there is honour killing in many countries – in Jordan, Pakistan, Iraq. They can do this, or they stop doing journalism. So, maybe the statistics show something but [they] don't show the real thing. No one tells us how many women walk away out of this profession. And I'm speaking about women because the gender here is very important with the culture.[2]

Even though online violence has increased since the pandemic, large parts of our industry still consider it a peripheral issue. The very fact that it exists online means that virtual threats are rarely given the same consideration as 'real life' ones, despite there being evidence that online and physical violence do co-exist. Furthermore, those who are targeted also tend to be people who are historically marginalised by our industry, which may reinforce the barriers to speaking out, while those who make the safety, commissioning and deployment decisions in newsrooms tend to come from identities that are less marginalised. The fact is that normalising conversations around online violence and the impact it has on people would go a long way.

Because physical, psychological, and online safety all interconnect, newsrooms should recognise the need for more holistic approaches, not least due to the knock-on impact on journalism itself. Where voices are silenced, media plurality is compromised, and in turn press freedom and its role in supporting democracy are undermined. The most substantive piece of research to date on this issue is *The Chilling: a global study of online violence against women journalists*,[3] which found that misogyny and sexism intersect with racism, ableism, transphobia and homophobia. The UNESCO-commissioned research, led by the International Centre for Journalists, draws on the testimonies of more than 850 women journalists, includes more than 100 recommendations, and has helped feed the development of an early warning system to combat online violence. The study, undertaken in 2020, found that almost three-quarters (73%) of women surveyed had experienced online violence. Threats were physical and sexual in nature, with a fifth of the women respondents saying they 'had been attacked or abused offline in incidents seeded online'. Online violence was shown to be having a significant impact on the mental health of the women respondents:

> The women journalists who participated in our survey identified mental health impacts as the most significant consequence of the online violence exposure that they had experienced (26%). And a substantial number (12%) said they had sought medical or psychological help in response. Another 11% said they had taken time off work to recover, and a number of our interviewees experienced severe psychological injury, including PTSD. Indeed, many of our interviewees broke down while discussing their experiences with us, describing how important it was for them to be listened to.[4]

In 2022, The Taking Care survey[5] in Canada surveyed 1,200 journalists on issues related to their mental health and found that online harassment was having a psychological impact.

> Women encountered harassment and violence at every turn – by email, on social media, in the field and in the newsroom – and were more likely to receive sexual harassment, hate speech, threats and intimidation. Women reported the highest likelihood of being psychologically harmed by this harassment. And, when compared to men, at least twice as many women reported increasing security at work or home, leaving their home city/region/country, changing their phone number or email address, or quitting social media at least twice as often as men reported.

It quoted one journalist:

> The discourse online on social media has a hugely damaging effect on mental health, and I believe for members of the media, in particular. We are the focal point for a lot of the hate and vitriol, targeted specifically for being 'fake news' or 'mainstream media' for reporting on facts that don't agree with the altered worldview of those who target us.

Marianna Spring was the BBC's first specialist disinformation editor. She is attacked daily on social media. In a podcast episode with Headlines Network,[6] she explained that although the relentless abuse affected her mental health, she had found coping strategies.

> It sounds slightly clichéd, but I think the way I do cope with it is because I love doing my job and I think it is so important to be exposing the harm that's caused by online disinformation, to be speaking to the

people affected, to understand the effect that trolling has, to speak to the people who are doing the trolling themselves. But it's not easy. Particularly during the pandemic there was a real onslaught of hate and abuse directed at me often, everything from really serious threats, rape threats, death threats to 'silly little girl', to very sexualised comments, every kind of gendered slur under the sun, very much focused on me for being a young woman. There are many people I have interviewed about the online hate they experienced. I am lucky not to be targeted with racist, homophobic [or] other forms of hate, but it's not always easy to cope with. In some ways, I think I have probably become slightly desensitised to it.

Spring credits friends, family and colleagues in helping her too:

I think a lot of it is about having really good support networks. I'm really lucky to have brilliant family and friends. If I ever wanted to talk to them about it [I could], or if I ever felt worried, [. . .] I'm very well supported by the BBC. I work with a brilliant team who have a really good understanding of this – editors who understand what it's like to be subjected to this, who help me to feel safe if I'm ever worried about my personal safety, and [. . .] I'm incredibly grateful for that.

Online violence is aimed at attacking, undermining, intimidating and silencing the people it targets. If we consider that those who are most likely to be affected are also the least represented by and in our global news media, then this is a threat to media plurality. Too often, individuals who are attacked self-censor, sometimes avoiding coverage of specific stories, sometimes stepping back from social media. A 2023 survey[7] by Women in Journalism and Reach plc found almost a fifth of respondents had considered leaving the media industry because of the threat of online harm. Even prior to the pandemic, there was evidence that individuals who might otherwise have thought about being journalists decided against a career because of the threats, therefore affecting future recruitment to the industry.[8]

Caroline Drees is Senior Director, Field Safety and Security at NPR. As part of her job, she works with her colleagues to ensure they are aware of how best to manage their digital hygiene, and to understand the potential negative repercussions of things they put online. But she said that as well as awareness and training, organisations need to make sure that individuals have the time to put into practice the risk mitigation tools required to reduce some of the threats of online violence:

A lot of individuals are not fully enough aware of things like doxxing. They might not know exactly what it means, or they may not be aware enough of the risks, for example, of putting a photo of their child with all the picture's location metadata online. In addition to creating that awareness, employers should ideally ensure staff have the time to engage in digital hygiene, because it can be very time-consuming to do it right – especially if you're also completing all the other mandatory company training, acknowledging various company policies, rebooting your computer as needed when new patches have been installed, changing passwords regularly, using multi-factor authentication, etc., and doing your regular job. Good digital hygiene is incredibly important to keep you safe, but it's also a time commitment and hard work to make sure it's where it needs to be.

At the same time, the threats and harassment are growing and growing and growing. We know that a lot of these threats don't stay in the cyber realm, but when they do, the emotional damage can be horrific. We also know that women and people of colour are targeted disproportionately, and the attacks are particularly ugly and vile. In journalism, the attacks also go to the essence of our mission, because diversity, equity and inclusion aren't just buzzwords. In journalism, you need to have a multifaceted lens through which you're observing the world, otherwise you're only going to get a tiny window into what's going on. By disproportionately targeting one subset of journalists, cyber-harassers are attacking and seeking to silence diversified voices and nuanced, complex reporting.[9]

It's reassuring to speak with leaders like Drees. She sees online safety as a shared issue between the individual and the institution, much as it is in the physical sphere. Preparation is key, in terms of ensuring not only that individual journalists have the right training and tools to protect themselves, but also that they have an open line of communication with colleagues who are managing them, to identify and mitigate the risks they face.

It's encouraging to see some news organisations taking seriously the issue of online violence, addressing it with the same focus as they might physical safety, where they consider what to do before, during and after the event. But even for Drees, the fact that online harassment is constantly evolving means it always feels like playing catch-up:

Cyberthreats are a big challenge for a whole gamut of reasons. They are a very nuanced challenge. It's not like you can just say, 'It's a challenge because it's increasing online' or because it's finding new forms. It's a challenge for all those reasons and more. You can't just plug one hole; it's like playing Whack-a-Mole.

Unfortunately, some newsrooms seem deterred by that Whack-a-Mole nature of the threat, and rather than recognising the need to iterate their policies, programmes and approaches, they'd prefer to bury their heads in the sand.

The Chilling made it clear that the news industry needs to do more to support those targeted by online violence. I have spent several years working as a media consultant, specialising in journalism safety, and regularly consult with news organisations on online harassment. At the time of writing, I have been facilitating a regular industry forum on this issue for two years. In these sessions, representatives of global news organisations collaborate by sharing some of the challenges in combatting online harassment and what they are doing in response.

Yet, even if there is a collaborative aspect to some conversations, sometimes violence against journalists is incited by other organisations. On occasions, an individual or story from one news organisation will criticise someone from a rival newsroom, resulting in an internet 'pile-on', where the journalist is inundated with online attacks orchestrated by a competitor organisation. These attacks may be motivated by the desire of one organisation to gain more of a foothold in the media market. One expert, who did not want to be quoted, said it was one of the biggest issues her company had to deal with from an online perspective. However, she acknowledged that 'the good thing is, it's very easy to contextualise, which is really helpful for people with mental health'.

From a good practice perspective, it is reassuring to hear that some newsrooms are offering specific training and resources for their journalists. At least two newsrooms have recruited individuals with a specific remit in this field. The Australian Broadcasting Corporation (ABC) has a digital wellness advisor, while Reach plc in the UK has an online safety editor, the UK media industry's first dedicated individual in this role. To have someone really taking ownership of an issue, in a leadership role, is a valuable step towards showing people in that organisation and across the industry that this is being taken seriously. Nicolle White is at ABC, where she says the creation of her role reflects a broader move to taking seriously issues related to the wellbeing of journalists:

> As an organisation, we've brought in a social media wellbeing advisor, specifically, which I think creates a space for people to feel comfortable, not only in social media, but it reflects broadly that wellbeing is really prioritised by the organisation and so we really have seen an uptick in staff feeling comfortable.[10]

ABC's peer support network has been particularly beneficial for moderators who encounter a lot of online vitriol:

> This isn't in the context of moderators, but we did some surveying recently where I asked them what they're exposed to and what's useful, and peer support and manager check-ins were the two things really seen as invaluable. Good managerial support where people feel safe is so vital [. . .], whether that's informal or formalised.

As White explained, ABC has created guidelines to help managers understand what their roles should be in supporting moderators:

> We say, it's not necessarily [about] asking, 'Are you okay?', because nine times out of ten, probably staff are going to say, 'Yeah, I'm fine.' But [by] asking, 'Okay, what have you been banning people from the page for this week?', you actually get insight into what folks are exposed to, and then they might start to open up. Then, [you might] open up as well and say, 'That would impact me.' Or some managers will say, 'Hey, it's my lunch break, I'm going for a run now' – if you're not working in the office together, and you're working from home – to really normalise that [kind of] self-care. And so, it really has to be managed and led because you can have a health and safety team, but it's all good and well for us to come in and say, 'It's a safe space – talk about your wellbeing.' But that really has to come from the individual editorial programmes.

At Reach plc, the online safety editor Dr Rebecca Whittington has developed a network of online safety representatives that trains selected individuals to be able to support their colleagues, as well as launching a new reporting system that triages cases, to bring in the relevant staff members to help.

> We know how prevalent and toxic online harms against journalists can be. Whether it is the regular occurrence of personal comments or a significant event such as a threat, backlash or being doxxed, the toll of not only the events themselves but also the burden of being vulnerable in online work spaces, and the trauma of online harm, can cause significant mental health impacts. It is vital employers give due recognition to these issues and do not dismiss them as being 'part of the job'. Ideally, employers will put training and protection in place to help employees protect themselves and make themselves less vulnerable to harm. There also needs to be a response to online harms which gives agency and control to the affected individual while also supporting them in their recovery.
>
> The issues that can arise from a failure to address online harm include burnout, stress, and ultimately people may choose to leave their jobs. We also know online harm is directed more at women and protected groups, so the ultimate impact could also be a decrease in diversity of the workforce at a time when [the] industry has recognised its need to diversify more.[11]

As part of her work to support those affected by online harassment, Dr Whittington has also set up an initiative called Reach Hive, which brings together a group of individuals to flood a person's timeline with positive messages if they are targeted.

Reach Hive is a support swarm of volunteers from across the business who send positive tweets to staff members who find themselves in the midst of a backlash on Twitter [now X]. We usually swarm a person when they are due to return to the platform after taking time back to allow the backlash to die down. We agree a time and date for their return and then we deploy the Hive to tweet them directly, starting with their handle, just before that return time so that the tweets drive negative notifications out of their timeline. The Hive creates a positive community and space for that person to return to and means they feel less isolated and vulnerable as a result. We never mention the backlash and the tweets never refer to the topic which triggered it, so the risk of reigniting the backlash is decreased.

In Kenya, Catherine Gicheru of the *Nation* newspaper and founder of Africa Women Journalism Project is concerned about online harassment of women journalists. Without effective policies and support from her newsrooms, she has developed a system of mobilising people to provide support when an online attack happens:

> If somebody trolls or attacks you online, you mobilise friends or get friends and relatives and other women to help and push back against the trolls. I call it *raining* on somebody. All of them will come to your support and drown out the stupidity or misogynistic trolling. And they will push back against this individual on my behalf. Because if [you] engage with the attacker, you're just adding fuel to the fire.[12]

It's a model she would like to see news organisations adopt to better support journalists who are targeted online.

> It doesn't cost any money to just say, for example, if Catherine or any other journalist is attacked online, the full weight of all the media organisations will come to their defence. You also have the support of friends, family and other journalists who will come to your defence. This would show that I have an army behind me. And once you do that once, twice, three, four or five times, those idiots will hopefully learn that this individual journalist is not alone. She's not alone. She's got a whole army behind her. What we see is her, but she's the general of an army that is huge and powerful. It's just that she doesn't brag about it, but she knows.

She said she felt this way when her newsroom supported her when she was in physical danger:

> It should translate online. It gave me the confidence to confront powerful individuals with hard-hitting questions and pursue my investigations, knowing that the news organisation I'm working for is standing behind me. Imagine now if there was that kind of confidence that I would get the same support if I'm trolled online.

Solidarity is so important. I frequently facilitate conversations with journalists targeted by online harassment, listening to their experiences. They say they want their news organisations to recognise what they have been through and support them visibly. Many colleagues at national news organisations told me they felt targeted specifically because they worked for a public broadcaster. They received the full weight of the ire of the harasser, whose anger is against the organisation the journalist represents. Online abuse is one of the main reasons that ABC employees access the trauma programme – proof of the impact the abuse has on their mental health. As Australia's public service broadcaster, ABC is held to a high level of scrutiny. 'One thing we really see is the immense pressure that you are held to, particularly by other media,' said White:

> There's this sense of, if you make the slightest misstep, that's going to be in the media. That's an immense pressure for journalists to be under. And if it's in the media, then there's going to be a social media pile-on. I think that causes a lot of anxiety, day to day, for staff who are making a lot of editorial decisions.

She noted that journalists who work in smaller communities are often even more exposed to online harm. Again, this is something that rings true around the world; where that individual has a relatively high profile in a community, they may become more of a target and potentially also more exposed to physical insecurity. In some ways, they are the mouthpiece of whatever organisation they work for, held up to high scrutiny, and a legitimate target for many. White explains:

> That's something I've been grappling with, particularly from an online abuse perspective, because if you're having the audience come at you for something that you've written, and you're in a capital city, you're a little bit more anonymous, in the sense of day-to-day walking down the street, whereas in a small town, it's a very different experience.

As with many situations where people's mental health is impacted, it can be beneficial to speak with others who have similar stories. It is also really important for journalists to know that they are not to blame for the harassment they receive and that it is no measure of their ability as a journalist. One of the most common points I hear from journalists who are threatened online is their desire that managers acknowledge what they are going through, so they feel seen as human beings, not as cogs in a machine. It's a similar story across all conversations to do with mental health. News leaders need to learn to listen to their colleagues, hear what they are going through, and, while recognising they won't always be able to fix everything, take action to support them. They need to recognise that certain people are more at risk than others and create spaces where people feel safe sharing their experiences without judgement.

As discussed in the previous chapter, journalists are at risk of real emotional distress if they feel they do not have the support of their news leaders. It's not just about talking the talk. News leaders need to walk the walk.

But managers are challenged too. Many lack training to understand the nature of online violence and mitigate it, to understand their responsibilities to support their colleagues, and how to signpost them to additional support. Unfortunately, too often I hear from colleagues who feel their newsrooms could do more, and that, in some instances, those who are speaking about online harassment are only paying lip service to it. Gicheru is the first female news editor of the Nation Media Group, the largest and most influential media group in East Africa. She told me that conversations have been happening around online violence and specifically what women go through.

> But my problem is that they do the lip service, but they don't do anything. They say, 'Oh, we're going to support you or we're going to provide support', but they really do nothing. Their newsrooms, at least in Kenya, I know, they have very beautiful policies, but they have very nonsensical implementation strategies. So, we are against online violence. We want to protect our women journalists from online violence. How is that going to happen? What are we going to do? What needs to happen? We as a newsroom, what is our position? We know we are against it, but what are we going to do if Catherine is harassed or trolled or whatever? What is our response to it? So, there is a lot of nonsense, beautiful talk, very little action.

In conversations with news leaders, it is clear many editorial executives want to do something but are not sure what. They feel as though their hands are tied, because – as one senior media executive said to me – 'It's like shooting a moving target.' As noted above, this may make it tough to tackle, but it is not a reason to do nothing, and not acting is failing in one's duty of care to journalists. I worry that some newsrooms are still burying their heads in the sand. When it comes to the impact on journalists, including the emotional toll, I do see and hear a desire to do something from those who recognise the reality. However, this is often stopped in its tracks by legal departments, who don't want to acknowledge the fact that online harassment exists because this would force them to recognise it as a safety issue and potentially open up the company to liability. I think it is only a matter of time before they see that this is not a defence.

So, the onus, unfortunately and wrongly, as *The Chilling* notes, is often on the individual. They are expected to report the attacks, often without sufficient support, and may therefore be re-exposed to traumatic material. When they do report it, they may encounter members of law enforcement who lack awareness of the reality and repercussions of online harassment, and who – in many cases – may be male. It's important, if people do have to report their experiences, that they have someone they can trust who can help them document what has happened, and – if they are in the fray of harassment – who perhaps can take over their social media passwords, to give them a break.

Online harassment is significantly under-reported. Some of the most common reasons are that individuals believe nothing will be done if they do report it, they fear that speaking about their experiences will impact their reputation, roles or career progression, or they have been conditioned to accept the attacks as part and parcel of their jobs. These are all reasons I have heard from journalists anecdotally, and it plays out in the findings of *The Chilling*, which notes that only a quarter of incidents were reported by journalists to their employers:

> The responses that the women survey participants reported receiving when they did report online violence to their employers were, on the whole, very unhelpful. They illustrate the enduring failures within many news organisations to respond appropriately or effectively to the crisis. The most common response received was that no action was taken; the next most frequently identified response was gender-insensitive advice such as 'toughen up' or 'grow a thicker skin'.[13]

To this end, journalists are experiencing misogyny in their own newsroom. The absence of assertive action by newsrooms will exacerbate the emotional burden carried by journalists targeted by online violence, who are very often the same journalists historically marginalised by and in the media. The consequence of a failure of our news leaders to act against online harm will impact on our industry's ability to do real journalism.

Fortunately, some work is being done to mitigate, counter and prepare people for the risk of online harassment, as well as to deal with it when it happens. This includes a realisation by a small number of organisations that online harassment can hurt people psychologically, and an acknowledgement that support is needed in the short and long term too.

Online harassment hurts the whole industry. It's been really interesting, in facilitating a conversation that includes several news organisations, to see the similar challenges that are faced globally, and what happens when solutions are shared, and solidarity built. Online harassment is not going away. As an industry, we have a valuable opportunity to come together to take it seriously, and to better support those who are targeted, for their mental health and for the future health of journalism.

Notes

1 Author WhatsApp conversation with Patricia Devlin, June 2023
2 Author interview with Abeer Saady, November 2022
3 Julie Posetti and Nabeelah Shabbir (eds) *The Chilling: A Global Study On Online Violence Against Women Journalists*, International Center for Journalists, 8 March. Available at: https://www.icfj.org/our-work/chilling-global-study-online-violence-against-women-journalists
4 Ibid

5 Matthew Pearson and Dave Seglins (2022) *Taking Care: A report on mental health, well-being & trauma among Canadian media workers*, Canadian Journalism Forum on Violence and Trauma. Available at: https://static1.squarespace.com/static/60a28b563f87204622eb0cd6/t/628556ab6053c80a9e1d668d/1652905646075/TakingCare_EN.pdf
6 Headlines Network, (2022) *Behind the Headlines*, Episode 5: Marianna Spring, [podcast]. Available at: https://audioboom.com/posts/8084971-marianna-spring
7 Women in Journalism (2023) *Research report 2023: Online harms against women working in journalism and media*. Available at: https://www.womeninjournalism.co.uk/research/report-2023-online-harms-against-women-working-in-journalism-and-media
8 Dalia Faheid, (2020) 'Online Harassment New Frontline for Journalists, Report Says', International Women's Media Foundation. Available at: https://www.iwmf.org/2020/12/online-harassment-new-frontline-for-journalists-report-says
9 Author interview with Caroline Drees, February 2023
10 Author interview with Nicolle White, December 2022
11 Email exchange between author and Dr Rebecca Whittington, June 2023
12 Author interview with Catherine Gicheru, May 2023
13 Julie Posetti and Nabeelah Shabbir (eds) *The Chilling: A Global Study On Online Violence Against Women Journalists*, International Center for Journalists, 8 March. Available at: https://www.icfj.org/our-work/chilling-global-study-online-violence-against-women-journalists

Reference list

Faheid, D. (2020) 'Online Harassment New Frontline for Journalists, Report Says', International Women's Media Foundation. Available at: https://www.iwmf.org/2020/12/online-harassment-new-frontline-for-journalists-report-says

Headlines Network, (2022) *Behind the Headlines*, Episode 5: Marianna Spring, [podcast]. Available at: https://audioboom.com/posts/8084971-marianna-spring

Pearson, M. and Seglins, D. (2022) *Taking Care: A report on mental health, well-being & trauma among Canadian media workers*, Canadian Journalism Forum on Violence and Trauma. Available at: https://static1.squarespace.com/static/60a28b563f87204622eb0cd6/t/628556ab6053c80a9e1d668d/1652905646075/TakingCare_EN.pdf

Posetti, J. and Shabbir, N. (eds) (2022) *The Chilling: A global study on online violence against women journalists* International Center for Journalists, 8 March. Available at: https://www.icfj.org/our-work/chilling-global-study-online-violence-against-women-journalists

Women in Journalism (2023) *Research report 2023: Online harms against women working in journalism and media*. Available at: https://www.womeninjournalism.co.uk/research/report-2023-online-harms-against-women-working-in-journalism-and-media

Their story – Rana Ayuub[14]

Rana Ayuub is the global investigations editor for *The Washington Post* newspaper. A Muslim Indian woman, and a critic of her country's prime minister Narendra Modi, Rana is regularly attacked online for her journalism. She has faced repeated threats of death and rape, as well as frequent false accusations about her finances, her family and her personal life. She has been detained physically and charged with money laundering by Indian authorities, attempts which are designed to destroy her reputation and silence her.

Living in India, historically one of the most violent countries for journalists, Rana faces danger constantly. And after the murder of her friend and fellow journalist, Gauri Lankesh, who endured a campaign of online violence against her, Rana survives new threats, trauma and fears every day. Despite this, she is driven by a mission to speak for those who are marginalised, doing a job that she says she does not have the luxury to stop.

Her friends are scared to meet her in public. Her family have been impacted too, charged with aiding and abetting her. Her brothers lost their jobs because of their relationship with her. She has been unable to find employment in India and is forced to work for international publications because of the extent of political pressure against anyone who might consider hiring her. Threats and violence have taken a significant toll on her mental and physical health, leading her to contemplate hurting or numbing herself on more than one occasion.

In April 2023, Rana, spoke with me from her home in India about the impact of the violence on her mental health and how she experienced frequent anxiety attacks and was on medication. She recounted a period of weeks in 2022, during which police filed charges against her in several Indian states; a relentless campaign of propaganda pointed the finger at her on primetime television and other news outlets, and the online violence against her spiralled. There were drones sent to film outside her building, and members of the media at her home, despite security refusing them access. Friends and family of hers were being hounded on social media, asked if she was guilty of money laundering and if they had profited from it.

'I called my brother,' she told me 'I said, "I don't think I'm gonna survive tonight." It was the worst kind of depression, anxiety. I couldn't eat anything. And I was just throwing up everything that I was eating, even a sip of water.' During this time, she did an interview with *The Economist* for a film they were making on press freedom:

> When I look back at it, I'm like, I did it with *The Economist*; I did it in my nightwear, which I had not changed in three days and [I had] not brushed [my teeth] in three days. I had no idea what I was talking about. I cried during the interview. My eyes were swollen. At that point, my doctors [said] I literally dodged suicide by a bullet. And then, the doctor gave me very strong sleeping pills, saying, 'Just allow her to sleep for the next three days.'

For Rana, one of the worst things was the lack of solidarity from Indian media.

> It's not about me. I fear [for] the unsung journalists in India. I speak at every interview about them. But still, the moment I speak about myself, some of the well-known journalists in India will be like, 'Oh, stop playing the victim all the time. Everybody else goes through it.' It's like victim blaming all the time: I cannot talk about what the government is doing to me; I cannot talk about the way it's attacking me and my family. Both my brothers have lost their jobs because of me. I can't explain the mental toll. But imagine sitting at home every single day feeling the guilt of literally ruining your entire family and not being able to tell the world and not getting an inch of solidarity from your own countrymen.

She explained how Jodie Ginsberg, president of the press freedom group the Committee to Protect Journalists, told her that the filing of money laundering cases was a relatively new tactic used by governments and other bodies to plant suspicion in the minds of people:

> Because unless proven otherwise, these things stick, right. They've done it with Maria Ressa, they've done it with journalists in Russia, they're doing it all over the world. I was feeling like a culprit, you know, in my head – every accusation that has been repeated against me, I was internalising that allegation.

In late February 2022, a group of international news organisations and press freedom groups took up Rana's plight and released a front-page press freedom advert in *The Washington Post*.

> I was in a very dark space. And somebody said, 'Okay, we believe you.' That just got me functioning back again. It made me more functional. I could take a shower. I could brush my teeth. People don't understand it. When something like this happens, your ability to function, even do the basic things, like brushing your teeth, like changing your clothes, becomes a huge task. It's not the same for everybody. It's not a one-size-fits-all. But in my case, I just become motionless. I just stop eating, even the taste of water feels bitter to my tongue. I stop everything. And then all I do is throw up, so the body just becomes weak.
>
> In the scheme of things right now, it might not look very important. But when somebody reaches out to me and says, 'Your journalism made a difference to me' [as well as] the friends around you and the allies who say, 'We believe you' – that is the biggest anti-anxiety thing that ever helps me, besides switching off, besides just doing something which is completely not journalistic, going and eating something with family

members or just going out or just meeting a friend or just going for a movie – just disconnecting completely.

Despite everything she has endured, Rana believes she has an element of privilege. When I asked her what she would say to those who dismiss the mental health toll of online violence, she answered:

> People believe that as long as a journalist is not killed, is not behind bars, they're okay. And when you tell them the problem, they look at other journalists. They do not realise that they are killing me – as Maria [Ressa] says: death by 1,000 cuts every single day.

Her desire to raise awareness of the emotional toll led her to record a podcast, calling on her audience to talk about mental health and specifically how those who are less well known than her have been impacted by online violence.

> I felt like, it happened to me, who is so famous in the country? What about those who are facing it without a voice and without the clout? So, I did a podcast on my Substack: 'Are we going to talk about the mental health of journalists?' And so many of my friends reached out and I said, 'If ever you feel like you're in the dumps, know that what you see – the internet trends – are sponsored; they are not you, they're not the reality.'

I say, you have to realise [that] besides the legal warfare, this is the new warfare. Others we will fight through legal cases. But the idea behind this one is to mess with your mental peace and make you mentally so fragile that you cannot even pursue those cases. So, I want to tell anybody out there that what you're feeling is real. But you have to understand that these people exist to bring you down, which means you are doing something terribly right. If you even google my name right now on the internet, the stories that I write take a backstage and all the first three pages are the cases against me and the allegations against me today. Because I was one of the voices in the country talking about India to the world. So, they had to kind of discredit me.

Rana's journey into journalism was inspired by the injustices she experienced as a child and those she saw experienced by fellow Muslims in India. She had polio at the age of five, which left her physically weak and unable to join the police as she had hoped later in life. As a child, anti-Muslim riots in Bombay meant that she and her sister had to flee their home overnight.

> We were forced to live in a ghetto, where there was absolutely no sanitary health. We were forced to live between a slaughterhouse of animals and a dumping ground. That's where Muslims were supposed to live. I felt like, as a journalist, it was my obligation to tell the world the lived experience and to report on those whose voices are not heard by the

mainstream media: the marginalised. That was my reason to be in journalism, why my entire career of the last 16 to 17 years has been focused on the marginalised, the ones whose stories we do not talk about. The reason why I'm pursuing Prime Minister Modi is because he was the chief minister when a thousand Muslims were killed under his watch. Right now, he is the prime minister and Muslims are being treated as second-class citizens. They want to convert the democracy into Hindu nation. And I believe it's my moral responsibility. Because I'm with *The Washington Post*; I have international publications who I write for. When journalism in my own country has been so captured, then the stories need to be told to the world. And that's the only reason that is driving me right now to do what I do.

Despite her experiences, Rana is determined to continue her journalism and that she does not have the luxury or choice to remain silent. Hers is a mission-driven life of work.

Note

14 This case study has been drawn from the author's interview with Rana Ayuub in April 2023

10 Journalists and burnout

Burnout has become a regular refrain in journalism in recent times. Yet until a few years ago, this condition was shrouded in stigma and a sense that those who experienced it were to blame. Burnout is used to describe 'a large collection of experiences caused by unmanageable stress at work', according to Drew Berrie, head of workplace wellbeing at Mind, the mental health charity in England and Wales: 'Ultimately, burnout can affect mental health, it can affect our physical health, it can affect how we feel about ourselves, and it can impact how we feel about others.'[1]

In 2019, the World Health Organization classified burnout for the first time as a 'workplace phenomenon'[2] or occupational hazard. Before this, it had been seen as a stress syndrome. This move by WHO was an important step that should theoretically have moved the onus of responsibility from the individual to the workplace, encouraging organisations to consider how their systems and workflows were wounding their workers. But less than a year on from WHO's classification, the Covid pandemic struck, and the change to deep-rooted journalistic practices did not evolve from a desire to protect people from the real health impacts of burnout, but rather from a global health crisis that forced our industry to reinvent decades of practice in days.

Still, this enforced evolution offered news organisations an opportunity to reconsider workflows, processes and systemic practices that had for so long piled pressure on journalists. Some took notice, and conversations around journalists' mental health moved up the agenda. Unfortunately, we have not yet seen real systemic change. Instead, after the relentlessness of the preceding few years in journalism, the pandemic opened the floodgates to cases of burnout in the industry. The rise in such cases doesn't mean that, all of a sudden, journalists have become unable to cope with the demanding nature of news. Journalism always has been an industry where people worked with a certain amount of pressure – something that is important, because, without it, Berrie noted, we can become bored and unmotivated:

> When there's a little extra pressure, that's where we find our comfort zone and we're challenged, we're able to realise that maximum performance. And we know we best perform in the longer term when we're

DOI: 10.4324/9781003344179-10

able to kind of oscillate between that period of being stretched and then being able to return to that comfort zone and able to recharge and when we're not able to recharge and that pressure continues to build, that's where we experience strain and that's ultimately what causes stress.

Stress is manageable if we are aware of what the pressures are and what support will benefit us. However, where stress is sustained over a long period at unmanageable levels, burnout can occur. Experiences of burnout differ, although – as mentioned previously – there are some common symptoms, including cynicism, self-doubt, a lack of motivation and an inability to prioritise. None of these are conducive to quality journalism or healthy working practices. So, when an individual burns out, they simply aren't going to be able to do the kind of journalism they need to do.

People with burnout may share some of the symptoms of PTSD, such as difficulty concentrating, anxiety and a sense of withdrawal, intrusive thoughts being particular to the latter. It's important to recognise that burnout can take its toll. Since early 2021, it has become almost synonymous with the journalistic condition, forcing some journalists to quit, others to take time off. Many of those who are leaving are journalists of colour and women. Others stay on, financially unable to leave, dealing with burnout in silence.

In March 2021, Stacy-Marie Ishmael left her job at *The Texas Tribune*, tweeting:

> So: I'm taking a break. I'm stepping down from @TexasTribune, where I've spent the last year operating at a relentless and breakneck pace to ensure that our journalism could rise to the demands of this moment.
> It did. We did. And in the process, I *totally* burned out.
> — stacy-marie ishmael (@s_m_i) March 30, 2021[3]

The same month, Megan Greenwell left her job as editor at Wired.com, citing exhaustion, while her colleague Scott Rosenfield also stood down from his Wired.com[4] job, where he had been in charge of digital strategy.

In 2023, noting the rise in cases of burnout across the industry, Headlines Network,[5] the company I founded, created a resource for journalists, based on conversations with colleagues from across the industry, as well as experts, including Berrie, mentioned above. We spoke with several journalists who had experienced burnout themselves. Kari Cobham, a Trinidadian writer, editor and digital strategist based in the US city of Atlanta, told us:

> During the pandemic, when we were all working from home, I was also short-staffed, and so I went through a period of several months where I was just really overworked. For me, the signs of burnout started to show where, even though I loved the work that I did, working with journalists and mental health, I started to not enjoy showing up to work. I was really anxious. The things that usually brought me joy did not

bring me joy. I just wasn't happy. I think the best way to describe it, I told somebody at the time, was that I was feeling a little crispy around the edges. And then the crispy began to spread until I was barely able to function at work. And so, for me, the signs that I was burning out were just like beyond being down and just being completely unmotivated to do anything related to work, having a lot of anxiety around work, just not wanting to show up at all. And it got to the point where I just really couldn't function and I ended up having to take leave and take time off so that I could build myself back up again and get to a place where I could function at work.[6]

Despite feeling utterly exhausted, freelance journalist Dhruti Shah explained that she kept working harder rather than taking a break:

It involved waking up at three o'clock in the morning and then trying to find out why was I waking up at three o'clock in the morning and then going into a rabbit hole, especially when it came to social media. It involved sometimes thinking that nobody wanted me around, and feeling very, very lonely about the world, and involved feeling quite hopeless too. For me, burnout was about trying to fill something that just couldn't be filled.[7]

This same sense of exhaustion was felt by journalists experiencing burnout at Agence France-Presse, said Phil Chetwynd, the news organisation's Global News Director. For the previously referenced Headlines Network resource, he described his colleagues becoming overwhelmed, leading to a sense of panic and consequently struggling to carry out simple tasks. Despite this, many seemed unable to stop working, he said:

One of the things that we see is a huge tendency to overwork, really struggling to see any kind of boundary between work life and home life, to be connected all the time. Difficulty in prioritising because everything becomes extremely important, [an] inability to really decide what's worth it, and what's not worth it, and probably with that, especially with managers, an inability to delegate and inability to prioritise. I think the two things probably go together, which leads to a sort of vicious circle [and the person] can't get out of that. I think, especially in our industry, it's [due to a] connectedness, [a] hyper-connectivity to things. I think, on an emotional level, [. . .] we see [. . .] people getting angry, people being on edge, people taking things extremely personally. [There's] a sort of mixing, in a sense of home and professional things, where everything becomes the fault of the company or the profession around you, when sometimes, clearly the issues are much wider.[8]

Digital overwhelm and unrelenting workloads are among the key factors that came up in conversations around what contributes to people's stress, exhaustion and burnout in newsrooms. Burnout is also synonymous with the struggle to create and maintain boundaries. These are the limits we set to protect ourselves, and when established and communicated, they can help others understand how we wish to be treated. When we have trouble setting and maintaining these boundaries, burnout can result. Therefore, healthy boundaries can be a protective mechanism, but it's important to note that they can often feel at odds with our work cultures.

Mar Cabra, who also experienced burnout in her journalism, now works to help colleagues explore and apply tools to support their own mental health and that of colleagues. In an interview with her, she explained to me how important it was to recognise that those leading teams were at risk of burning out.

> I think we also need to rethink the workflows around what managers do, or maybe add the skills and the time that they need to develop them, because [we don't], it's very frustrating; and what we're seeing is that middle managers and top managers are among the first to burn out and to have mental health challenges.[9]

As a manager, you're not going to be able to support your colleagues unless you're looking after yourself. Drew Berrie explained it like this: 'Thinking about [a] metaphor, it's about putting on the oxygen mask before you go and support the person next to you.' He elaborated:

> That means making sure that you are setting appropriate work boundaries, you're giving yourself protective time for breaks, you're scheduling your time appropriately to really think about the tasks that you've got to achieve, what those deadlines are, and giving yourself the space and headspace to really complete that work to the best of your abilities.

While Kari Cobham agreed, she pointed out that it can be hard for managers to deal with their own burnout when they are trying to watch out for others:

> Because you don't really have anything left. That's why you're burnt out. I think if you're a manager and you're at that level of burnout, well, I hope that you wouldn't allow yourself to get to that point of burnout, but it happens, right? Because journalism. But I would say, if you are a manager, and you are feeling burnt out, I think one of the most important things that you can do is be honest about it. Because we operate in newsroom cultures, where it's not always acceptable for you to talk about how are you [sic] feeling and what your mental health is, and, as managers we want to be strong for the team; we want to seem like we're steady, but at the end of the day, we're also human.

Managers talking about their feelings, their struggles and what they're doing to deal with their burnout helps normalise those conversations in the newsroom and lessens the sense of stigma, shame and isolation that others might feel. Cobham continued:

> Being honest with people about where you are [at], I think, is a big step in any newsroom when you're a manager, because you're setting the tone for the newsroom and then for the folks on your team, who may also be dealing with burnout themselves. And so, if they see that their manager is also struggling with it, and is also being open about it, I think it will make folks feel a little less alone.

Self-compassion is crucial when managers are burnt out, according to Shah, because it allows for a more open culture, in which leaders are role models:

> How are you going to help those whom you're managing, if you're not helping yourself, at the same time, or even before? And one of the key things when it comes to burnout, is being able to have open conversations.

We need to get beyond this stigma and shame, to normalise conversations, create spaces where people can speak about their experiences, give them time to recover; and we need to acknowledge that burnout is real. It is impairing people's ability to do their jobs. It is making it hard for them to function productively, for them to support themselves and those around them.

Burnout has an opportunity cost for the journalism industry, Berrie pointed out:

> The cost of presenteeism and absenteeism and staff turnover are well documented, and newsrooms will see these costs arrive specifically in relation to burnout. That means less-focused journalists, maybe journalists missing deadlines, staff calling in sick or maybe falling out of employment altogether, because they don't feel able to cope. And this might not go unnoticed by your external audiences. Again, they might see a reduction in the quality of your output. If they're being interviewed, they might notice your employees feel less prepared or they're making errors. And again, this means you're not producing your best work. And again, your organisation's maybe not being viewed in the best light.

Cobham changed jobs after she experienced burnout and is now the director of fellowships at The 19th, an independent not-for-profit newsroom in the United States, and a digital news leader:

> Burnout is costing our industry, and it is in all of our best interests to really look to prevent it proactively and manage it where it arises. If journalists aren't able to look after themselves, or if they are not given the space to look after themselves, it will affect them, those around them, the work they do and the communities they serve. We need to be relatively

healthy, and we need to be in a place where we can cover the news and tackle difficult topics and get the information to folks that they need. I think the impact of burnout on one journalist is so significant because it doesn't just impact them and the people around them; it impacts entire communities and beats.

Amantha Perera is based in Australia but works with journalists across Asia Pacific, and noted that digital overwhelm was a real barrier to people doing their jobs healthily in communities that rely on journalists for life-saving information. He developed training for journalists around healthier relationships with technology, drawing on his experiences from working as a journalist in other hostile environments.

I think that the challenge for me is essentially to first get journalists to realise and understand that digital trauma is real, a real danger, and that its impact has increased in the last two and a half years. And it's unlikely to diminish. We need to have safety measures in place that are going to make our workplace safe and to go to the core of it, and say, 'Look, this is not a pragmatic conversation. This is a workplace safety issue. Right, the workplace that you and I work in now is the screen. The moment we open the screen, wherever we are physically, whether we are travelling in the bus, sitting at home or at the dinner table, and looking at the phone under the table, it's the workplace. So, we need to kind of have those safety precautions in place that will allow us to work safely.'

I was talking with a group of journalists from East Asia [. . .]. The easiest way for me to describe the screen as a potentially hostile reporting environment was to draw parallels with my conflict-reporting days. When you go into a conflict zone, there are these physical signs that either volume up or remind you that you are entering the business end of things: that beyond a certain point the bullets are going to be flying all over the place and it's going to be dangerous. In Sri Lanka, it was the no-man's-land with the ICRC flag; you knew that as you got nearer to that, the houses on the side of the road became less and less and less and less. The armed men and women on the side of the road got more and more. You were reminded of the changing threat vector without any ambiguity. But when you're working in the digital realm, there's no markings like that; there are no skull-and-bone signs in red, unless you consciously put them there: that is the trick.[10]

I was struck by these analogies to conflict, which I saw echoed in an article called 'The Burnout Year'[11] by Alexandria Neason, published in *The Columbia Journalism Review* at the end of 2018. In it, the author wrote:

The feeling I'm left with at the end of a frenetic 12 months reminds me of the 2013 radio documentary by veteran war correspondent Kelly McEvers.

In the documentary, *Diary of a Bad Year*, she chronicles a violent, dangerous year for journalists working abroad. McEvers – who found herself uncharacteristically emotionally volatile, crying uncontrollably – repeatedly ran headfirst into the firestorm, recorder in hand, against her better judgment. The symptoms of trauma and exhaustion she described feel familiar, and her central question – why am I doing this? – is one I repeated to myself that night last year, and many nights since.

That deep-seated disillusionment, that questioning of our work, in an industry that many of us enter, driven by a desire to make a difference, is really at the heart of burnout in the media. Clearly, the system, not the individual, is at fault. In a series of articles[12] for the American Press Institute, Jane Elizabeth explained how journalism newsrooms should consider revamping their work design in order to create healthier working environments for everyone. In one article, she wrote:

Journalism has never been quick to adopt practices from the business world, and when it does happen, it can be half-baked and clumsy. (An editor in one of my former newsrooms had people doing 'trust falls' from the top of their desks, about two years after everyone else stopped talking about trust falls.) But some of the concepts of corporate work design are worth examining for their potential in today's newsroom, from redistributing work to reconsidering work hours.

At Agence France-Presse (AFP), leaders have invested time in gaining a better understanding of how workflows and processes can be adapted to improve support in terms of their journalism and their journalists. This is necessary given how considering how our industry has evolved in recent years, according to Phil Chetwynd:

I've been very conscious of the pressures of the changing nature of our job, you know, the kind of real-time digital, mobile, all-social media environment. That's something that's been on my mind a long time and the industry's inability to adapt to that with regards to mental health, [an] inability to put processes in place where people [can] control the amount they work, control their level of interaction. Because the way of doing journalism changed so completely, your whole process of information gathering has changed so completely. So much is through this one object, on your phone; so much of your profile as a journalist is building your identity through social media. So there was this complete change in the way of doing journalism. But it meant people might have no disconnection at all.[13]

It's particularly important for first-time managers to know they have support, because moving up to a more senior position can typically bring many more stresses and, as we have seen, expose them to burnout, which in turn has a knock-on impact for those around them. Chetwynd went on:

> I think one of the real challenges of management is how [to] rise above all the little day-to-day things to really clarify what is massively important, and really, what doesn't matter till the next day or the next week. And that's something I focus on a lot. The reality is, very few things matter that much that you have to do them right now. Or that you can't delegate, or that can't wait till tomorrow. And I think that's a huge point to make. We live in such an intense, digital-first, mobile phone-first, real-time reality that everything seems so important. So I focus a lot with managers and myself in trying to say, 'I will answer that thing tomorrow. I will deal with that tomorrow.'

His suggestions chime with what experts call the 'four Ds' of effective time management: do, defer, delegate, drop. More news leaders would do well to follow these techniques. In her American Press Institute series, Jane Elizabeth uses the following quote:

> An organization that goes through massive transitions faces the question of what are the things that we want to hold on to? And what are the things that we want to let go of? Where do we see an opportunity to bring in something different and better? [. . .] We ask ourselves, what must be rebuilt, and what must we build anew?[14] — psychotherapist Esther Perel, 'Breaking News Has Broken Us'

Unfortunately, breaking news continues to break us. It's not easy to implement new work designs. Journalism has often dragged its heels and managers will always encounter some individuals resistant to change. But if we don't evolve to make our environments healthier for those at risk of burnout, we will put more people at risk. In the chapters that follow, we will consider how newsrooms should see safety issues as interconnected, and good mental health and wellbeing as contributing to more sustainable journalism. I will show how some of the good practice around hostile environment reporting can be used to mitigate the risks journalists face, and to encourage more open conversations that should foster environments where people can do their jobs better because they feel more supported. So much of safety is about preparation. This is the same with burnout. Shah echoed this when talking to Headlines Network:

> A lot of situations, when it comes to burnout, [are] actually about risk mitigation. And it's about saying, 'Let's put this in place so that we don't end up in a situation where burnout happens. So, let's make sure that people have time to step back. Let's make sure that the journalists have time to talk to each other and that they feel comfortable in terms of the

dynamics of the team, or the wider newsroom.' To be able to say, 'Hold on a minute, this situation where we've had multiple terror attacks, multiple natural disasters, multiple climate situations – have we incorporated time for people to rest? Have we incorporated time for people to say, "This is affecting me in this way?" Have we incorporated time for people to acknowledge that, actually, these are significant stresses?' And if you foster a culture that does that, then, honestly, surely, you're less likely to be on a path where everyone's going get burnt out.

Notes

1. Headlines Network interview with Drew Berrie for burn-out resource, Headlines-Network.com, published September 2023
2. WHO (2019) 'Burn-out an "occupational phenomenon": International Classification of Diseases', 28 May. Available at: https://www.who.int/news/item/28-05-2019-burn-out-an-occupational-phenomenon-international-classification-of-diseases
3. Jaden Edison (2021) 'Why Stacy-Marie Ishmael doesn't see leaving a job as a failure', Poynter, 5 August. Available at: https://www.poynter.org/business-work/2021/stacy-marie-ishmael-quit-every-job-shes-ever-had-including-at-the-texas-tribune-heres-why
4. Keith J. Kelly (2021) 'Two top Wired.com staffers resign, citing "burnout" and "exhaustion"', The New York Post, 15 April. Available at: https://nypost.com/2021/04/15/two-top-wired-com-staffers-resign-citing-burnout-and-exhaustion
5. www.headlines-network.com
6. Interview with Kari Cobham for Headlines Network burnout resource, 2023
7. Interview with Dhruti Shah for Headlines Network burnout resource, 2023
8. Interview with Phil Chetwynd for Headlines Network burnout resource, 2023
9. Author interview with Mar Cabra, February 2023
10. Author interview with Amantha Perera, August 2022
11. Alexandria Neason (2018) 'The burnout year' *Columbia Journalism Review*, 13 February. Available at: https://www.cjr.org/special_report/burnout-journalism.php
12. Jane Elizabeth (2021) 'Journalism managers are burned out. Is it time for a work redesign?' *American Press Institute*, 7 September. Available at: https://americanpressinstitute.org/journalism-managers-are-burned-out-is-it-time-for-a-work-redesign
13. Author interview with Phil Chetwynd, March 2023
14. Esther Perel (ND) How's Work? with Esther Perel, Breaking News Has Broken Us, Episode 6 [podcast] Available at: https://www.estherperel.com/podcasts/hw-s2-episode-6-breaking-news-has-broken-us

Reference list

Edison, J. (2021) 'Why Stacy-Marie Ishmael doesn't see leaving a job as a failure' – Poynter, 5 August. Available at: https://www.poynter.org/business-work/2021/stacy-marie-ishmael-quit-every-job-shes-ever-had-including-at-the-texas-tribune-heres-why

Elizabeth, J. (2021) 'Journalism managers are burned out. Is it time for a work redesign?' *American Press Institute*, 7 September. Available at: https://americanpressinstitute.org/journalism-managers-are-burned-out-is-it-time-for-a-work-redesign

Headlines Network, Burnout Resources. Available at: https://headlines-network.com/f/headlines-network-launches-burnout-resources

Kelly, K. J. (2021) 'Two top Wired.com staffers resign, citing "burnout" and "exhaustion"', *The New York Post*, 15 April. Available at: https://nypost.com/2021/04/15/two-top-wired-com-staffers-resign-citing-burnout-and-exhaustion

Neason, A. (2018) 'The burnout year' *Columbia Journalism Review*, 13 February. Available at: https://www.cjr.org/special_report/burnout-journalism.php Elizabeth, Jane. Journalism managers are burned out. Is it time for a work redesign? – American Press Institute (2021)

Perel, E. (ND) How's Work? with Esther Perel, Breaking News Has Broken Us, Episode 6 [podcast] Available at: https://www.estherperel.com/podcasts/hw-s2-episode-6-breaking-news-has-broken-us

World Health Organization (2019) 'Burn-out an "occupational phenomenon": International Classification of Diseases', 28 May. Available at: https://www.who.int/news/item/28-05-2019-burn-out-an-occupational-phenomenon-international-classification-of-diseases

Their story – Mar Cabra[15]

I was an investigative journalist specialising in data. I used to lead the team at the International Consortium of Investigative Journalists and was in charge of the whole data and technology aspects of large cross-border investigations, such as the Panama Papers. I spent seven years working non-stop on project after project, the next project bigger than the previous one, up to the point where we get to the Panama Papers, which was back in 2015/16: the largest leak in journalism history, the largest cross-border investigative collaboration at the time, with about 400 journalists working around the globe. And the stakes were very high, right?

I was connected, glued to my computer, and to my phone, all the time, from the minute I woke up to the minute I went to bed. And I thought I was doing great. I thought I was excelling at being hyper-connected and being able to pull so many people and complex things together. The reality is that when the project got out, and after few months touring the world, talking about the Panama Papers, I started feeling very exhausted, physically and emotionally, and very detached from what I was doing. I started being cranky. I started being negative. I started not liking what I was doing. And I was like, 'Well, I should be happy. But I'm not. I feel empty inside. I feel like my gas tank is completely empty, too. And I don't like what I'm doing. And I don't know why. Because there's no reason why.' Because I had a great team. I was working for an amazing organisation. I could work on anything I wanted. I mean, there were not political pressures, [I didn't feel] like there were some topics I couldn't cover. No, I had all the freedom in the world. And yet, there I was, unhappy, empty, lonely, sad.

That was a turning point for me, when I decided that I couldn't be all those things in my early thirties and with a Pulitzer Prize. That's when I quit my job and started doing a process of recovering. I didn't know, but it turned out I was burnt out and that all these symptoms I just described are burnout, by definition. I basically started recovering from burnout. Recovering my energy first took me many, many months; then I started to see what I wanted to do, and I didn't want to go back to doing the same thing that I was doing. I always explain it, as, when you like chocolate cake, and they bring you a chocolate cake, and you eat a lot of chocolate cake, and then you spend the whole night vomiting. And then the following day, you're, like, 'No more chocolate cake for me my whole life . . .'

I started figuring out something else I could do, and I specialised in digital wellness, initially, to help people around the world connect with technology in a healthier way, regardless of their profession. But the reality was that at the beginning of the pandemic, a lot of colleagues from journalism from all around the world started to contact me and say, 'Mar, you've de-stressed. You feel more calm. You're better now. So, what did you do, because I feel the same way?' That's when I called my former personal development coach Kim Brees, and we started, with another colleague from Spain who joined, Aldara Martitegui, an initiative called The Self Investigation,[16] to help journalists with their stress management, for many things – their work, but especially also the stress coming from technology, because at the beginning of the pandemic, a lot of people were overwhelmed. So that's how we started. It was a pandemic project, I would say. And as we kept going, we started seeing hundreds of people wanting to join our courses in English and in Spanish. And the conversation in different countries progressed around the importance of wellbeing and mental health, and a year and a bit later, we realised we needed to register as an entity. We've been registered as a non-profit since November 2021; since then, The Self Investigation [has been] a foundation, and we are working towards building an organisation that can help journalists with wellbeing and mental health. I'm very happy that we can now say 'mental health', because it was such a taboo term before.

Notes

15 Extracted from author interview with Mar Cabra, February 2023
16 https://theselfinvestigation.com/

11 The pandemic and a perfect storm of pressures

If Covid brought one of the biggest news stories in living memory for many working in the news media and forced a reinvention of the industry, it did not emerge from a period of relative serenity for journalism or journalists. The years preceding the pandemic brought a rise in attacks against our profession, some licensed by elected leaders. From the United States to Turkey, Hungary to India, the Philippines to Brazil, politicians and officials directly undermined the news media with populist and polarising rhetoric, and there was a rise in physical and online violence against journalists. Online harassment, the focus of Chapter 9, ballooned, with women journalists targeted disproportionately.

Trust in mainstream media decreased, with the proliferation of social media providing many more sources of information. Journalists were fighting for credibility, drowned out by misinformation, and trying to verify even greater volumes of views and news sources. Many legacy media organisations were accused of being out of touch, and struggled to grapple with how to better reflect the audiences they were supposed to serve.

The global pandemic exacerbated stressors that journalists were already facing, brought new pressures, and created a perfect storm of challenges to the mental health and wellbeing of our colleagues. 'The game changer for me, looking at it from the outside, has been the pandemic,' said Professor Anthony Feinstein, who carried out a survey in June 2020 in association with the Reuters Institute for the Study of Journalism (RISJ). 'I think the pandemic basically said to people: you can't ignore mental health any longer. And I think journalism was very open to that message.'[1] The study found a significant number of journalists reporting on Covid-19 showed signs of anxiety and depression,[2] and that 'even experienced reporters working for large, well-funded media organizations are often struggling to cope with the demands on reporting on the pandemic'. While the data offered a warning to newsrooms, it also underscored the value of practical support for journalists, with Feinstein noting it 'showed in real time that if newsrooms put into place therapy, journalists are less anxious'.

In the months that preceded the survey, our industry saw decades of work practice reinvented. Many journalism workspaces were designed to encourage spontaneous collaboration and community across open spaces with a central

DOI: 10.4324/9781003344179-11

hub. But, suddenly, newsrooms became almost entirely remote, or hybrid. The chat across the news desk with colleagues, the water-cooler moments where we could check in with each other, that served as the birthplace for many ideas and connections, were no longer.

During the pandemic, journalists began their careers, changed jobs, and became managers, sometimes without ever meeting their new colleagues in person. Our industry, which has always been built on connection, much of it in person, became disconnected. We adopted new processes of working, of communicating, or collaborating, adapting to technologies we had scarcely considered prior to 2020. We became increasingly reliant on our phones and digital devices to stay connected with the world. Our calendars became filled with back-to-back meetings and because they were remote, we no longer walked between them, no longer had the space to reflect, process and prepare. We no longer commuted, and the bridge between home and work became non-existent. We were hyper-connected and disconnected simultaneously at work. Movement outside of people's homes was restricted in many countries, with schools, businesses, leisure activities and travel curtailed. The pandemic brought unprecedented uncertainty that affected everyone, albeit in different ways.

Joyce Adeluwoye-Adams MBE, Editor, Newsroom Diversity at Reuters and whose remit also includes mental health, said of the pandemic: 'It really did help us normalise the conversation around mental health, and it also helped us have more conversations about how we were feeling during this really difficult time, where it felt like the world was all going through the same thing.'[3] The pandemic made it easier for Reuters to prioritise mental health offerings, such as their regular mental health week, as well as training and sessions for colleagues:

> I think getting journalists to talk about their trauma during the pandemic made it easier for them to reach out and seek help. The amount of people that have reached out to therapists and who have attended mental health sessions, you sort of wonder whether or not that's a good thing or a bad thing. It could cut both ways. Yes, it might be an indication that we're more stressed and need much more support around this. But also, for me, I'd like to think it is because we are normalising the conversation, that people feel now they can come out about their mental health, and what is impacting on them.

Because there were a lot of things impacting them. Around the world, many journalists, with little previous experience of enduring physical threat, found themselves covering a constantly shifting story in their local communities, in which risk and danger were present, but often difficult to detect. They had little preparation for this. They weren't travelling to some far-off hostile environment, and the rhetoric – including in the UK, where then prime minister Boris Johnson frequently used language more akin to that used in conflict – certainly made it seem as if they were working in a war zone.

It is unsurprising that some journalists also described the situation with terminology traditionally reserved for war zones. It was the closest many of them had come to covering a hostile environment, and that brought intense pressures for individuals and the industry. In a podcast episode for Headlines Network, my colleague John Crowley and I spoke with Victoria Macdonald, the Channel 4 News Health and Social Care Editor, and Emily Morgan, the ITV News Health Editor.[4] Emily told us:

> It's difficult as a health journalist to say that, but it certainly was a war and it felt like the battlefield had come to suburban hospitals, I think in a sense in the way that we had to reserve our energy and ensure we were constantly assessing our mental wellbeing and checking in ourself, and making sure we had the energy or ability to continue what we were doing. That was very important. We didn't have flak jackets, but of course we had PPE [personal protective equipment][5] and that became our armour, if you like, in the hospitals. In the same way [with] a conflict, you go in, and you don't know what to expect, you don't know what is round the corner – I think that was the same.[6]

Needing to report from the front lines of the pandemic in what was the biggest story of her career, Morgan explained how she had to navigate concerns she would infect her loved ones, while knowing members of the public were relying on her and continuing to bear witness amid great uncertainty.

> The first time I went into a hospital, I had to have a conversation with my family; it was. 'Okay, they've asked me to do this. We have to do this, we need to do it – there was no question about that – but should it be me?' And at this time, we didn't know very much about Covid and what it did. My husband is in his fifties. I had to have conversations about whether he was prepared for me to take that risk and bring anything home, potentially any infection. I've got children. I had to think about them, so all those initial decisions had to be made and, of course, once we were there, it was a hostile environment.

Both Morgan and McDonald spoke candidly about the toll their work took on their mental health and how important it was for them to be able to speak about this and gain support from each other and their ITN colleagues. Their insights chime with some of the points made by Stephen Jukes, Karen Fowler-Watt and Gavin Rees in their article, 'Reporting the Covid-19 pandemic', which notes how significantly the practice of journalism changed. The authors corroborate much of what I have heard over the past few years: in terms of the emotional labour of reporting the pandemic, the relentlessness of it, the fact that journalists were unused to covering a disaster of such magnitude on their doorstep, that they felt they were 'always on', and – as Morgan noted – that they were covering something in their own communities, while trying to navigate personal and professional boundaries.

The digital environment made journalists accessible to the public, but also accentuated the sense of 'always on'. They found themselves fielding approaches on social media and following up links sent to their mobile phones. These journalists painted a picture of emotional labour that is relentless and exhausting, where professional and personal boundaries no longer existed and where feelings of personal vulnerability were intensified. The sense of precarity was most marked for those with fewer economic resources, for example, those from minority backgrounds or with underlying mental health issues. Some were concerned about job security.[7]

If one of the underlying principles of ethical journalism is accountability, our industry found itself forced by Covid to confront the inequities within its own structures and institutions, something this article also noted. In addition, the pandemic brought a renewed focus on the health and social inequities faced by many Black people as a result of systemic racism. In early 2020, the killing by police in the United States of George Floyd ignited the Black Lives Matter movement. Both Covid and this killing of another unarmed Black man highlighted the additional emotional and professional burdens carried by Black journalists.

In October 2021, Jessica Gold wrote a piece for *Forbes* entitled 'We need to talk about the experience of Black journalists.'[8] In it, she cited the experience of Stacy-Marie Ishmael, mentioned in earlier chapters earlier in this book, who left her job as the executive editor of *The Texas Tribune* in March 2021, after 'an absolute brutal year for many people, and especially for non-white people'. Within the *Forbes* article, Gold also linked to a piece by Patrice Peck in *The New York Times*, entitled 'Black Journalists are exhausted'.[9] With the subtitle, 'but we keep on keeping on', Peck explained:

> As we've heard again and again, these are extraordinary times. However, it's an especially peculiar time to be a black journalist. The pandemic has laid bare many of the same racial inequities that generations of black journalists have been covering since 1827 when the Freedom's Journal birthed the black press. While this pandemic is unique, the waves of trauma crashing down on my community are not.

The pandemic underscored just how interconnected the issues of diversity and inclusivity are with mental health. It highlighted the need for newsrooms to recognise that people experience mental health differently and for them to provide a range of support. But, critically, because everyone was impacted in some way, it was an invitation to lessen some of the taboos around talking and extend the conversation to other areas affecting the psychological wellbeing of journalists. 'I think Covid lit a fire, under conversations, and for us at the ABC, under just reducing stigma and increasing awareness around mental health,'[10] said Nicolle White, Social Media Wellbeing Advisor for the Australian Broadcast Corporation.

Covid has been a massive change. I think, as an organisation, we've brought in a Social Media Wellbeing Advisor, specifically, which I think creates a space for people to feel comfortable – not only just in social media, but it [also] reflects broadly that wellbeing is really prioritised by the organisation and so we really have seen an uptick in staff feeling comfortable. Even for me personally, I certainly feel much more comfortable in the workplace, speaking about the way that my work impacts me, than perhaps I would have two years ago, which is great, because we are then able to get to places where we can be proactive around it, instead of people being injured through their work.

Covid accelerated the conversation around mental health in the Asia Pacific region, according to Amantha Perera, the Sri Lankan journalist and project lead for Dart Centre Asia Pacific.

Words like trauma, mental wellbeing, words like distress – they've come more into common circulation. So you get that kind of conversation going in places like Sri Lanka, Nepal, Bangladesh, the Pacific Islands, more often than we saw before, and that's kind of made it easier for those like me to push the other idea we've been also pushing, which is, 'Look, we need to talk about the mental wellbeing of journalists.' You can't have a journalist reporting on a pandemic stuck in their house, in fear of getting infected, writing about this without talking about how it is going to have an impact. And it has allowed us to kind of go beyond that. I'm working on a long-term project, concentrating on Sri Lanka, and it has allowed us to talk about historical issues in Sri Lanka having an impact on the journalism community. The impact of the civil war in Sri Lanka – for years, we never spoke about this. Covid pushed it into the journalism conversation. And when we created that space, colleagues opened up about how difficult it has been at different levels, when the very social fabric they belong to appears to be melting around them and you just don't talk about it. Why? because that is what journalists do. Covid changed that.[11]

In Mexico too, Covid has proved to be a watershed moment, said Ana Zellhuber, a Mexican psychologist and emergency psychology expert:

I think that, now, people talk about it. Now, people are interested in the subject. Before, it was really hard. I mean, most people were like, 'Yeah, a little thing here, a little bit there', but not really into it. It was like there were other pressing matters, always something more important. They didn't understand that mental health was the thing that was corrupting all the rest. Because if people are not in a good state of mind, they're going to take more risks, and they're going to put their lives at risk, and they're going to work less, and they're going to get sick more. So mental health is like a pillar. And I think people are starting to understand this.[12]

Despite the pandemic's indisputable impact on many journalists' mental health, Australia-based journalist and workplace mental health trainer Dean Yates gave little credit to the pandemic in terms of shifting conversations.

All Covid has done is made media organisations respond by saying, 'Oh, we better get a training course organised, we better have someone come in and show a few slides.' I don't see any evidence of any media organisation really taking this issue seriously and implementing a serious mental health strategy that has clear policies, that has clear input from staff, that has external advice spread over three or four years, that's got evaluation built into it. I don't see anything like that at all. So, anything else is just window dressing – which is not to say that a bit of training can't help.[13]

For many months, India was one of the countries that was worst affected by the pandemic, as highlighted by Tanmoy Goswami, a journalist, suicide prevention and mental health advocate, and creator of Sanity, an independent, reader-funded mental health storytelling platform.[14]

I talked to a bunch of journalists who said that, individually, one or two editors helped them out. Some people lost their parents during Covid and one or two editors helped them out. But they said that, at the same time, 'We were shocked we didn't receive a single email, even from the head office, or from the top brass, acknowledging what a crazy time this was for reporters to go out there and put their lives at risk, and then come back and, you know, start working after personal bereavement.' And there were many reporters who fell ill because their newsrooms had not given them any sort of basic protection in Covid, so all of that happened.[15]

At the same time as the global pandemic, there was an infodemic, defined by the World Health Organization as 'too much information including false or misleading information in digital and physical environments during a disease outbreak'.[16] This meant there was an overwhelming volume for journalists to sift through, process, verify and, at times, debunk, even as data, details and decisions kept changing. Simultaneously, the public service role of journalism was more important than at any time in living memory, and those who sought to detract, undermine and attack our colleagues also did so at unprecedented rates, through an explosion of online threats and harassment. Those at the forefront of fact-checking and on the front lines of online violence were often very vulnerable to mental health impacts, as discussed in Chapter 9.

In early 2022, I facilitated a conversation for an international news organisation. One of the participants was a young Indonesian journalist, who was isolated in her Jakarta apartment because of a stringent lockdown but constantly connected to her phone. She explained how she felt her mental health was suffering because of the intensity of some of the conspiracies she was facing in her fact-checking, while she used the same digital device to connect with friends and family. On the other side of the world, in Europe, I spoke with young journalists, during the early months of Russia's invasion of Ukraine, in 2022. They were working, exposed to graphic material, from the same rooms where they slept. Unable to forget that content, they were isolated and at risk of their mental health being impacted by this vicarious trauma.

Authorities responded to the global pandemic in different ways, some of them using draconian emergency measures to clamp down on press freedom under the guise of protecting people from the pandemic. In Turkey, Hungary, Brazil and elsewhere, journalists were arrested and attacked for doing their work, their reporting called into question, reputations undermined and pressures piled on them that went beyond direct reporting on the pandemic. For other journalists, it meant that the work that defined them was on hold. Travel was curtailed in many parts of the world, meaning those used to going overseas to cover conflict and crises were stuck at home. So too were those who covered entertainment, sports and other events restricted by Covid.

Egyptian journalist Abeer Saady spent years travelling extensively in areas of high risk, and explained how the pandemic forced her to take a break: 'I think I was running all the time, always doing things, travelling from country to country, doing, doing. But [the pandemic] put me home and got me out of the survival mode, so I had depression for the first time during the pandemic.'[17]

Something similar came up in an industry meeting I facilitated early in the pandemic. News leaders expressed their concern for the mental health of some colleagues who, unable to travel to cover conflict overseas, felt a sense of identity loss and a lack of purpose that impacted their mental health profoundly. Then, as the months went on, certain governments employed extremely strict lockdowns. These brought a real personal toll for many journalists, particularly those working in countries a long way from their families. In China, for example, journalists were stuck far from home for many months, either in distant provinces or overseas. They faced the daunting prospect of extensive isolation if they left to see loved ones and then returned to where they worked. On top of this, the cost of travel became prohibitive even when lockdowns lifted, which became an extra source of anxiety for people long separated from families and friends. Aleluwoye-Adams reflected on how the pressures of the pandemic changed as the months went on, with journalists working harder, even as they grew increasingly exhausted:

> During the pandemic, a lot of journalists felt like they couldn't get home. So they were stranded and isolated without their communities, their family and support, their friends around them, which added an additional pressure. [There was] hyperconnectivity, the 24/7 news cycle,

particularly during the pandemic, where everybody felt the world was shutting down – but not in journalism. Everyone was working much harder, I would say. So we needed, as journalists, to find a way to re-charge and switch off, whilst dealing with that digital overload as well. Online harassment, especially in this geopolitical environment, we find ourselves in – that has gone through the roof as well. [There's] the severe bullying and explicit threats, particularly of a sexual nature that women and women of colour seem to be a target of, and obviously, the racial unrest with George Floyd and Covid. Navigating the challenges of covering a global story that is both personal and professional – all of those things have added up.

Dr Sian Williams, the broadcaster and counselling psychologist, echoed the sentiments of Adeluwoye-Adams, in terms of the cumulative nature of the pressures:

There has been an awareness that somehow the personal and the professional can blend and that you can be in a state of high alert for a long time. And I think we all became aware, with people working from home, with people being impacted by the pandemic, as well as having to report on it; that psychological flex I've talked about before, that ability to bend, has gone a bit.[18]

For a global newsroom like Reuters, there was value in being able to offer support to journalists in a flexible way. They ran workshops, training and webinars and offered services through platforms that really came into their own during the pandemic. Zoom, Microsoft Teams, Google Hangouts, all of these – and more – provided visual remote connections that could bring journalists together with their sources, story subjects and each other. They were far from perfect, of course, and brought their own stressors, but they also brought positives.

At Agence France-Presse, conference tools had been used prior to the pandemic, but Covid prompted AFP to use them more effectively and they came to play an important role in mental health conversations across the international company, as described by Phil Chetwynd:

We regularly do 'town halls' with the entire newsroom, where you can choose the things you want to talk about, and you can also let people ask questions. It's a game changer, because they can actually see that the person at the top of the tree believes this stuff, because they're not just reading a note – they can see the way you speak, your tone, the priority you give to something. The large-scale appropriation of conferencing tools is incredibly positive in our ability to humanise management in a global company, to be able to push stuff like this that would be harder through notes and messages and so on. Because they need to hear the empathy in your voice, need to hear that it's for real. They need to hear that it really does matter to you.[19]

Certainly, for global news organisations like AFP and Reuters, these platforms, used effectively, provided an opportunity to offer flexible training, workshops and access to resources, enabling people to connect at times that suited them given their location and altered circumstances, while also linking colleagues in different parts of the world.

These platforms also allowed journalists to see beyond the colleague, to the person behind the job. While we were physically distanced, we became more aware of other aspects of our colleagues' lives. We knew about their immediate environments, if they lived alone, or shared space with children, parents, house mates, partners, pets. At least until people started using computer-generated backgrounds, we knew something of their surroundings, tastes, backgrounds, preferences. Covid blurred the boundaries between our home and work lives, for a long period of time. Yet if Covid taught us a lot more about our colleagues than we knew previously, for those who did not belong to newsrooms, the isolation was often extreme.

'If we're going to talk about the journalism workplace, we're also talking about hybrid newsrooms and the increased freelance community, the terrible toll that working remotely has caused for many journalists,'[20] said Jane Hawkes, co-founder of the Canadian Journalism Forum on Violence and Trauma.[21] In response to the specific emotional burden experienced by different groups of journalists, conversations began that connected affinity groups to each other, building solidarity and a sense of support. Organisations like the Society for Freelance Journalists[22] were founded, recognising both the growing number of freelance journalists around the world and the need for a supportive community when people feel disconnected. Hawkes explained:

> Covid, however horrendous, brought support groups, and people who are advocates for journalists' health, together in a different way. I think that's changed the conversation, I really do. Because I don't know what anybody thought was normal before Covid. I don't know if anybody's gone back to 'normal', whatever that was. If that means going back to a toxic workplace, that's not okay. I think Covid was a sort of pivotal moment in how those conversations could be framed. There's something existential there; when you've got a global pandemic, it sharpens your thinking about how you support each other.

At the time of writing this book, many newsrooms are navigating what that 'normal' might look like, trying to find a balance in a world that has shown that award-winning journalism is possible when working remotely, while exposing the downsides of digital hyper-connection and the importance of social connection. In the meantime, we've become acutely aware that any response must be flexible to people's needs. It feels too important a lesson to ignore. In global terms, the consensus is that Covid changed the way we speak about mental health, but it did not do away with taboos entirely. When we were forced to reinvent our ways of working, we were given a chance to reshape the cultures of our newsrooms and create spaces where people feel safer speaking about their experiences. We were offered an opportunity to lead empathetically in ways that recognised the toll recent years had taken, and the very necessary work journalists have done through the pandemic.

Notes

1. Author interview with Professor Anthony Feinstein, July 2022
2. Meera Selva and Anthony Feinstein (2020) 'COVID-19 is hurting journalists' mental health. News outlets should help them now', Reuters Institute for the Study of Journalism. Available at: https://reutersinstitute.politics.ox.ac.uk/news/covid-19-hurting-journalists-mental-health-news-outlets-should-help-them-now
3. Author interview with Joyce Adeluwoye-Adams, MBE, January 2023
4. Sadly, Emily Morgan passed away in May 2023, from cancer at the age of 45
5. Personal protective equipment
6. Headlines Network, (2022) *Behind the Headlines*, Episode 9: Emily Morgan and Victoria Macdonald, [podcast]. Available at: https://audioboom.com/posts/8135047-emily-morgan-and-victoria-macdonald
7. Stephen Jukes, Karen Fowler-Watt. and G. Rees, (2022) 'Reporting the Covid-19 pandemic:
Trauma on our own doorstep'. *Digital Journalism*, 10(6), pp.997–1014.
8. Jessica Gold (2021) 'We need to talk about the experiences of Black journalists', *Forbes*. Available at: https://www.forbes.com/sites/jessicagold/2021/10/31/we-need-to-talk-about-the-experiences-of-black-journalists/?sh=72343b9a44ff
9. Patrice Peck (2020) 'Black journalists are exhausted'. *The New York Times*. Available at: https://www.nytimes.com/2020/05/29/opinion/coronavirus-black-people-media.html
10. Author interview with Nicolle White, December 2022
11. Author interview with Amantha Perera, November 2022
12. Author interview with Ana Zellhuber, May 2023
13. Author interview with Dean Yates, September 2022
14. SanitybyTanmoy.com
15. Author interview with Tanmoy Goswami, August 2022
16. https://www.who.int/health-topics/infodemic
17. Author interview with Abeer Saady, November 2022
18. Author interview with Dr Sian Williams, October 2022
19. Author interview with Phil Chetwynd, December 2022
20. Author interview with Jane Hawkes, February 2023
21. https://www.journalismforum.ca/
22. https://freelancesoc.org/

Reference list

Gold, J. (2021) 'We need to talk about the experiences of Black journalists', *Forbes*. Available at: https://www.forbes.com/sites/jessicagold/2021/10/31/we-need-to-talk-about-the-experiences-of-black-journalists/?sh=72343b9a44ff

Headlines Network, (2022) *Behind the Headlines*, Episode 9: Emily Morgan and Victoria Macdonald, [podcast]. Available at: https://audioboom.com/posts/8135047-emily-morgan-and-victoria-macdonald

Jukes, S., Fowler-Watt, K. and Rees, G. (2022) 'Reporting the Covid-19 pandemic: Trauma on our own doorstep', *Digital Journalism*, 10(6), pp. 997–1014.

Peck, P. (2020) 'Black journalists are exhausted'. *The New York Times*. Available at: https://www.nytimes.com/2020/05/29/opinion/coronavirus-black-people-media.html

Selva, M. and Feinstein, Prof. A. (2020) 'COVID-19 is hurting journalists' mental health. News outlets should help them now', Reuters Institute for the Study of Journalism. Available at: https://reutersinstitute.politics.ox.ac.uk/news/covid-19-hurting-journalists-mental-health-news-outlets-should-help-them-now

Their story – Kari Cobham[23]

Kari Cobham is a Trinidadian writer, editor and digital strategist based in the US city of Atlanta. A survivor of a devastating car wreck, and a journalist, who for years covered tragedy in her local community, Kari is a staunch advocate of changing the way we speak about mental health in our journalism communities and coverage.

> When I was a 24-year-old journalist, and I was running out and covering fatal car accidents and shootings and stabbings and that kind of stuff, I was not thinking about the vicarious trauma of interviewing families in grief. And it wasn't until I was having a hard time, and even then, I didn't want to be seen as weak, right? But I was thoroughly unprepared.
>
> We can't have folks coming into the industry without a clear awareness of the mental health impact of the work, and some tools to deal with that, because folks are going to struggle, or they're going to burn out. And if you already live with mental health disorders, those are going to get worse. And so, I'm just really passionate about preparing folks before they even get in the industry, about what they're going to face. And what the tools are that they need to cultivate to survive.
>
> One of the things that's super important to me is preparing young journalists to go into the newsroom, so journalism schools. And for folks who don't go to J-school, but they're in a newsroom anyway, there needs to be training around trauma, and vicarious trauma and moral injury and mental health reporting and the mental health of journalists. I remember talking to a journalist for a story that I was doing on how trauma affects journalists. And he said, and I'll never forget it, 'You know, we don't send a journalist out to cover baseball, if they don't understand the game.' But we're sending journalists out in the field, who have no clue about how their work is going to impact them. So, you're already putting them at a disadvantage.
>
> It's just understanding what it is, what the different terms are. So, what is trauma? What is vicarious trauma? What are all the terms that we hear being used around mental health? So, by definition, understanding what those things are, and then how it connects to the work that we do. How does trauma affect you? What kind of impact does it have? How do you identify that you were traumatised after a story? What kind of stories can you expect to have an impact on you? And then what can you do about it? How do you mitigate that?
>
> For example, there are stories that people know or consider to be difficult stories. Like mass shootings. It's a no-brainer that this is going to be a difficult story to cover. I'm probably going to cry. I'm going to be stressed-out. And people already know by dint of how big the news is, or how difficult the news is, that it's going to be hard. But folks don't always recognise that the smaller, quick-turn, daily stories that we have

to cover also do have an impact. Like, the car accidents and the stabbings and the shootings are maybe part of the daily news that folks may go out and cover but the impact of that work [accumulates]. I think that a lot of journalists don't recognise that.

She says there is inconsistency across the industry with regard to how different organisations deal with mental health. Newsrooms vary in the way they address it with their staff, what policies they have and how they are communicated, the culture and to what extent conversations are normalised, as well as how senior leadership prioritises mental health. Kari sees responsibility around mental health awareness as being two-fold:

Some part of it is on the journalists, and part of it is on the leaders in the newsroom. So, for the issues that you're aware of, there needs to be some sensitivity around that. I'll give you an example. When I was 24/25, I was on my way into work and I had a really bad car accident on the interstate, and my car rolled over a few times. I shouldn't have walked out of it. After that accident, I became obsessed with other accidents on the road, specifically rollovers, and people who lived and people who died and what was the difference between the two? I was out of work for about two weeks because I was all banged-up. And then probably less than a month after I came back, a teenager at a local school had taken a car and gone joyriding with friends and the car rolled over. I think some of the kids died. And they were having a memorial outside of the school. My editor at the time thought it was a good idea to send me to cover it. Because I was good at drawing people out. People will come up to me and just tell me everything. So he sent me out to cover this story. And at the time, I was, like, 'This car accident isn't going to stop me. I'm going to go out there and show them that I can still do my job.'

But in retrospect, I'm like, 'What the fuck was he thinking?' He knew that I had just been in a rollover, and now he's sending me to cover a fatal rollover. That was the most insensitive, thoughtless thing that he could have done. And so that was an error on his part, as a news manager: aware of the issue, yet still would send me out to do this.

The same goes for when coverage is happening around racism and race – you becoming the 'go-to' person in the newsroom to either cover these stories or help folks understand what the issues are, or the exact opposite, which is [that] you can't cover the story because you're Black, you know, and that keeps you from being objective.

From the news managers' side, they also need to have an awareness of the impact of certain news and certain coverage on various communities. So if you're talking about abortion [or] trans bills in the House [of Representatives], when they're having Black Lives Matter protests, when there's another police shooting of a Black man – those are going to impact the journalists in the newsroom who are tied to that community, and there needs to be an understanding of that from the editors' perspective, and the impact of the work, and so there is responsibility.

The other piece is the responsibilities of the journalist and their own mental health, being able to say no and having the agency to say no. I didn't have the agency, when my editor sent me out to do this story, to say, 'No, this isn't good for me.' That's not where my head was at. And I think even if your head is there, folks just feel reluctant to say no. But it's okay to say no.

I'll give you another example: when I worked at this newspaper in Florida, I had a cop shift, and I did it once a week. And then the person who covered that beat full-time left, and [the editors] basically were like, 'We're going to slot you into this shift. And that's going to be your new beat.' And I was, like, 'I cover this shift, one day a week and I feel like it breaks me and I'm on antidepressants. So, I promise you that if you put me in the shift full-time, it's not going to be good for my mental health, and that ain't gonna happen.'

And so, I fought that tooth and nail, because I just knew that I wouldn't survive it. I had no choice but to fight it, because the alternative was not something that I wanted to consider. All of which says that if you're a survivor of sexual assault, and the person who's assigning this story doesn't know, it's going to be on you to say. You don't even have to say why, like, 'I'm a survivor. I can't do this story', but [rather], 'I am not comfortable doing this story' or 'This story isn't for me.' Some of the responsibility as a journalist [is] to identify where they are and have the tools to be able to do that and say, 'No, I'm not going do this.'

Note

23 Based on author interview with Kari Cobham, October 2022

12 Self-care and supporting others

Self-care is not selfish and yet in the busy world of journalism, we often forget to look after ourselves. Unless we find time to support our own mental health, we will not be able to help others, and when our mental health suffers, so too will our journalism. However, it is important to recognise that the onus for wellbeing should not sit squarely with the individual. Self-care needs to be complemented by other support strategies in our newsrooms and industry, including more specialised help where needed.

This chapter is not a substitute for medical advice or therapy. It draws on conversations with colleagues and clinicians, offering practical suggestions for journalists on self-care. It also offers tips on how we can support colleagues, not as mental health experts, but as compassionate human beings. It recognises that, just as everyone experiences mental health differently, some strategies may work better for some people than for others.

In some cultures, there is a tendency for all the responsibility for mental health to be put on the individual, rather than seeing it as a collaborative thing. For me, there is a fine balance. If 'wellbeing' begins with letters 'we', then perhaps this offers a reminder that this is a collective effort. Similarly, I like to remind people that 'mental health' begins with two letters that spell 'me', and therefore we do need to prioritise ourselves. This might be tough to get our head around in an industry that conditions us to run after the story, often at a cost to our health. We may want to consider incorporating self-care into our routines, making it non-negotiable, as we might other forms of physical self-care such as brushing our teeth, or scheduling it into our diaries, ensuring we intentionally factor in breaks or other practices that support our wellbeing. Otherwise, there's a risk we will become the last on our own lists, because the times we need it most may be when we are busiest or feel we least deserve it.

Self-care doesn't need to be a big gesture that costs lots. With practice, it becomes easier to integrate into our regular activities. It can begin with choosing to spend five minutes outside, deciding to stop checking notifications, singing along to a favourite song, walking before work, limiting the number of apps, platforms and communications channels that keep us almost constantly connected. It's about recognising what will make us feel better in ourselves,

DOI: 10.4324/9781003344179-12

even if some of the activities – like stepping away from social media – might initially seem hard or counter-intuitive.

As mentioned by Drew Berrie of the mental health charity Mind in Chapter 10, safety demonstrations on aircraft remind us to put on our own oxygen mask first before helping others. We won't be in any fit state to help others if we don't have access to what keeps us well. Of course, if we are very unwell, this might not be possible, and this is where it is important that others are able to look out for us, support us and help us get help. This idea of prioritising ourselves is a particularly important one for news leaders and will be discussed in Chapter 13.

We probably all know the person who ignores their own mental health and in so doing affects those around them. I refer to it as the mouldy satsuma in the fruit bowl. If the piece of fruit is allowed to go mouldy, it can spread quickly to damage others around it. Likewise, one person can bring down the morale of the whole newsroom. But in an industry that has traditionally thrived off burning the candle at both ends, where we are told to not become the story, how do we make ourselves a priority? And in a world of digital overwhelm, how do we disconnect without losing touch, and take a break without the news breaking us?

The first step in self-care is giving ourselves permission to prioritise *us*. Self-care is not a 'nice to have'. It is a 'need to have'. When we are stressed, or under pressure, lots of things may seem beyond our control. Early in the pandemic, Professor Anthony Feinstein and I were talking about how many journalists, including me, felt anxious and overwhelmed. He told me that worrying about things over which we have no influence wastes energy. Now, I try to focus on what I can control, and worry less about what I can't, be that the behaviour of others, government policy, news events, the weather. It is not always easy, but it has lifted a weight off my shoulders.

Dr Cait McMahon, the founding managing director of Dart Centre Asia Pacific, explained how we can use a similar strategy when we feel overwhelmed by major news stories, specifically ones that involve issues of inequity. She suggested we ask ourselves: 'What can I focus on here? Where can I do a good job? Is there something specific I can choose that really gets my juices going? Is it women and climate change? Do I look at the violence that happens when people are in poverty?' She elaborated:

> Find what gets you going, because that's going to engage you. And then find how you can report your best on that small aspect. It's the same stuff that Anthony would say: find that small aspect that gives you a sense of purpose and meaning, where you feel that you might be able to inform the public, about this little bit here, and then you might want to put it in a global context or whatever, but just so you don't get so overwhelmed, take small chunks that are controllable.[1]

Dr McMahon also noted the importance of purpose and meaning, and how reminding ourselves why we do our work can be very helpful for our mental health. Some journalists see it as holding power to account, shining a light in the darkness, fighting against injustice or inequity, or amplifying the voices of others. Some call it 'bearing witness'. Tasmanian journalist and workplace mental health trainer Dean Yates has reminded colleagues of this, to help them deal with some of the distressing things they encounter:

> For these journalists who find themselves in this weird world that we have today, where you've got half the population hating you, your job is to bear witness. That's what I would say to them. My job is to bear witness. Someone was asking me how they should deal with this distressing imagery that they were having to edit, and I said, 'Your job is to bear witness, your job is to make this horrible shit palatable for your audience. You are doing a public service. By doing this, you are bearing witness, as if you're out in the field; you're bearing witness to this stuff, so that everyone else out there doesn't have to view it.'
>
> You obviously need to use strategies and techniques like minimising sound and all that sort of stuff, but that's your mission. Yeah, that's a journalist's mission, to bear witness, and, I don't know, maybe that's something that the younger journalists can keep in mind.[2]

Journalists may feel they have no right to complain because they chose to do their jobs, regarding their experiences as inconsequential compared with the experiences of those whose stories they tell. But the trauma faced by one person does not invalidate the trauma faced by someone else. Comparison can be a real obstacle in terms of people seeking the support they might need. It can also eat up a huge amount of our energy, yet we persist, and social media compounds the compulsion to compare, based on an incomplete picture. Everyone is different; their history, perspective, identity, emotional load and coping strategies are different, and we can never know exactly what someone is going through.

Everyone has a right to support for their mental health. Everyone owes themselves compassion. The past few years have been tough. Awareness of what we have gone through or what we are going through is a helpful step towards self-compassion, and will help us better respond to additional stressors. One analogy used is a cup of tolerance, or the idea that we have only got so much capacity before our cup overflows. Some people use the idea of a bucket or jar. For me, the analogy of a pan helps. We need to be aware of the things that happen in our lives that take up space in these vessels, and recognise how to deal with them. There have been times when I felt as though there was so much boiling water in my pan it was close to overflowing. Equally, if I left the heat on for too long, all the water would evaporate, causing the bottom of the pan to burn. Self-care for me has been about identifying what I need to keep that temperature manageable, what adds extra volume to my pan or heat to the element. It is about adding and subtracting based on where I am at any given time. It is about learning to recognise what helps and what hinders and how I respond.

138   Self-care and supporting others

The BBC correspondent Clive Myrie was a guest on the Headlines Network podcast in early 2022, shortly after returning from Ukraine. He shared his self-care tips:

> I think it's about being honest with yourself and truthful with yourself that perhaps you've reached a certain limit, that perhaps you can't go on any more, that perhaps now is the time to stop, reassess, refocus, so that things don't get worse, and it's not about battling through that and being able to tell yourself you're a hero because you're doing that, or tell your employer you're a hero, because you're doing that, Actually, being heroic is being around for your family and friends and the people that love you. That's the most profound truth, I think, and if you're honest with yourself about that, then you'll be happier.[3]

It is important that individuals recognise when they have had enough. However, they may not always feel as if they have the agency to say no if someone more senior asks them to do something. The more I have focused on mental health, the more I have become attuned to my body's emotional climate – when things do not feel quite right and when they are going well. Dr Sian Williams, broadcaster, author and psychologist, told me that she suggested journalists think about their emotional load: 'red flags, which mean that your normal coping strategies or your normal levels of resilience might be tested'.[4] It is also important that we are able to access support elsewhere, from friends and within our newsroom. Our mental health and physical health are two sides of the same coin, meaning we should look after our bodies. We may feel unable to tear ourselves away from the desk, but making time to eat lunch in a different location is beneficial to our mood and productivity. Likewise, staying hydrated can do the same, so we should try to drink sufficient fluids, limiting our sugar, caffeine or alcohol intake.

For many journalists, alcohol has been a temporary fix. Historically, journalists have ended up in the bar after a particularly draining story, sharing experiences over several drinks. There is less of a heavy-drinking culture now, but there is still a tendency to over-rely on alcohol in some parts of our industry. It is best to avoid alcohol if possible, because it can make us feel worse, affect our mood, our sleep, our physical health, our work, relationship and finances.

Physical activity is an important part of self-care. Biologically, exercise of a certain intensity releases feel-good hormones, known as endorphins, which can boost our energy levels, and make us more productive. But any kind of physical activity can benefit us. It doesn't need to be a marathon that you run, and you can start small. The important thing is that you start. If you exercise outside, connecting with nature and the world around us can also be beneficial, because it takes us away from the screen and offers a sense of perspective and an alternative view on the world beyond our work. Some people find it easier to exercise with a friend. Others prefer to do so alone. Some people thrive off challenges that can accompany exercise, setting themselves goals and targets, celebrating the achievements they make. These needn't be huge and, on days when you might take a step back, it's important to recognise this isn't failure, but a temporary blip, pause or diversion.

Running has been a powerful medicine for my mental health, along with writing. However, I know that when my mental health is on a downwards trajectory, I tend to exercise too much. I have learned this is a warning to ease back and listen more to my body. As with many forms of self-care, exercise is best in moderation.

Sleep is one of the most important barometers of our mental health, according to Professor Feinstein. Yet it is often one of the first things to suffer when our mental health is compromised. When our sleep suffers, we are less able to cope with stressors. Our ability to function is compromised, our resilience lessened and our immune systems can be affected. And yet ensuring a decent night's sleep is easier said than done.

It can help to disconnect some time before we go to bed. Some people find it helpful to practise relaxation activities, like reading, meditating, listening to music, practising deep breathing, taking a bath. Speaking with colleagues from around the industry, it is clear that sufficient sleep is a major issue for journalists. Reuters is one news organisation that now offers sleep workshops, run by Charlie Morley, who describes himself as 'a lucid dreaming teacher and author who helps people wake up in their dreams and harness the power of sleep for psychological growth'.[5]

The pandemic blurred boundaries between our personal and work lives, increasing our reliance on digital connections in the absence of physical ones. Journalists are not the only people in society with an unhealthy reliance on our devices, a reliance that is affecting our wellbeing. It's often difficult to acknowledge that many of us are addicted to our phones, and that self-care also includes building a better relationship with technology. Of course, we need our devices for work. For digital natives, the idea of being without one's phone may be completely implausible. Many journalists have a real sense of FOMO, or 'fear of missing out', which heightens our attachment. The number of journalists who have told me that they sleep with their phone under their pillow or under the bed is astonishing. We worry we can't possibly step away from our phone in case we miss a breaking story. But we do not need to be connected all the time and being so can be detrimental to our mental health. We need to be in control of the digital tether, said Amantha Perera, journalism trainer for Dart Centre Asia Pacific:

> I think the heavy reliance on digital resources and online resources has given another opportunity to talk about this: that you're so reliant on these digital interface resources that their impact needs to be spoken about – the whole idea [of] where does the personal and the professional connect or disconnect. In places like Sri Lanka, and during the height of the protests in Myanmar, that was a big issue, because we kept telling journalists: 'Look, if your phone is your work phone and your personal

phone, and you take it to bed, and if there are these intense events happening in your country, you're never going to get any break. And how are you going to have a proper night's sleep, let alone do your job properly, and take care of whatever else that you need to take care of, if this is the way that you're dealing with this?' You need to have these kinds of interventions.

We are now beginning to understand the concept of context collapse with journalists and their digital usage. Because our personal and professional digital profiles are collapsing on to one another, we are unable to differentiate which is which. We react to situations that are entirely professional as if they were personal, because of this digitised blindness at play.[6]

It's often easier to start small. This might mean turning off notifications, deleting apps, or disabling Wi-Fi. It might mean stepping away from one's phone for a few minutes and building up to larger breaks. Mar Cabra, an expert in digital wellness, calls this creating 'friction', making it more difficult for us to connect digitally, where we put in place a barrier to the mindless scrolling that many of us do, and the knee-jerk reactions we have to every notification.

Many journalists need to be accessible outside of traditional working hours, by email, phone or other messaging devices. However, we still need to have protected personal time. News leaders can play an important role here, modelling behaviour. As members of a team, we can also have conversations with our colleagues about how and when to communicate outside of office hours, which channels to use when there is something urgent, and what constitutes urgent. Before social media, and 24-hour news, there was an on-call system for covering stories. One set of people, or hub, was responsible for monitoring breaking news and tasked with alerting relevant people if the story merited their additional involvement. For the others, it meant they had time to rest and disconnect, but they knew they would be informed if needed.

I vividly remember a conversation, however, at the start of the pandemic where a bureau chief of a major global news organisation told me he expected all his journalists to have their phones on at night. We need leaders to recognise how unhealthy this is for individuals, for organisations and our industry. We need them to give others permission to power off, even just occasionally. Because if they act this way, then they are role-modelling unhealthy behaviours that others may feel compelled to follow.

A lot of this is about boundaries, establishing digital ones to allow us to disconnect. In a world where there is often limited delineation between our work and personal time, there are other things we can do to demarcate those boundaries. Since working from home more regularly, I often go on a fake commute between my bedroom and home office. This creates a bridge between my personal and professional life and allows me physical activity before sitting at a screen all day. As mentioned in Chapter 7, ceremonies may be helpful – an idea shared by Drew Berrie – an activity to mark the beginning and end of one's working day. It might constitute covering up or putting away one's laptop, lighting a candle or something else meaningful.

As well as ensuring we have boundaries, we need to factor in breaks. It can be easy to spend hours in front of a screen without consciously taking time away. Sometimes actively scheduling those breaks can be helpful, especially now we need to work with less of the sense of spontaneity we had pre-Covid. 'Don't forget to breathe', we hear sometimes, which might seem like a rather obvious thing to say. But there is one kind of breathing, the snatched, ragged kind that most of us do when we are fraught, when time is tight and we are juggling too much. It's the kind where we are breathing more from our chests and our mouths. Then there is the breathing that babies, animals and some people do: from the belly, slower and often more from the nose. In May 2023, I was at the Media Strong Symposium in Belfast, where Nicola Doherty, lead psychologist for the regional trauma network across Northern Ireland, described the difference in this way. Almost every night since, I have practised breathing by placing one hand on my belly and one on my chest. focusing on trying to breathe like a baby.

Breathing is often overlooked as a form of self-care but done right it can bring vast improvements to our wellbeing, help us feel more relaxed and give us more energy. We can reach for it if things threaten to become overwhelming, a tiny window of respite in a hectic day. The charity Mind developed a breathing technique for people working in high-pressure environments that takes just 90 seconds, and is done by focusing on a square shape such as a laptop screen or window. To do it, you trace a line clockwise with your eyes, taking a deep breath in and out as you follow each line, keeping your breathing slow and steady. It involves the following:

Breathe in through your nose and out through your mouth. Try to keep your shoulders down and relaxed and place your hand on your stomach – it should rise as you breathe in and fall as you breathe out. Position your feet square on the ground, hips' width apart.

Count as you breathe. Start by counting 'one, two, three, four' as you breathe in and 'one, two, three, four' as you breathe out. Try to work out what's comfortable for you. Repeat the cycle four to five times. Give yourself a moment to reflect on how more relaxed you feel. Stretch and gather your thoughts before returning to work.[7]

Meditation or mindfulness allows us to connect with the present, clear our minds of worries and feel more grounded. Traditional forms of meditation and mindfulness are often dismissed by cynical media people, but the practice doesn't necessarily have to constitute sitting still and meditating, and it is a great form of self-care. Gina Chua, the executive editor of Semafor and a guest on the Headlines Network podcast, explained what it meant to her:

> I used to think of meditation as clearing your mind of things. It turns out that's not the case, at least not for me. When I tried to meditate, it would be like, 'My leg itches', 'Why's that fly around?' and so on. When

I draw, time just stops. There was a very good professor I had at university, and he wrote a book called *Flow*; flow is when you are so engrossed in [an] activity and you don't realise time and you look up, and it's eight hours later and you've forgotten to eat. Drawing is like that for me: two, three hours of complete immersion – you can't think because your brain is fully occupied with one thing. And it's been fantastic for me throughout the pandemic. If you don't want to meditate and you don't want to sit in a lotus position and do yoga, I think finding [an] activity that so fills your mind is one of the ways you can help prepare yourself for the rigours of the world.[8]

It is healthy to have a pastime that enables us to switch off from professional life, particularly a creative one where we can focus on other things, or one that allows us to be active. For me, these pastimes include writing, running and cycling. For other journalist colleagues, they are as varied as the individuals: jazz, yoga, computer games, t'ai chi, drawing, playing or watching football, baking, making music, building models. My advice to people is to find what makes their heart sing.

In April 2023, I was at the International Festival of Journalism in the Italian city of Perugia, where I attended a panel by Ana Zellhuber, the Mexican psychotherapist. She encouraged people to take time daily to dance, sing or engage in another activity that brought us joy. There was laughter from the audience, a sense that a taboo had been bridged, a reminder that joy can be a valuable antidote, especially when there is so much darkness in journalism.

When our mental health is poor doing anything to help ourselves can be difficult. We feel more isolated, and connecting with people can be hard. But we know that spending time with others does help a lot of people. Self-care is also about connecting with others. It is about finding people we want to spend time with, whose company we enjoy, those we trust. It may help us to speak with colleagues too if things are tough. It is not always easy to have those conversations at work, but if you feel comfortable doing so, you might want to think about discussing your mental health with your manager. In turn, they might be able to help you identify coping strategies and advise you of what your organisation can do. Therapy is another way of supporting your mental health. We do not need to wait to be unwell to seek help in this way. In our Headlines Network podcasts, we ask each of our journalist guests to share a mental health tip. Bryony Gordon, the award-winning author and journalist, said:

Connect, connect. Connection, connection, connection. Do the thing your brain tells you [that] you don't want to do, like get outside, connect with people, even when you don't want to, *especially* when you don't want to. Mental illnesses tend to tell you that you don't have them, or you're being silly or you're being dramatic, or you're being whatever. It's really important to know that often our brains will lie to us; our brains are not always telling the truth.[9]

Bryony's reminder is important. Our mental health may make it harder for us to do what we need to, to feel better. It is another reminder of the importance of having people we trust around us, who will notice when we are not quite ourselves, who check in with us, who make it easier for us to tell them that we're not doing okay. Sometimes, we need additional support. Dr Khaled Nasser works with journalists in the Middle East and Africa, and his first step in supporting them is helping them with their identity.

> I make sure that they develop a healthy perception of their 'I', of who they are. Self-esteem, self-confidence, self-efficacy, in essence, their capacities and their resources, to give them the sense of confidence, you pass through difficult times, and you find solutions, the problem-solving aspect, to remind them you can take care of yourself, not to lose hope in yourself, at least.[10]

One of the most important things I've learned is that some days are darker than others. It helps me to notice that and accept it's okay to not feel okay. Weather analogies can help when we think of our own mental health. Sometimes there will be storms, rain or clouds, and sometimes there will be sunshine. So too, every day the sun will set and every morning the sun will rise again, whether or not we see it.

On certain days, we might be less productive, or find it more difficult to achieve certain things. I often think about something said by Kathy English, the chair of the board of the Canadian Journalism Foundation and former public editor of the *Toronto Star*, who talked about giving ourselves permission to have days of lowered expectations. For this to work in journalism, we need to have strong enough relationships with our colleagues so we all know that we can cut ourselves and each other some slack at times, allowing for an occasional reduction in pressure on individuals and broader teams. It's a way of recognising we are all human.

Journalism is a vocation for many of us. It is a mission-driven profession, and that brings with it challenges. It means it can be even harder to cut ourselves such slack, to lower, even temporarily, the extraordinarily high standards to which many of us hold ourselves. Indian journalist Tanmoy Goswami is convinced we should be less wedded to the notion that ours is a job for life:

> All journalists have some incredibly, incredibly valuable skills, and there is no reason for us to sort of feel beholden to any one industry, because ultimately you are accountable to your family; you have to safeguard your own interests. I think there is no need or reason for journalists to feel that somehow the responsibility of saving the world is on their shoulders.[11]

It's refreshing to hear this attitude, but the reality is that, for many, journalism risks defining and consuming us. It demands sacrifices and compromises, leaving little space for other things in our lives. This being so, it's even more important that self-care includes ensuring we have something in our lives unrelated to work. ITV News' Health and Science Editor Emily Morgan, who passed away in May 2023, was a former colleague of mine who appeared on our Headlines Network podcast with her Channel 4 News colleague Victoria Macdonald, their Health and Social Care Editor. Speaking in 2022, Emily told us:

> Keep a tiny bit of your life that has absolutely nothing to do with the job, whether it's exercising or walking, spending time with your children, your husband, your family, your wife; just reserve that one thing that makes you happy and never, ever, ever, give it up.[12]

Anna Blundy, who co-founded The Mind Field, which offers psychotherapy to journalists and aid workers, also noted that sometimes we need help before we can practise self-care:

> This is why you need psychotherapy. The trouble is, if you feel incredibly guilty about your position relative to the people that you're interviewing or dealing with, and if you feel worthless yourself and have to perform to be loved, have to perform to get any kind of sense of validation or affirmation at all, then it's impossible to look after yourself because you need to work 24 hours a day. You can't just think, 'Right, now: sandwich, bottle of water, an early night.' Because you're running on guilt, masochism and worthlessness and a feeling that you need to perform to be loved. So, these aren't choices that you can make for yourself until you are mentally healthy. That's the problem. [13]

But therapy isn't appropriate or accessible for everyone. Catherine Gicheru, the first female news editor at the Nation Media Group and the founding editor of the *Star* newspaper in Kenya, would like to see self-help taught to all journalists as part of a broader process of raising awareness around mental health in the industry, as well as tackling some of the taboos in Kenyan society and more broadly across Africa. Kiran Nazish, founding director of New York-based Coalition For Women in Journalism, noted that in other parts of the world, Western-centred approaches to psychotherapy can do more damage than good, especially where trauma is a constant in society and in their work:

> When your body is used to a certain system of regulation or coping mechanisms, and you suddenly throw in mental health support, and you get people to do therapy, they break. I know a lot of journalists who break this way, and I myself I broke after therapy. I mean, I broke even harder after my therapy started. Because there was this new narrative introduced to my coping mechanisms, called protection, and my body

was used to coping without protection. If you look at it from a neuroscience perspective, it can challenge the critical motor skills your brain has developed to survive.

I think one thing that can really work, to get through this transition of developing new mechanisms in your brain, is journalling. Journalling is a form of you walking through your own neural pathways, channelling your inner language and temperament and the emotion that makes the most sense to you as a journalist and a human being. It helps you identify your feelings, responses to situations, etc., without having the fear of being wrong or right. That is when you can explore the state of your mind, in the secure and trusting environment of your own head. In fact, it is most likely that you will come out of journalling creating new neural pathways, and uncovering new abilities unknown to you before. Which is why journalling is a crucial journey of self-exploration I recommend to all journalists.[14]

This goes back to the idea of making sense of our own stories, owning our own narratives and ensuring we come to see them as valid as we work through a process. Connection and community are protective for our mental health. Journalists often think of themselves as part of a 'tribe', distinguished by a sense of camaraderie and a recognition that we speak the same language. Some news organisations have formal peer networks, others informal ones. Unfortunately, in many parts of the industry, support structures are patchy, or non-existent.

The next chapter considers how managers can have conversations with their colleagues. But what if we don't supervise people, yet want to ensure we are decent humans, and are concerned about saying the wrong thing, uncertain how to establish and maintain boundaries, and don't know what to look out for?

In terms of spotting if someone has poor mental health, this differs from person to person, but one of the first things to look out for is if that individual's behaviour is different from normal. They might be working much longer hours or taking greater risks, be more absent or restless or display an attitude of resignation. They may be tearful, have lost their motivation or humour, or have thoughts of suicide. Physically, they may feel cold, have body aches, or be more – or less – energetic than usual. This is not an exhaustive list. We are not mental health experts and should not be expected to be so.

If you think a colleague is having a difficult time, you might want to approach them. Before you start a conversation, it helps to find an appropriate time and place that works for them. Remote working makes this more complicated. In one of our 2022 Headlines Network workshops, one participant said they invited people to go for a walk with them and talk by phone even though they were in different locations. Something that is so simple but is worth asking and then repeating is, 'Are you okay?' and then, 'Are you okay, really?'

Ultimately, a lot of this is about being a decent human being, particularly at a time when another person may feel isolated and in need of someone to check in on them. It's important to recognise when we might not be the right person to support a colleague, which could be for all manner of reasons. In this instance, we could point them to someone else they can trust, or in other instances to more specialist help. Checking our privilege and being mindful of power dynamics can be especially helpful when people are experiencing poor mental health.

Natasha Hirst is the president of the National Union of Journalists in the UK. From her perspective, 'Sometimes it can help if you talk about your own mental health first. Talking about your own mental health demonstrates that it's safe, it's okay for them to talk about theirs and you're somebody who will have empathy.' She was contributing to a video[15] for Headlines Network on 'Supporting Colleagues', and in the same resource, Marcus Ryder, of the UK's Lenny Henry Centre for Media Diversity, explained that empathy and a listening ear were important: 'Properly, constructively listening, not rushing to solutions, maybe explaining things that have helped you cope, and then enabling that person to process that in their own time.'

Jon Birchall, the director of editorial strategy at LADbible group, valued the time his colleagues gave him:

> I think the main thing that worked in terms of support from my colleagues was having time. I wasn't pressured to feel better or ready to work when I had been in a difficult place. Working through that can be a particularly difficult period. It can be a long process and it's not something you can rush and never should be.[16]

Supporting colleagues means offering them space to speak if they wish, yet reassuring them that they do not have to, if they are not ready. During any conversation, we should offer our full attention, minimise interruptions, listen in active and non-judgemental ways, and avoid casting any sense of blame when we speak, while also respecting their privacy.

It is a good idea to discuss the next steps the person might take. You can encourage them to seek help, either from their personal doctor, if they are experiencing a mental health problem, or from their line manager. It is worth knowing where to signpost people for that additional help, outside your organisation and, if the company has a safeguarding policy, what it offers, such as an employee assistance programme. Resources vary greatly from country to country and region to region, so any list will not be conclusive.

Since this chapter began with speaking about *self*-care, it is worth returning to that, because when we support colleagues, we still need to consider ourselves. We need to maintain boundaries in terms of the time we can offer others and our own responsibilities, and we need to recognise when we may also want to seek support ourselves.

Notes

1 Author interview with Dr Cait McMahon, August 2022
2 Author interview with Dean Yates, September 2022
3 Headlines Network, (2022) *Behind the Headlines*, Episode 3: Clive Myrie, [podcast]. Available at: https://audioboom.com/posts/8060240-clive-myrie [42.54]
4 Author interview with Dr Sian Williams, April 2023
5 https://www.charliemorley.com
6 Author interview with Amantha Perera, November 2022
7 Headlines Network (2022) *Managing Our Mental Health: A guide for journalists and media professionals*. Available at: https://img1.wsimg.com/blobby/go/6ca5410e-ac1d-4642-b85f-b717e6a71453/downloads/Managing%20Mental%20Health_April%202022.pdf?ver=1649153848550
8 Headlines Network, (2022) *Behind the Headlines*, Episode 6: Gina Chua, [podcast]. Available at: https://audioboom.com/posts/8096662-gina-chua
9 Headlines Network, (2022) *Behind the Headlines*, Episode 4: Briony Gordon, [podcast]. Available at: https://audioboom.com/posts/8072452-bryony-gordon
10 Author interview with Dr Khaled Nasser, October 2022
11 Author Interview with Tanmoy Goswami, August 2022
12 Headlines Network, (2022) *Behind the Headlines*, Episode 9: Emily Morgan and Victoria Macdonald [podcast]. Available at: https://audioboom.com/posts/8135047-emily-morgan-and-victoria-macdonald
13 Author interview with Anna Blundy, July 2022
14 Author interview with Kiran Nazish, July 2022
15 https://headlines-network.com/our-work
16 See video above

Reference list

Csikszentmihalyi, M. (2002) *Flow: The Psychology of Happiness* (Rider & Co, UK)
Headlines Network, (2022) *Behind the Headlines*, Episode 3: Clive Myrie, [podcast]. Available at: https://audioboom.com/posts/8060240-clive-myrie
Headlines Network, (2022) *Behind the Headlines*, Episode 4: Briony Gordon, [podcast]. Available at: https://audioboom.com/posts/8072452-bryony-gordon
Headlines Network, (2022) *Behind the Headlines*, Episode 6: Gina Chua, [podcast]. Available at: https://audioboom.com/posts/8096662-gina-chua
Headlines Network, (2022) *Behind the Headlines*, Episode 9: Emily Morgan and Victoria Macdonald, [podcast]. Available at: https://audioboom.com/posts/8135047-emily-morgan-and-victoria-macdonald
Project SIREN, Centre for Mental Health Law & Policy. Available at: https://cmhlp.org/imho-siren/team

148 *Self-care and supporting others*

Their story – Tanmoy Goswami[17]

Tanmoy Goswami is an Indian journalist and founder of Sanity, an independent reader-funded mental health storytelling platform. A self-proclaimed 'accidental journalist', who started out working as an English teacher to MBA aspirants, his entry into the conversation around journalism and mental health came about in around 2016. At the time, the media industry in India was going through significant job cuts, and he saw how many of his colleagues were personally affected. In response, Tanmoy took to social media, to share how affected he was by the episode and offering suggestions from his experience.

> I wrote this long thread on Twitter about the need for journalists to de-risk their careers and become a little detached from the idea of being a journalist, because most of us are fiercely wedded to that identity. And it was quite clear back then that journalism jobs were becoming more and more insecure, along with all the other crap that comes with being a journalist, including, you know, the stress and the trauma and the lack of institutional support.

When he woke the next day, the thread had gone viral, with lots of influential Indian media people having shared it.

> It had still not crystallised in my head that I was talking about mental health in journalism, per se. But clearly a lot of the themes that I had tackled in that thread were about how to de-stress your life as a journalist. And then I wrote a post on LinkedIn about living with depression, suicidality and anxiety. And it was very rare – actually, I don't know any other journalist who, at that time, spoke openly about living with mental illness. But, again, that post went viral. I started getting a lot of messages from complete strangers from all over the world.

At this stage, Tanmoy was already doing some informal individual advocacy work around mental health.

> I started being on the lookout for an opportunity where I could do this full-time, but of course, nothing like that existed. And then our child was born in 2018. And that was the really definitive, decisive push that I needed. You know, parenthood brings all sorts of epiphanies. By then I was working at a very large business newspaper in India. I was in a senior role and my life at that point was all about, you know, 'One day, I have to be the editor of some big publication and get that corner office or whatever.' But then, soon enough, I realised that's not really what I want to do.
>
> A lot of my colleagues and peers, because they knew that I was open about it, would come and confide in me about the struggles of their job. And some of the stories would be very personal, about family issues, or how the job left them with no time to spend with

their family or friends, or whatever. Also, [there was] the second-hand trauma that a lot of reporters were sort of soaking up. But equally, there was this moral wounding that was happening, I think, where a lot of journalists felt that [in terms of] the values they stood for, their employers weren't necessarily walking the talk [sic]. And so, they could not live with that sort of duplicity and hypocrisy. A lot of people would come to me and say, 'You know what, this is not why I wanted to be a journalist' – from across different companies.

In 2019, he started working full time as a mental health journalist.

Even then, I never really separately thought about mental health in journalism. But I think six months or so into my job, mental health in journalism. But I think, six months or so into my job as a correspondent, I got a call from an acquaintance who had been hounded out of the job after they disclosed their mental health condition. And it was one story too many, you know; I was just filled with disgust at that point, really.

One of the ways in which I thought I could help was by helping the media become more accountable in the way they report on these issues.

He started working with the Centre for Mental Health, Law and Policy[18] in India, and together they started training journalists on the responsible reporting of mental health and suicide, hoping, 'by osmosis, some of those values would also start seeping into the work culture in these organisations'. That work culminated in Project SIREN, India's first ever monitoring mechanism for suicide reporting, which has an annual award for reporting on suicide. Goswami noted that the coverage of mental health, previously equated with violent crime, has become a little more sensitive. However, the increase in mental health coverage hasn't been matched by greater sensitivity in newsrooms.

I still get calls and messages from burnt-out colleagues. You know, people were just constantly doing Covid. I talked to a bunch of journalists who said that individually one or two editors helped them out. Some people lost their parents during Covid and one or two editors helped them out. But they said that at the same time, 'We were shocked that we didn't receive a single email', even from the head office, or from the top brass, acknowledging what a crazy time this was for reporters, to go out there and put their lives at risk, and then come back and start working after personal bereavement. They said it felt very much like a lone editor waging war against a sort of anti-newsroom culture, because there was not even an email acknowledging this. And there were many reporters who fell ill because their newsrooms had not given them any sort of basic protection in Covid.

So I don't think, culturally, things have changed a whole lot. But I do think that, on balance, some things have shifted towards the right side of the scale. People think that organisations don't know what they need to do. You know, if only somebody could write a nice PDF, with ten bullet points and send it to the editors and CEOs? Surely, they'll see the value. Surely this is not going to be so hard for the organisations to implement.

This is not a problem of knowledge. I refuse to believe that CEOs and editors overseeing multimillion-dollar companies don't know the basic principles of humanity and kindness and dignity. It is just the lack of will, and looking at human beings as expendable. And this is not only true of journalism; it is true of every industry. I think if there's one thing that companies can do relatively easily, I would say: learn from some other industries, where the first week at any job is orientation week.

I used to sort of scoff at it when I was younger and more rebellious. I used to join these organisations and then they put you through these boring week-long sessions where every function head would come and talk to you and you got the organisation's mission and vision, and there'd be an HR day, a finance day.

[But] that needs to happen. I think that's easily doable, right? So, you talk about why the hell are you here, why do we exist? And try and be as matter of fact, as practical, as possible. One of the big cognitive dissonances I see is that people join this industry expecting something very different. I think that becomes too much of a disconnect for young people; they get disillusioned very rapidly, and then that sort of spreads very quickly within the organisation. But within the newsroom, if organisations can stop encouraging the silo culture and get the desk and the reporters to work together more cohesively, that could take away a lot of the feeling of being isolated, at least.

Tanmoy rails against the idea that the individual should be the one to find solutions:

We need to stop talking about what individuals can do. In India, there was this workshop: something to do with how journalists can take care of their mental health. And every time I see a title or a headline like that, I cringe, because journalists can't do jack shit. I mean, how is a journalist supposed to do that when their job is on the line? They're asked to report on high-stress topics with zero institutional support. How is an individual supposed to go up against this system and feel empowered? It's just not possible and it is a perverse thing to ask of people.

It is clear to those of us who have been in the industry for any length of time that jobs are becoming more and more insecure. I think one thing that individuals can and must do is to start thinking of how they can use the skills that they have in other professions, in other industries, and start building a portfolio approach to [their] career. Because you should be prepared that you may not have this job in two years, or five years, or ten years, or whatever, [given] the rate at which things are changing. So you should do yourself a favour and start thinking of yourself not as a journalist alone, but as a storyteller, or a connector of dots.

All journalists have some incredibly, incredibly valuable skills, and there is no reason for us to sort of feel beholden to any one industry, because ultimately you are accountable to your family; you have to safeguard your own interests. I think there is no need or reason for journalists to feel that somehow the responsibility of saving the world is on their shoulders.

So put yourself ahead of your job sometimes, you know; this idealism can be the death of you, literally. Balance your idealism with some self-interest, I would say.

Notes

17 Taken from author interview with Tanmoy Goswami, August 2022
18 Centre for Mental Health Law & Policy (cmhlp.org)

13 Managing with empathy, and effective leadership

Good journalists do not necessarily make good managers. This is a frequent refrain in my conversations with colleagues. And yet rarely are journalists who become managers offered the relevant training and resources to enable them to feel equipped to support the diverse needs of the journalists who report to them, and to deal with the demands that they face from higher up the news organisation.

Since the pandemic, pressures on managers have become more pronounced. Many seem to be stuck in what I've heard called 'a stress sandwich', responding to the needs and demands of those they manage, as well as the expectations from those more senior. Recent years have brought additional pressures, particularly for first-time managers, positions that are frequently tough to take on. Many have missed out on mentoring themselves, and have to supervise people remotely. Those who became managers during Covid have probably been disconnected from support structures at work. And aside from professional stresses, managers often carry significant personal responsibilities, with caring roles for elderly or young family members, or both.

Pulled in so many directions, it is little wonder many managers seem to have lost sight of their own needs. I run a regular industry conference, attended by news leaders from several major media organisations. I vividly remember asking them at one stage who was looking out for their mental health, and the answer: nobody. Many managers feel they do not have time to make themselves a priority. But they must, and they would do well to remember airline safety briefings and put on their own oxygen mask first. If they don't, they won't be able to support others, and, even worse, they may start having a negative impact upon their work environments and colleagues.

But it is hard to juggle so many things when the demands of journalism are intense, resources scarce and workflows unrelenting. Mar Cabra, founder of The Self Investigation, an organisation providing tools to support media workers' wellbeing, has witnessed this herself:

> You become a manager because you were a good reporter. And you are promoted, and you have no training on how to lead people and how to manage people. They need to be trained about mental health issues, but

DOI: 10.4324/9781003344179-13

they also need to be trained about basic leadership, managing people skills, and that's quite a challenge.[1]

Although she was referring specifically to Spanish-speaking countries, the same is true elsewhere:

> One of the things that we know from research that helps teams, is doing one-on-one meetings. But a lot of leaders that we've trained in the past years tell us, 'Yeah, all these things about one-on-one meetings are great; how do I fit it in my schedule?' And that is because they are doing just too much. We also need to rethink the workflows around what managers do, or maybe add the skills and the time that they need to develop them. Because [without this], it's very frustrating, and what we're seeing is that middle managers and top managers are among the first to burn out and to have mental health challenges.

Phil Chetwynd is the Global News Director of Agence France-Presse, where a lot of thought has been given to how they can make use of workflows to support the wellbeing of their staff and their journalism. He explained how they had been trying to find ways to reshape the news processes to ease some of the pinch points where managers become overwhelmed, saying:

> Of course, even with the best will, it can be a challenge for managers. I see so much going on, people being overwhelmed all the time; somebody steps up for the first time and takes responsibility, and then is plunged into, 'God it's limitless and it's all on my shoulders and what if, what if, what if.'[2]

In the past, AFP has used coaches to help managers when they encountered trouble, but they are now using them proactively:

> Now we're thinking, [when] someone steps up into a position for the first time, they need a coach to tell them how to manage this environment, things you take for granted when you've got more experience [like], 'It's an earthquake, I know how this works', instead of a void of, 'Oh my God, there are so many things [to do].'

This multitude of 'things' can prove an obstacle to ensuring conversations are had around mental health. In an intensive, deadline-driven news environment, managers may want to consider the best ways of checking in with their colleagues, explained Dr Sian Williams, broadcaster, author and psychologist:

> I would say we need to rethink how we're viewing support. When we say, 'a mental health conversation', that to me sounds really heavy. And

> I'm not sure whether as a journalist working to a deadline – which I've always done, because I've always worked in daily news – I would relish somebody saying, let's have a conversation about mental health, about your mental health.[3]

That doesn't mean there isn't a place for a mental health conversation; however, certain news environments might not be conducive to opening up, particularly if people are feeling fragile. Instead, Dr Williams said managers should consider the best ways to help their colleagues understand that they are there for them.

> It's about sometimes holding difficult things as lightly as possible in a constricted, deadline-driven environment. You can't have open conversations about mental health in a newsroom, which is deadline driven. It's got to be the right space, and the right time, and you've got to be in the right frame of mind. And that's great if you've got all that. If you haven't got all that, get to it in different ways: 'If everybody's working really late tonight, I'm buying the pizzas; what does everybody want?' Sit around, let's just get 15 minutes and conversations come from that.

Santiago Lyon is the former head of photography for another global news giant, the Associated Press. He echoed the concerns of Cabra, Williams and Chetwynd around the relentlessness of the news industry and the related challenges in terms of mental health support.

> It seems like things are going faster and faster and faster, and people have less time to focus in on these kinds of things. As a result, maybe people who are exposed to traumatic experiences and need help processing those experiences don't get the time that they deserve, whether that's through organisational shortcomings, individual leadership shortcomings or just the frenetic pace of the news and this notion that it's urgent and something needs to be done.[4]

Having gone on to work for Adobe, he sees far higher levels of empathy and emotional quotient in his new industry, and attributes that to the rigour of and investment in recruitment and retention, something his former profession might learn from:

> I think that at the heart of any solid leadership lies empathy and the ability of leaders to engage with their employees in an empathetic way. And then organisational empathy, that allows people to take the time they need, provides the resources people need, doesn't stigmatise things.

Empathy has long been seen as an important attribute for leaders, one that came even more to the fore during the pandemic. A September 2021 article[5] by Tracy Bower for *Forbes* named this the 'most important leadership skill', citing research by Catalyst, which found empathy contributed to improvements in innovation, engagement, retention, inclusivity and work-life. It also said, according to another study by Qualtrics, that 'when leaders were perceived as more empathetic, people reported greater levels of mental health'.

As the former editor-in-chief of Reuters, David Schlesinger said he found it harder to establish empathetic connections in large newsrooms or bureaus:

> I think that the small bureaus are able to deal with it better than big bureaus. It tends to be more of a performance – in every meaning of the word – culture. Not only do editors look for performance, but journalists feel that they have to perform more to stand out in a big bureau. When huge layers of middle management have kind of been cut out of even the big organisations, then journalists tend to be part of much larger teams, and it's harder to have that empathetic, intimate connection that you might have in a small bureau or a small newsroom.[6]

Dr Khaled Nasser is a Lebanese trauma and mental health consultant, working with journalists across the Middle East and Africa. He sees leaders stymied frequently by systemic challenges that mean prioritising productivity is seen as being at odds with prioritising mental health.

> They will tell you, 'Yes, of course, we do this and that', but it's still at a very theoretical level for them. Because they are not used to this. They are coming from a different generational culture, mental mindset. And they think, [we need to be] on the ground, and the pace of work is really fast. The whole system is constructed, to kind of disregard the mental health.[7]

He said many managers were inured to violence, and their attitude to mental health was a barrier to normalising conversations:

> They don't understand that, actually, [they're] sending this person to cover this story, but this story is toxic in itself. So, you have this sense of desensitisation. Over time, we get used to blood. They don't have the empathy to consider or ask about their staff's mental health.

Catherine Philp has spent decades as a journalist for *The Times* newspaper, working often in hostile environments. She would like to see increased support within journalism, to feel there were more people 'down the phone', and believes 'a lot more training is needed for the people who are in head office, because it can't just be down to the journalist's family to help them'.[8]

Empathy is the idea that we can walk alongside someone without necessarily sharing their experiences. It is central to good journalism: the idea that we can hear someone's story, hold space for them, listen actively, without interrupting or trying to fix them. In amplifying their experiences, we can help them feel less alone. I remember early on in my journalism career being taught soft skills that would help me share the stories of others with my audiences. During my work in mental health, it has become increasingly clear that these same skills that make for good journalism also make for good managers and healthier journalism workplaces.

Empathy in leadership is crucial to creating and sustaining effective and inclusive cultures. Empathy does not divest us of efficiency. Instead, when it becomes part of a culture, it's more likely to encourage it. Empathy helps us recognise that we all go through stuff and that sometimes it is good to have company in the darkness, without that person trying to provide a crutch or a solution to someone's problems. Sarah Ward-Lilley, a former managing editor of BBC News, was awarded an MBE[9] for her services to mental health in journalism. From her perspective, managing people takes time, which journalists are short of, but it's better for journalism if we are more open to talking about mental health.

> It has to be a positive, that we are managing and working with human beings, who are doing journalism and taking their humanity into their stories. They can still be impartial, if that's what is required. They can still be highly professional. They can do their jobs better, if they are supported in their emotional life.[10]

Joyce Adeluwoye-Adams MBE is Editor, Newsroom Diversity at Reuters, where mental health comes within her remit, and she agreed that newsrooms needed to adapt to more empathetic types of leadership, believing that in turn, this would improve the overall health of newsrooms.

> If you're empathetic, you are allowing yourself to be vulnerable. And it's a choice because you're choosing to connect with the person you're talking to. And I think in a fast-moving industry like journalism, we have empathy with our sources, but actually we're not as kind to each other. Because there is an expectation that you don't necessarily show your emotions. And I would like us to do that a lot more as leaders, because I think that will help people feel they can come to us more, and it will help us identify and address their concerns around their mental health. It will also help create a mentally healthy workplace. I'd like to see a lot more work done around empathetic leadership when it comes to mental health, because I still feel that a lot of leaders really struggle with having these conversations.[11]

In workshops for managers at Headlines Network, we offered participants the space to role-play such conversations. We did this because managers very rarely have the chance to prepare for and think through difficult discussions in advance, but having the time and support to do so can help people become better managers. These conversations are not always easy, and it's tempting to fill uncomfortable silences, to try to fix or judge, rather than simply listen. This is something we grapple with in our news gathering. But we and our interviews with those whose stories we share as journalists would do well to remember that often the moments when we are silent are when the other person feels safe to share their story, as are the moments when we ask them, 'Is there anything else you'd like to share?'

Journalism and managing journalists are not the same thing, but we can learn from some of the skills that make us good at our journalism to make us better at other aspects of our journalism. We need to find a way to sit without judgement, to listen actively and to reassure the person that they have our full attention. Managers should also be mindful of the power dynamic and do all they can to make reasonable adjustments for this. And because managers are rarely mental health experts, they should be aware of their own boundaries and the need for self-care, and know how to signpost colleagues to additional support where necessary.

Much of this is rooted in the notion that we are all human beings. I often hear people say they are worried about making things worse: but the fact is that checking in with others rarely does.

I have facilitated conversations with hundreds of journalists from around the world. As an external consultant, I am often invited by managers to speak with their staff. The discussions take place under Chatham House rules, meaning that what is said cannot be shared in a way that will identify the individual. Afterwards, I draw together the themes of the discussion and share them with their managers without attributing the information to specific people.

In all the conversations, two things come up repeatedly, and it's clear that having more empathetic managers would help in tackling these points. The first is that people fear that any admission of distress will be regarded as weakness and have repercussions on their careers and their reputations. The second is that they wish their managers would treat them more like human beings and less like cogs in a machine. When asked specifically how they might do this, the overriding response is that people want to feel seen, heard and humanised. They're not asking for a lot but would just like to be thanked or for their managers to take a few seconds to express their appreciation for their work, or some recognition that a story was tough, or ask them how they are. None of this takes excessive time, but it's likely to be remembered.

Most of us can recall when a manager took the time; we also remember the managers who were the antithesis of this, who treated us as robots because they had been conditioned to suppress their emotions and only release them as anger, not empathy. Matthew Green, a journalist who has worked for the *Financial Times* and Reuters and is a co-host of the Collective Trauma Summit, gave his view:

> Certain people have a particular kind of trauma signature, which makes them ruthless, ambitious, unfeeling, unempathetic and – guess

what? – these are the people who tend to rise to the top of these organisations. I was fortunate and received very good support when I struggled with depression while working as a correspondent. However, I have also seen cases where people have been very badly let down. I think part of the problem is that, often, the people who run these organisations do not want to look at their own trauma history: they don't have the resources to go there. They may acknowledge pragmatically that they need to be seen to be doing something and, politically, it serves them to be paying their dues to mental health. But many of those best placed to make a difference have yet to cultivate the kind of self-awareness needed to actually engage with the subject in a genuine way. So that's the conflict we have: the leadership will allow a conversation about mental health to go to a certain point, but not beyond that point, because then it becomes uncomfortable for them. It's not just in the media, but across society. Those who wield the most power tend to be the most in need of healing.[12]

Perhaps these people are themselves traumatised, were never shown the empathy that might have helped them acknowledge the stressors of their work. Conditioned to put up and shut up, they become leaders of organisations, products of a vicious cycle where, without the resources to manage their own mental health, and without the training to support others, they reinforce unhealthy coping mechanisms and cultures that lack compassion.

One of the unanticipated outcomes of our Headlines Network workshops was the support that these managers found among their peers. Being a manager can be a lonely business, and it's important that leaders can access ways to manage their mental health and connect with people they trust, otherwise, they run the risk of becoming the bruised or injured piece of fruit in the bowl, growing the mould that negatively affects those around them.

Empathetic managers tend to recognise that the people who work with them are humans and not cogs in a machine, something that is vital in building a more open, healthier culture where people perform better because they feel seen and heard.

David Walmsley is the Editor in Chief of *The Globe and Mail* in Canada. He cut his journalistic teeth in Northern Ireland, coming of age in the Belfast newsrooms, where 'very many people didn't have any other life, apart from their work life and so, they'd lost balance, and they lost perspective'.[13] Thirty years on, he believes things have changed but that the industry still needs to get better at demonstrating understanding in situations when journalists do not consciously choose to cover stories.

That can often happen in a country that's very stable, that suddenly has a terrible moment where news desks themselves are not experienced in understanding it. So having empathy is a really important skill on the desk. I think [in designing] news desks today, it's best to build in an empathetic editor. Say you've got a traditional news desk, take a generic design, a backbench of assignment, commissioning editors, five to 25 people on that bench discussing things – you need to have that challenge function built into [it]. Somebody who's [still a] journalist, but is empathetic, has the duty of care reference point to challenge the assignment of an individual going off to do a story, or has the ability to say, 'Hang on, we're relying once again on John and Jane. And remember, they just came back from doing this and that, and they shouldn't.'

He said this person needs to be someone other than the commissioning editor who has the responsibility for that live breaking-news story:

Because their pressure point is not the individual; that pressure point is getting the story, and it's not realistic to think that that person is the one who's going to be able to give you the correct long-term staff answer. They're going to give you [the] very correct practitioner's short-term response, which will get the job done today. But at what [is the] cost cumulatively, when you do that again, and again and again? That has to be set from the top and that's about the design of your news desk.

Kari Cobham, the Trinidadian writer, editor and digital strategist, has spent a long time considering how to support teams, after early career experiences where she was badly impacted and felt unsupported by those in more senior positions.

I think managers need to be able to identify when things start to shift. Who is shifting? Who needs the most support? What are the resources that are available? Are those being proactively communicated? Are they being reinforced by leadership? Are managers talking about their own support systems and what are they doing to take care of themselves to normalise that conversation? Are they doing regular check-ins with the people who are covering difficult topics? Are they rotating out the folks who are covering the difficult topics? If all they're doing is covering crime and death, day in, day out, after a while that's going to wear on you, right? And so are the difficult assignments being rotated with easier assignments? Are there enough resources internally to really move the needle to support your employees? Because there's a difference between 'We're going to bring in dogs to the newsroom, because that is a form of therapy', versus letting folks know, 'You have six complimentary sessions with a therapist every year, and this is how you set that up.'[14]

For Kate Nowlan, psychotherapist, and former CEO of CiC, a provider of Employee Assistance Programmes, the idea that empathy can be built into the processes and workflow is critical in her interactions with news organisations:

> It makes a massive difference to be able to cascade down empathic and thoughtful interventions from an enlightened leadership, who believe in this stuff and actually want to deliver psychological support and don't see it as something that's woke and fluffy but rather one of the most powerful things you can offer.[15]

Chetwynd, Cobham and Aderuwoye-Adams are leaders who walk the walk and talk the talk: 'It's sort of liberating from the top to be able to speak to that [. . .] because you can set the tone and people are looking for you to do that. And it does have an impact, and it absolutely has to be led from the top,' said Chetwynd. 'Otherwise, there'll always be doubts people have in the back of their mind, because they will meet sceptical managers halfway down.'

Aderuwoye-Adams said she took seriously her responsibilities as a leader, someone to be a role model, but acknowledged the challenges of building a company-wide culture in which conversations about mental health didn't alienate people:

> Being a global organisation – I think we do this quite well at Reuters – making sure that we don't look at mental health through a Western lens – I think that's really important. Being of African descent myself, I know how difficult it is talking about mental health in Africa sometimes. It's getting better, but it's still a little bit of a taboo subject, which is why I try to be really open about my own mental health, because I want to bust that taboo as much as I can. But, also, in other parts of the world, Asia as well. I think we have got to understand that what works for us in the West may not necessarily work elsewhere. We have to make sure that the support we give is steeped in local knowledge.

Chetwynd, who is based in Paris and has spent many years in Asia, said for mental health conversations to be normalised in global news organisations, there needs to be backing from all regions:

> [Mental health] is obviously something that's viewed very differently in different places and cultures, and every region has their own cultures and ways of dealing with these issues. The challenge, as always, in a big organisation is being able to really communicate the message about these things because it has to trickle all the way down. You can say, from the top [of the organisation], and you can write: 'These [things] are important to us, these things matter, there's no stigma attached to it,

we're here to support.' But you need buy-in from your entire management structure, all the way down to the bureau chief in a small country, managing their team, because if that person either doesn't have the confidence to believe what you're saying, or doesn't agree with you, their team is not going to feel that this is a company, or a culture, where they can talk about these things openly and where the support [is].

The old adage might be that journalists don't necessarily make good managers, but there are many skills critical to good journalism that also underscore good management, principally connection, communication and empathy. For Dr Cait McMahon, former managing director of the Dart Centre Asia Pacific, the buck really does stop with managers – and so ensuring they receive the proper support is vital.

We know the research shows that journalists can put up with a lot of crap in terms of trauma exposure, if they are really supported properly by management, like, true social support. So we need to educate managers and organisations about their responsibility and what part they play in the trauma puzzle in terms of them having a real role, and they've got to get on board with this. It's not just an added extra – 'Oh, I'm too busy.' This is a really important part of the puzzle. We need to teach them psychological first aid [. . .] to give them those basic skills to be able to support or to prevent, in some cases, and not be assholes, basically.[16]

Notes

1 Author interview with Mar Cabra, February 2023
2 Author interview with Phil Chetwynd, March 2023
3 Author interview with Dr Sian Williams, April 2023
4 Author interview with Santiago Lyon, April 2023
5 Tracy Bower (2021) 'Empathy is the most important leadership skill according to research' *Forbes*. Available at: https://www.forbes.com/sites/tracybrower/2021/09/19/empathy-is-the-most-important-leadership-skill-according-to-research/?sh=7010fdaa3dc5
6 Author interview with David Schlesinger, February 2023
7 Author interview with Dr Khaled Nasser, March 2023
8 Author interview with Catherine Philp, April 2023
9 British Order of Chivalry awarded for outstanding achievement to a community, MBE is Member of the Order of the British Empire
10 Author interview with Sarah Ward-Lilley, January 2023
11 Author interview with Joyce Adeluwoye-Adams, MBE, January 2023
12 Author interview with Matthew Green, September 2022
13 Author Interview with David Walmsley, February 2023
14 Author interview with Kari Cobham, October 2022
15 Author interview with Kate Nowlan, February 2023
16 Author interview with Dr Cait McMahon. August 2022

Reference list

Bower, T. (2021) 'Empathy is the most important leadership skill according to research', *Forbes*, 19 September, available at: https://www.forbes.com/sites/tracybrower/2021/09/19/empathy-is-the-most-important-leadership-skill-according-to-research/?sh=7010fdaa3dc5

O'Neill, L. and Lindsay, C., eds (2022) *Breaking: Trauma in the Newsroom* (Maverick House, London)

Their story – Leona O'Neill[17]

Leona O'Neill is a journalist from Northern Ireland. In a career spanning more than 20 years, she has covered many difficult and distressing stories, including murders and court cases, as well as hearing the traumatic testimonies of those who survived the Troubles, the conflict in Northern Ireland during the late 20th century. In 2019, Leona was covering a riot in the Creggan area of Derry when the journalist Lyra McKee was shot dead beside her. But after Lyra's murder by dissident Republicans, the trauma didn't end for Leona. She was harassed by conspiracy theorists and targeted by paramilitaries.

> From that, I really struggled with trauma; I went to counselling. And after about a year, I don't know if my body just broke down, or what have you. I left my career. I burnt my career to the ground in journalism and I went off in a different direction to academia. That gave me the space to look at what had happened perhaps three years ago, 10 years ago, 20 years ago in journalism, and I realised that it was a terribly unhealthy, toxic environment for anyone who's struggling with anything. And, that made me want to make things better, I suppose.

Now head of the journalism school at the University of Ulster, she is determined to change the mindset of newsrooms, conscious she is sending young journalists into places where mental health is 'not even a priority, not even an afterthought. It's not thought of at all in a lot of cases.' She wants to show that journalists are humans too. Together with the BBC journalist Chris Lindsay, Leona co-edited *Breaking: Trauma in the Newsroom*,[18] which brings together 16 well-established journalists to talk about how the news broke them.

> They're talking about seeing someone being murdered, blown up or shot. But also, the inquests, the kind of court cases, the tragedies, the stories of human heartache, and the grim conveyor belt of doom that sometimes our local newsroom can be. We're not robots. These people have had experiences, and that has really broken down their mental health. And there's been no dealing with it. People just had to leave or go to a different job. It was never dealt with. They were never supported terribly well in the newsrooms.
>
> I'm trying to change the mindsets and the newsrooms, which are terribly unhealthy. The mindsets are very macho. You need to be a tough, hard-nosed reporter; if you have any weakness at all, if you struggle with anything, or if something has impacted you negatively, something lands on you, there's very much [an attitude of] 'Mask it, keep going, keep on doing the story, and if you show any weakness, you should get out, you should go into another job. You're not up for this. You're not capable.'

I would argue that there are plenty of journalists who are very strong, very resilient, and that we just need some support there. Just the fact that there is support there would help a lot of people.

Notes

17 From author interview with Leona O'Neill, November 2022
18 Leona O'Neill and Chris Lindsay, eds (2022) *Breaking: Trauma in the Newsroom*, (Maverick House, London)

14 Conclusion

When journalists thrive, so does journalism

Good mental health and wellbeing are necessary for good journalism. For too long, they have been an afterthought or absent from discussions about the success of our industry. We have ignored the fact that journalists are our industry's most precious resource. Journalism safety must be looked at holistically, with physical, online and psychological safety considered as intersecting parts. These should be integrated throughout the news-gathering process, from planning, through production, to publication and beyond. And this should be done in a way that allows flexibility as risks and responses evolve.

Journalism safety and wellbeing have long been viewed through a Western lens. We need to recognise that safety means different things for different people and in different places, and that, collectively, we can learn from each other. Joyce Adeluwoye-Adams MBE, in her role as Editor, Newsroom Diversity at Reuters, said she recognised the need for journalists to be more prepared for what they might encounter, but also noted the importance of ensuring that conversations do not default to a Western-centric perspective.

> I think we have got to understand that what works for us in the West may not necessarily work elsewhere. We have to make sure that the support we give is steeped in local knowledge. I think we do that quite well at Reuters. But I've noticed that whenever we talk about mental health in the West, it is very much steeped in a Western lens, so it automatically alienates a lot of people. So, we need to do better at that.

Amantha Perera, Sri Lankan journalist and PhD researcher in Australia and the project lead for Dart Centre Asia Pacific, said we need to get away from a sense of 'false universalism', or the idea that what applies in a place like Australia can be taken 'lock, stock and barrel' and used elsewhere: 'We need to have a conversation where we understand the social, cultural and other dynamics of those communities, and then work with them, give them that voice, give them agency and [continue to] work with them.' He believes that by doing so, connections can be made across cultures and countries: 'Then these whispers start going across the globe. And then it's not an isolated dialogue.

DOI: 10.4324/9781003344179-14

It's a global community dialogue, and then it's easy to go in and talk about these things and make sure we don't [make] the same mistakes that I did.'

In many parts of the world, any conversations around mental health are isolated. Elsewhere they are a privilege people simply can't afford: 'This is a country where you have community papers that don't really pay their reporters,' said Weng Paraan, the former head of the National Union of Journalists of the Philippines (NUJP):

> So, they definitely don't, and will not, provide for a mental health programme. And then there's the stigma still of being perceived as weak, if you are traumatised by an experience, so there are a lot of challenges. Newsrooms still have to develop that programme so they will be able to respond to their staff.[1]

One of the ways the mental health conversation gained traction in the Philippines was through the NUJP's safety programme. Run regularly for members, many of whom are freelance or work for small newspapers and stations, it includes a significant component that focuses on recognising and dealing with trauma. This, said Paraan, is 'very good because the statement you're making is that physical security is important, but mental wellbeing is also important and a press freedom issue, so they should not be looked at separately'.

Seeing these as interrelated issues is crucial in countries like the Philippines, where press freedom is under pressure. Where there is no guarantee of free media, there can be no guarantee of journalism safety: physical, digital or psychological.

Globally, for a long time, any safety discussions have been owned by a small population, but such discussions must be more flexible in their approaches, and less beholden to policies fixed by a privileged – often male – perspective which do not reflect the realities of those who are most vulnerable.

In Kenya, Catherine Gicheru has seen solutions developed by individual journalists and affinity groups. She would like to see decision-makers consider these seriously, because they reflect the realities faced by journalists, in particular women.

> Some of these interventions and conversations need to be more open to the realities of what 51% of the world is going through. And it's not going to happen in a month of Sundays, that we're going to be able to put everything in neat boxes. We need to deal with a mess; that is life. Therefore, these conversations need to be open to informal, unstructured responses, because I read the books and I read the guidelines, and I read the tip sheets and I'm, like, 'Yeah, it's not happening in Kenya. It's not happening in Africa. It won't happen in Ghana. Even if you prayed for it, it won't happen.' So how do we formalise the informal, so that it becomes part of our strategy in a global attempt to address the problems?

Those informal interventions need to be formalised in terms of being recognised as valid. I don't want you to validate my existence, but I need you to acknowledge that I have [created my own] intervention. I have taken agency in dealing with a problem in my own way. And because it doesn't fit your neat boxes, it doesn't mean that it's not scalable. It can be scaled up, but it's just not happening according to how you think.[2]

At CBC, Dave Seglins is the wellbeing champion, a role he combines with his journalism. He has noted a disconnect between policies and reality:

Wellbeing and mental health are thought of as being kind of an HR health benefit over here [in Canada]. It's not actually the core business of the newsroom. The disconnects – [resulting in] the programmes that get cooked up [away] from the newsrooms – are often so tone deaf and ignorant of the realities of the stressors of the news business, that they're kind of laughable. And [the programmes are] ineffective and non-responsive to the needs. Figuring out how to make sure that these initiatives are actually owned, and based in the newsrooms, driven by the people who know the challenges, is a major challenge.[3]

For Seglins, working within the newsroom has helped bridge this divide:

[My role] is not another management initiative. Because there's a lot of scepticism and toxicity and concern among journalists about revealing their state of mind, their mental health, I said, 'Hire me as a journalist and wellbeing champion. Let's try it out for a year.' And so, we've been doing it for a year.

His work has included consulting on major stories throughout their coverage, one-on-one sessions with leaders dealing with difficult coverage, and building a peer support network. He has helped change the conversation in CBC, specifically through lunchtime-learning sessions, an internal newsletter and a blog. Like many I spoke with in the research for this book, Seglins saw the value of a broader industry conversation. In safety terms, no individual or institution has all the answers; however, some organisations are more experienced and better resourced, while, as individuals, we all have different perspectives. Therefore, faced with an issue as varied and vital as mental health, solidarity and forging a global community are key.

I was motivated to found Headlines Network[4] because I wanted to help normalise conversations around mental health and recognised that we could benefit from hearing others' stories and sharing strategies. Even where there is traction, there are differences in approach and awareness. 'If you're moving from one organisation to another, you never know what you're going to get,' said Kari Cobham, director of fellowships at The 19th newsroom in the United States:

> You may come from a newsroom where they recognise the importance of mental health and they encourage folks to take time off and leaders [to] check in with their newsrooms, and they rotate assignments, and they do the things that are essential to having a healthy staff. And then you may go into a newsroom where that does not exist.[5]

This raises the prospect of a possible industry standard around mental health, akin to the principles supporting the safety of freelance journalists at the ACOS Alliance[6] or the code endorsed by members of the International News Safety Institute.[7] Universally, education is an important first step. Among journalists and aspiring media workers, it can increase their understanding of terms associated with mental health, as well as informing them of what they might be exposed to and what might happen if that includes trauma. 'I remember talking to a journalist for a story that I was doing on how trauma affects journalists,' said Cobham. She continued:

> He said – and I'll never forget it – 'You know, we don't send a journalist out to cover baseball, if they don't understand the game.' But we're sending journalists out in the field, who have no clue about how their work is going to impact them. And so, you're already putting them at a disadvantage.

Across the world, there are significant taboos around mental health, but the promotion of good standards in mental health reporting is tackling some of the stigma and outdated stereotypes. At the same time, when coverage improves, it tends to give rise to more conversations in newsrooms around mental health. Tanmoy Goswami is a journalist based in India, and the creator of Sanity,[8] India's first independent, reader-funded mental health storytelling platform:

> We started training journalists in responsible reporting on mental health and suicide. The idea was that, by osmosis, some of those values would also start seeping into the work culture in these organisations. We ended up training a few hundred people through live sessions, and then they turned it into a digital lesson that anyone could access. This culminated in a project called Project SIREN,[9] which is India's first ever monitoring mechanism for suicide reporting. And every year we give out an award for responsible reporting on suicide and I'm part of the jury for that. I have been told by many friends and peers that ever since we started doing this, some amount of accountability [emerged] – because earlier there was no conversation at all on these issues. People

in leadership roles are now talking about these issues, and they find it a little harder now to ignore these issues in their own workforce, which really was all that we had hoped for.

In Canada, MindSet[10] is a guide developed for journalists by journalists on reporting mental health with an associated set of awards: 'One of the by-products of [the guide] is that journalists have remarked on how it challenges their own ideas about their own mental health,' said Jane Hawkes, the co-founder of the Canadian Journalism Forum for Violence and Trauma,[11] which developed the guide:

> This idea about good mental health reporting is good for lots of reasons. One of them is part of what I would call journalists' self-care: turning that mirror around. I think if you're wanting to have frank, accurate conversations in your journalism, there is a benefit to the journalism, the journalists themselves and the journalism classroom and the newsroom.[12]

Research shows us that journalists are largely resilient. However, resilience is not about keeping on going regardless, according to Professor Neil Greenberg, a specialist in trauma risk management:

> It is important to recognise – and not just with media professionals – that rather than expecting people to not develop mental health problems, it is more realistic to accept that almost everyone may experience distress, and a minority mental ill-health. The sensible approach is to consider how you tackle difficulties early on and help people to move on or recover. Resilience isn't the same as resistance. We should not be fostering a view of 'I don't break'; rather, people should be encouraged to think, 'Yep, this one's too much for me, move on' and should be supported, if distressed, in a way that allows them to come back to their full role when they have recovered, with support from colleagues, supervisors, family or friends.[13]

Professor Greenberg said we need to change people's perceptions of what health and psychologically robust working looks like:

> It is not the same as 'I can stick it out longer than everybody else.' I believe that there has been a change in attitudes within the media over time; there are plenty of great media professionals who are willing, and able, to speak about their mental health experience and journey. But I think we need more of that, and we really need discussion of the emotional impact of the work to be part of the standard way of working.

A lot of this is about preparing people in advance. At Reuters, this has become an important part of their mental health work, said Adeluwoye-Adams:

> The one thing that we are really looking at is making sure we factor in trauma resilience. Before people go into the field. We're very good, I think, at catching them towards the end, but I would like to see more work done upfront, and that's certainly going to be a big focus of mine this year.

Before journalists are deployed, a risk assessment can help with recognising potential dangers and understanding what can be done to mitigate them, as well as ensuring a contingency and communications plan. As well as a risk assessment – which needn't cost a great deal of money or time – some news organisations and media support groups provide journalists with safety training if they are covering conflict or disasters. Often known as Hostile Environment First Aid Training (HEFAT), it can help participants recognise dangers they may be exposed to and how they might react. It is worth noting that some HEFAT courses have been overly focused on the safety issues faced by small populations of journalists at the risk of isolating those who might be vulnerable to identity-based violence, or in need of trauma support. In addition to training, the right equipment – like flak jackets, helmets and first aid kits – can help journalists feel better equipped to avoid danger and respond if necessary. Preparation, training, equipment and education are key to physical safety, and already a feature of many newsrooms. But, in mental health terms, there has been less pre-emptive work carried out in terms of mitigating harm. Dr Mark Grant, in his role as Head of High Risk, Safety and Security at Sky News, told me:

> We all take flak jackets to conflict zones. We all take medical care, we all do HEFATs; why are we not always made aware of what is there to support us now? It's okay not to be okay at times. I think you need to build [preparation] within the wider safety culture, otherwise, it simply becomes a tick-box exercise.[14]

Caroline Drees is Senior Director, Field Safety and Security at NPR, based in Washington, DC, and she agreed that conversations around mental health and physical safety need to be closely aligned. But, as has been heard throughout this book, when news leaders really take these issues seriously, it makes a real difference.

> It's not a box-ticking exercise. And you can do this in multiple ways, but also, really importantly, this has to be supported from the top down. [It is] something that needs to be mentioned at 'town halls' or whatever, by the most senior leadership – the importance of it. You need to keep reminding people. People forget, or there's high

turnover in the industry. So, [it's important to keep] reminding everybody of what's going on, what's available, how it's available. [I believe] hostile environments training, which is critical in the field-safety sphere, [should include] mental health and the support that's available to people, understanding triggers, understanding what happens physically in your body when you're stressed, or when you're traumatised. All of that has to be part of hostile environments training, in my opinion. You can't separate it. I know that we pack an awful lot into these training courses, and the courses get really, really dense and intense. But if you start separating [these aspects], you're separating [them] in people's minds too, as though it were two different things. And they're not.[15]

At NPR, journalists have a security conversation ahead of every assignment to what is considered a hostile environment. Drees said there is a wide range of such situations:

That would include going to cover a school shooting or going to natural disasters, etc. We talk about this ahead of time, and I say, the obvious: 'No story's worth a life. But note, no story is worth you getting hurt.' And they're not. Every story is voluntary. 'If you don't want to go or if, during the assignment, you decide this doesn't work for you, that's okay. You just have to tell us so that we can work on another way of covering it. But that's all. Just tell us, so we can plan.'

Even when a newsroom leader or policy explicitly states deployments and stories are voluntary, the ability to say no can differ depending on one's position within the newsroom. Ensuring journalists are reminded regularly that there will be no repercussions if they turn down deployments will reduce stigma. It may take a lot longer to diminish the competitive instincts or maladaptive behaviours that sometimes push journalists to keep going. David Walmsley, editor-in-chief of *The Globe and Mail* in Canada, said:

The instruction has to start inside the newsroom; it has to start at the top. Or it has to start with a growing swell of people who have mutual feelings of either being misunderstood or [who] think help can come and [who ask for] it to be done in an environment where it's safe, so people aren't feeling their careers are going to be affected. And it has to be done gently and always more slowly than you would ever want to do it. Because journalists, despite being massively urgent and busy, and my goodness, they don't have time, hate change.[16]

Drees makes an important point about the need to create an open dialogue with journalists while they are on a story. It helps ensure that the safety conversation continues throughout the news-gathering process.

Seglins mentioned the before, during and after approach. It is important that journalists know they are supported, and how they can access that support, even after a story has been published; this needs to be communicated regularly. Newsrooms need to put in place systems of support which recognise that individuals may need help long after coverage of an event, particularly if they experience PTSD, or if they are attacked online. From a mental health perspective, when journalists return from a difficult assignment, a debriefing offers space to discuss what went well and less well. Drees gave her perspective:

> During that conversation, I find it helpful to have someone doing it who is not your direct editor, because you might be afraid to say to that person how emotionally draining the assignment was after they've edited all your copy. But it should be someone who is in a position to help you and who could also speak to your editor or speak to your manager as appropriate.

Debriefings are good practice when journalists return from hostile environments. They are also beneficial for other stories that might impact their mental health, such as those where they are exposed to vicarious trauma, or where they face online harassment. Normalising the use of debriefings would benefit people's mental health. Ultimately, they are a way of checking in with colleagues to see how they are and what support they need, and to remind them what is available. They provide an opportunity for journalists to process their experiences. From an organisational perspective, debriefings can also help capture lessons and learning and help managers recognise when their colleagues might need time off to decompress, rest and recover.

At Agence France-Presse, after journalists have covered difficult stories, they transfer into more comfortable settings, such as sport. This works on several levels, according to Phil Chetwynd, AFP's Global News Director:

> One is to put [the person] in an incredibly convivial environment with their other colleagues and to have [a] sharing experience, which is important [so they] work on different types of content. [You] take them away from the daily work, if it's bang, bang – war and conflict and difficult things. It's not that we have unlimited budgets, but you can do that in the normal flow of news and stuff. That's something we've tried to work on a lot, and I think has really been a positive thing. One of the things you realise is that people really need validation and support of their colleagues. They feel then that they can talk more freely.
>
> These are often things that may seem simply symbolic, but if you can show staff that you care – it may not be the thing that they want, right – but that care goes a long way, because it means they then have the courage to ask for other things or to take one step further.[17]

From Professor Greenberg's perspective, the challenges major news organisations face are similar to the military on deployment:

> You don't want to deploy military personnel for extended periods, because that has a detrimental impact on their mental health. However, at the same time, troops who have been deployed for an extended period get very good at doing what they're doing. They can see what's happening more easily than rookies. So therefore, if you rotate troops too quickly, you keep losing that experience. Similarly, from a journalistic point of view, a media professional who's really good at speaking to people in the Middle East, who understands the Middle East political situation, is likely to be a much better Middle East reporter than a rookie. Having sufficient experience most often means better reporting.
>
> But on the other hand, staying in one area means you have to keep going back to the same areas, where the people who you made friends with have been killed, and it may increase the threats you face yourself. So one of the challenges is how do media organisations work out the right rotation schedule for keeping workers in these trauma-filled environments; they want them to be good at their job, but not stay so long that they become unwell. Of course, some media professionals live and work in environments of extreme trauma, and it can be difficult to separate the psychological impact of reporting on traumatic events from the effects of living in such a confronting environment. This too is a challenge.

This idea of rotations has been adopted by many news organisations who send journalists into hostile situations. Over time, most have reduced the duration spent in such settings. Rotations also work for journalists covering long-lasting stories, like the pandemic, or ones with a risk of online harassment or vicarious trauma. Again, it's important the journalist feels part of the decision-making process, that they know their work is valued, do not feel punished by being taken off a story, and – even if they are not going to be at work – that they have access to support.

All of these steps are about normalising conversations around wellbeing in the newsroom, recognising there are numerous intersecting aspects: physical, online and psychological safety, as well as diversity and inclusion. And once this becomes normal, it can be more easily integrated throughout the organisation. At ABC in Australia, where Nicolle White is the Social Media Wellbeing Advisor, there has been an organisation-wide approach to reducing stigma. These include regular 'RU OK?' days,[18] 'where people at different levels of the organisation speak about their experiences, so that everyone feels safe to be themselves at work and show up in whatever way that they are'.

At Reuters, ensuring a mentally healthy newsroom is part of the organisation's overall strategy. Adeluwoye-Adams said:

> [This is] a priority, and I will be putting together a strategy around mental health for our newsroom. Because we've got all of these great things that we do, but I want to make sure we are being strategic so it's really embedded into our practices as well. For us, that's a really big step and it's fantastic. I think that all newsrooms should be doing this. In the same way that [a company has] a business strategy, a diversity strategy, we should have a mental health and wellbeing strategy, so it's not just words – it's bedded into our practices, as well as everything we do when it comes to our journalism, so that we're actually moving the dial on this. We've also got a mental health committee, which is made up of reporters and editors, so we can really get to what some of the issues are, and, again, all of that will feed into a strategy.

Reuters was one of the pioneers around mental health conversations in newsrooms. As well as its editorially led work around wellbeing, it has been working with CiC, an Employee Assistance Programme (EAP) provider, for many years. Kate Nowlan is the former CEO of CiC and believes that these functions need to work side by side:

> For good practice, it's the relationship with any provider that is key. We will always work with those at a senior level initially to ensure the programme is thoroughly integrated into the organisation and we make sure that key stakeholders really understand what initiatives are available to improve mental health and wellbeing at all levels. We will offer very practical solutions, which might include a global 24/7 helpline, a network of professional and expert clinicians in all regions, specialist training or peer support programmes that include rigorous assessment and supervision. All programmes should be monitored regularly, and it is essential that clinicians and peer supporters are supervised by professionals experienced in working with the journalistic community.
>
> In recent years, we have provided resilience modules to hostile environment training, and these are now seen as an essential component of the sessions. The ongoing relationship between the newsroom and the clinical provider is of the greatest import, as the provider will always need to be aware of changing dynamics in a fast-moving organisation that will have an impact on its staff.[19]

Like many I spoke with, Nowlan noted the need for more support for freelancers, and greater access to therapy. At the time of writing, the Dart Center ran the Journalism Trauma Support Network, training therapists to offer support to US-based journalists dealing with trauma and occupational stress. The Rory Peck Trust also had a therapy fund[20] covering the cost of treatment for psychological support. Still, there is a real lack of therapists who 'get' journalism, while around the world, therapy often provides little benefit to journalists, being either unaffordable or too reliant on Western forms of practice.

In terms of peer support networks, Reuters was one of the first to establish a formal one. Other organisations have followed suit. At ABC in Australia, the peer network has been especially helpful for moderators, said White, who often encounters online vitriol as part of their work.

> While EAPs are great, they don't necessarily understand the intricacies and the particular pressures of these roles. So having someone that you can speak to that does is so useful, [as is] being able to refer on if you need more specific psychological support.

Although this is a company network, across the industry are identity-based, affinity groups and informal communities that connect. While there are benefits in professionalised systems, it is not always possible to put them in place. The value of communities and conversations where journalists can share their stories and strategies in a trauma-informed way should not be underestimated. There is an incredible wealth of wisdom when we bring together communities of practice to share insights into their safety and wellbeing. What's more, when connections are created between people and stories shared, it can help others feel less isolated, build solidarity, overcome stigma and normalise conversations. According to Cait McMahon, the founding managing director of Dart Centre Asia Pacific: 'We need to start re-empowering human beings, journalists, [so] that we can be good allies to each other, good supports. When you've got that, you've got the skills to be [there for each other,] human to human.' She noted that she says this even from her position as a trauma therapist: 'It's about really empowering human beings to know that they can trust their gut instincts to support their buds.' [21]

It is important to recognise that the same mental health solutions don't apply to everyone. In order to determine how better to support different people, investment should be a given, said Kiran Nazish, who launched the Coalition for Women in Journalism after realising that many other women lacked the support to help them overcome obstacles in our industry.

> I think mental health support for journalists should be just as important; we should have the same resources in it as we have for, say, stationery in a newsroom, right? You need to have a budget for every newsroom for mental health support for the reporters. The reason I say that is not, 'Oh, we should have these resourced', but the fact that we can start getting into the nuances [of what people need] as regularly as possible, if you take it so seriously.[22]

Investment in journalism makes sense, not least from a financial perspective, as noted by Jane Hawkes, of the Canadian Forum for Journalism and Trauma:

> I believe that nobody will ever be able to argue against the fact that mental health investment is still a good business model, if you're only looking at it as a business model, let alone the sort of moral obligation you have to keep your people safe from crashing and burning. But it is a business model issue.[23]

Despite this, some newsrooms still cannot see that investment in mental health support will help efficiencies, and without taking stock of unhealthy workflows, they will remain in a vicious cycle, unable to adequately support their journalists' wellbeing. Dave Seglins highlighted this:

> The news business, in its current downsized, cut-to-the-bone state, doesn't have the resources to allow constructive discussion and proactive planning; everybody's running around with their hair on fire, every single day, putting out fires and trying to make deadlines. I think that one of the big underpinning challenges in this industry is that we have worked for far too long, far too hard, with far too great a workload, unable to engage this kind of conversation, because we don't have time for it.

This is a reminder that our industry needs to undergo a fundamental review of its processes and practices before breaking news breaks journalists beyond repair. It is worth repeating the following paragraph from the start of this book. The costs of not doing something about mental health are great. The costs of not addressing mental health are great. Also great are the costs of not ensuring that conversations around wellbeing are positioned front and centre in our work. Where journalists are not safe, they will take greater risks at work, their journalism will suffer, and so will their journalism colleagues. Where journalists are not safe, journalism will see reduced performance and productivity, rising presenteeism, problems with retention and increasing costs in terms of sickness and injury, as well as increased pressure and payouts related to staff turnover.

When journalists are not safe, the social contract between us and our audience will start to fray, those most marginalised by our media industry will feel less supported and we risk losing talented and diverse individuals with ties to the communities we have long failed to reach. When journalists are not safe, our reputation as a profession is not safe, because our journalism will not be as accountable, accurate, independent, impartial and empathetic. When journalists are not safe, press freedom and media diversity will suffer, democracy will be more fragile, the grip of autocratic regimes more secure.

It might seem a large leap from the failure to take seriously issues of journalists' wellbeing to the collapse of democracies, but the two are linked.

Taking seriously the mental health of our media colleagues can only be good for them, for our newsrooms, our industry, for all of us.

Notes

1. Author interview with Weng Paraan, February 2023
2. Author interview with Catherine Gicheru, May 2023
3. Author interview with Dave Seglins, January 2023
4. www.headlines-network.com
5. Author interview with Kari Cobham, October 2022
6. https://www.acosalliance.org/the-principles
7. https://newssafety.org/insi-safety-code/
8. https://www.sanitybytanmoy.com/
9. Project SIREN: https://cmhlp.org/imho-siren/team/
10. https://www.mindset-mediaguide.ca/
11. https://www.journalismforum.ca/
12. Author interview with Jane Hawkes, February 2023
13. Author interview with Professor Neil Greenberg, August 2022
14. Author interview with Dr Mark Grant, April 2023
15. Author interview with Caroline Drees, February 2023
16. Author interview with David Walmsley, February 2023
17. Author interview with Phil Chetwynd, December 2022
18. Caitlin Shea (2017) 'R U OK? Day: How Gavin Larkin's memory lives on through his family and the movement he started', ABC News, 3 September. Available at: https://www.abc.net.au/news/2017-09-04/r-u-ok-day-the-true-story-behind-the-creation/8865546
19. Author interview with Kate Nowlan, January 2023
20. https://rorypecktrust.org/how-we-help/therapy-fund
21. Author interview with Dr Cait McMahon, August 2022
22. Author interview with Kiran Nazish, July 2022
23. Author interview with Jane Hawkes, February 2023

Reference list

ACOS Alliance (ND) 'The Freelance Journalist Safety Principles'. Available at: https://www.acosalliance.org/the-principles

Canadian Journalism Forum on Violence and Trauma. Available at: https://www.journalismforum.ca/

Centre for Mental Health Law and Policy, Project SIREN. Available at: https://cmhlp.org/imho-siren/team/

International News Safety Institute (ND) 'The INSI Safety Code'. Available at: https://newssafety.org/insi-safety-code/

MindSet (ND) *Reporting on Mental Health – Guide*. Available at: https://www.mindset-mediaguide.ca

Sanity by Tanmoy. Available at: https://www.sanitybytanmoy.com/

Shea, C. (2017) 'R U OK? Day: How Gavin Larkin's memory lives on through his family and the movement he started', ABC News, 3 September. Available at: https://www.abc.net.au/news/2017-09-04/r-u-ok-day-the-true-story-behind-the-creation/8865546

The Rory Peck Trust, Therapy Fund. Available at: https://rorypecktrust.org/how-we-help/therapy-fund

Index

9/11 attack, impact on newsrooms 9–10

ABC *see* Australian Broadcasting Corporation
accountability 124
ACOS Alliance 29
Adeluwoye-Adams, Joyce 72, 122, 127–128, 160, 170, 174
AFP *see* Agence France-Presse
Africa 14–15, 39, 44, 47, 143–144, 155, 160, 166
Africa Women Journalism Project 37, 100
Aftershock (Green) 81
Agence France-Presse 21, 26–27, 82, 111, 115, 128–129, 153, 172; bolstering management training 27; conferencing tools 27–28; streamlining news-gathering 26
The Age newspaper 29–30
'alarm state' 45–46
alcohol 11, 34, 138
American Press Institute 115–116
American Psychiatric Association 56, 69
American Psychological Association 81, 86
amygdala 44–45, 48, 50–51
anxiety 21, 47, 49, 69, 101, 110–111, 121, 127, 148
APA *see* American Psychological Association
assignments 31–32, 38, 47, 49, 159, 171–172
Australia 91, 114, 165, 173, 175
Australian Broadcasting Corporation 98–99, 101, 124, 173, 175
avoidance 55
Ayuub, Rana 93, 94, 105–108

Balkan Wars 5
battle fatigue and combat stress reaction 56
BBC 8, 12, 18, 61, 95–96; High Risk Team at Television Centre 12; journalist 5, 44, 59; trauma training at 12
behaviours 39, 47–50, 55, 58, 68, 80, 136, 145; empathetic 37; maladaptive 34, 49, 55, 171; and mental health 145; and newsroom cultures 48
Behrakis, Yannis 82–84
Berrie, Drew 74, 109–110, 112–113, 136, 140, 141
bio-physical responses 48
Black journalists 124, 130; emotional and professional burdens carried by 122; health and social inequities 122; online harassment of 97
Black Lives Matter movement 122
Blundy, Anna 28, 57
body and brain, connection between 47–48
boundaries 3, 27, 36, 57, 72, 80, 111–112, 123–124, 129, 140–141, 145–146, 157
brain 2, 44–45, 70, 72, 142, 145; and body, connection between 47–48; reacting to extreme pressures 48
Brayne, Mark 6, 12
breaking news 21, 24, 116
Breaking: Trauma in the Newsroom (O'Neill) 36
breaks 26–27, 38, 73–75, 88, 110–112, 116, 127, 134, 135–136, 140–141, 144, 169; limited 24; lunch 99; natural 27; scheduling 74
breathing 45, 139, 141

Index 179

burnout 3, 16, 21–22, 99, 109–119; causes of 115; classification of 109; definition of 109; factors contributing to 111–112; of managers 112–113, 115–116; opportunity cost of 113–114; pandemic impact on 109; rise in cases of 109–111; stress and 110; struggle to maintain boundaries 112; symptoms 110; tools to support mental health in 112
'Burnout Year, The' 114–115
Buzzfeed 24

Cabra, Mar 17, 112, 119–120, 140, 152
Canadian Journalism Forum on Violence and Trauma 129, 169
CBC 6, 38, 48, 53, 167
Chetwynd, Phil 21, 26–27, 75, 111, 115–116, 128, 153, 154, 160, 172
Christchurch massacre 72
Chua, Gina 75
churnalism 26
CiC 16
Coalition For Women in Journalism 25, 37
Cobham, Kari 36, 110, 112–114, 113, 130, 132–134, 159, 160, 168
cognitive dissonances 23
collaboration 18–19, 121
Committee to Protect Journalists 5–6, 11
communities 2, 7, 15, 22, 28, 39–40, 49, 57–59, 78–79, 88, 101, 113–114, 121, 123–124, 127, 133, 145, 165–166, 175–176; informal 175; journalistic 174; positive 100; supportive 129
company-wide culture, challenges of building 160
compassion 3, 37, 39, 137, 158
compassionate leaders 2
competition 21
complex PTSD 56
conditioning 38–39
conferencing tools 27–28, 128–129
confidence 43, 65–66, 100, 143
confidentiality of patient 56
conflict zones 16, 72, 114, 170
connections 1, 24, 27, 29, 39, 48, 50, 85, 122, 127, 129, 140–142, 145, 156, 158, 165, 175; and community 145; empathetic 155; in-person 28; professional 139

context collapse, concept of 140
coping mechanisms 57, 144–145, 158
coping responses 47
coping strategies 36, 41, 47, 138
corporate work design, revamping 115, 116
counselling, access to 56
countries dangerous for journalists 6
coverage of traumatic stories, moral injury risk with 88–89
Covid-19 pandemic 3, 7, 21–23, 25, 27–29, 53, 55, 60, 72–73, 85–86, 93–94, 96, 109–110, 120, 121, 123–130, 136, 139–140, 142, 149–150, 152, 154, 173; authorities response to 127; conferencing tools used in 128–129; impact on burnout 109; impact on spontaneity 27; moral injury inflicted by 85–86; prioritising mental health offerings 122; professional pressures of managing through 22; sense of community lost during 28; stresses exacerbated by 29; support to journalists in 128; vicarious trauma risk in 72–73
Covid-19 pandemic, pressures of reporting on: cumulative nature of 128; emotional labour 123–124, 129; extensive isolation 127–128; from front lines of pandemic 123; health and social inequities 122; hostile environment 122–123; infodemic 126; lockdowns 127; mental health issues 121, 122, 124, 127; normalising conversations 122, 125, 126, 129; online threats and harassment 126, 128; prioritising mental health in 122–123, 125–126, 129–130; reliance on digital devices 122, 124; support to resolve 124–125; uncertainty 122; vicarious trauma 127; war zone like situation 122–123
CPJ *see* Committee to Protect Journalists
c-PTSD *see* complex PTSD
Cramer, Chris 8, 13, 58–60
cultural change, for mental health 37–39
cultures 2, 14, 25, 34–42, 70, 73–75, 78–79, 91, 94, 117, 130–131, 135, 155–156, 158, 160–161, 165; anti-newsroom 150; generational 41, 155; heavy-drinking 138; inclusive 156; open 28, 113
cyberthreats 97

Dart Center for Journalism and Trauma 10, 18, 25, 54, 69, 78
decisions 22, 32–33, 35, 83–85, 101, 126
defences and protective mechanisms 61
democracies 94, 108, 176
depression 17, 49, 69, 82, 121, 127, 148, 158
Devlin, Patricia 93
Diary of a Bad Year 115
digital devices, reliance on 122, 124
'digital frontline' 68
digital hygiene 96–97
digital interface resources, reliance on 139–140
digital overwhelm 111, 114
digital wellness advisor 98
disconnect 23, 38, 136, 139–140, 150, 167
distress 39, 68, 84, 87–88, 125, 157; journalistic 64; moral 87–88
distressing material, interaction with 67–68; concern about 75; impact on journalists 69–72; limiting time of 74; psychological injury risk 69; in remote working 72–73; as unavoidable part 75
diversity and inclusion 37
doxing 93, 96–97
Drees, Caroline 96–97, 171–172
duty of care 17–18, 59, 102

EAP *see* employee assistance programme
earthquake in Turkey and Syria, moral injury risk with coverage of 88
Edison, Jaden 22
education 18, 23, 56, 61, 168, 170; around PTSD 56–57; to react in stressful situations 47
effective communication 85
effective leadership 152–163
effective time management, 'four Ds' of 116
Elizabeth, Jane 115, 116
emotional avoidance 42
emotional burdens 17
'emotional flak jacket' 47
emotional impact of refugee crisis 82–83
emotional labour 123–124, 129
emotional load 73, 142
emotional quotient 154
emotions 35, 37, 42, 44–46, 50, 55, 80, 145, 156–157
empathetic connections 155

empathetic managers 157–158
empathetic types of leadership 156
empathy 2–3, 22, 25, 27, 39–40, 70, 129, 146, 154–155, 155–159; built into processes 160; and compassion 3; in leadership 156
employee assistance programme 16, 26, 32, 52–53, 56–57, 146, 160, 174–175
exercise 74, 138–139
exhaustion 21, 110–112, 115, 117, 119
extensive isolation 127–128

'false universalism' 165
Feinstein, Anthony 5, 8–9, 11, 13, 15, 18, 21, 24, 32, 54, 56–58, 60, 68, 69, 81–82, 85–86, 121, 136, 139; on education around PTSD 56–57; on global pandemic 21; on investment in mental health conversations 24–25; on moral injury risk 86–87; PTSD in war journalists 57; on stigma 13–14; tools to detect moral injury 86; on women are liability 58; work shaping medical health conversation 15
fight response 45, 48
financial insecurity 24
first responders 46–47, 80
flight response 44–45, 48
flop response 45
Floyd, George 122
Forbes 124, 155
Freedom Foundation 8
freelance journalists 6, 29, 68, 129, 168
freeze response 45, 48

gal-dem 24
Galizia, Daphne Caruana 94
Gicheru, Catherine 35, 37–38, 100
good intent, expressions of 2
Goswami, Tanmoy 23, 126, 143, 148–151, 168
graphic and sexualised threats 93
graphic videos 74
Greenberg, Neil 12, 169
Green, Matthew 81, 157
grief and trauma 52
guilt 57, 70, 80, 82–83, 87–88, 106, 144

Hawkes, Jane 129, 169, 176
Headlines Network 38, 74, 95, 110–111, 116, 123, 138, 141–142, 144–147, 156, 158, 167

HEFAT *see* Hostile Environment and First Aid Training
Hirst, Natasha 146
honour killing 94
Hostile Environment and First Aid Training 5–6, 48, 170
hostile environments 2, 5–6, 16–17, 47, 71, 73, 93, 114, 116, 122–123, 155, 171–172; reporting, good practice around 116–117; training 5–6
Hughes, Stuart 6, 59–60
human migration 81–82
hybrid newsrooms 129

identity: and gendered violence 72; identity-based violence and inequity 2; and trauma 73
impunity 6–7
Indian Ocean tsunami, coverage of 84–85
inequity 2, 58, 124, 136–137
infodemic 126
in-person connection 28
INSI *see* International News Safety Institute
intentional spaces 27
International Centre for Journalists 94
International News Safety Institute 6, 11, 13, 18, 59, 82, 168
International Society for Traumatic Stress Studies 12
intrusive memories 54–55
Iranian Embassy siege in London 58
Iraq 6, 12, 60, 94
Ishmael, Stacy-Marie 22–23, 110, 124
isolation 29, 72, 113, 127, 129
ISTSS *see* International Society for Traumatic Stress Studies

job cuts 24
journalism 1; attacks against 121; external drivers influencing 29; and trauma 10, 18, 25, 54, 68–69, 78, 89, 176; *see also* mental health
journalism safety 5–6, 11, 13, 59, 84, 98, 165–166; and mental health 11; movement 8; and wellbeing 165
journalistic injury 4
Journalists Under Fire: The Psychological Hazards of Covering War (Feinstein) 9
journalling 145
Jukes, Stephen 11

Kenya 3, 7, 15, 35, 57, 100, 102, 144, 166

Lankesh, Gauri 93
leaders *see* news leaders
leadership 2, 22, 34–35, 156, 158–159; attitude 36; empathetic 156; empathy in 156; enlightened 160; macho behaviour 35; roles 34, 98, 169; shortcomings 154; skill 155; toxic tendencies associated with 35
LGBTQI+ journalists, online harassment of 93
Lister, Gwen 35
lockdowns 127
Lyon, Santiago 31–32, 34, 154

Macdonald, Victoria 123
macho culture 10, 35, 58
maladaptive behaviour 55
management training and personal coaches 27
McEvers, Kelly 114–115
McMahon, Cait 17
media safety 58, 93
mental health 1, 3–4, 8, 12, 15, 24, 54, 107, 133, 165; conditions 2; costs of not addressing 1; crisis 25; expenditure, World Health Organization map of 14; good practices to improve 25–26; obstacles to advances in 30; prioritisation in pandemic 122–123, 125–126, 129–130; reasons preventing talking about 60; support 29; and wellbeing 17, 84, 121, 174; *see also* journalism
mental health conversations 1–7, 5–20, 11, 13–19, 23, 24, 34, 36, 37–38, 56–58, 59, 60–61, 64, 66, 68–71, 73, 81, 84, 87–88, 91, 98, 101–102, 109–111, 113, 120, 122–126, 128, 129, 133, 135, 140, 142, 145–147, 152–154, 153–154, 156–160, 165–170, 166, 172, 174, 175–176; advocating 37–38; appetite to talk 7; broadening around medical health 16–17; change in newsrooms 17; collaboration 18–19; company-wide culture, challenges of building 160; countries dangerous for journalists 6–7; discrepancy in 25; in education 18; emotional safety 6, 12, 14; Feinstein's work shaping 15; history of 2, 4; importance of 2–3;

informal interventions 166–167; need for investment in 24–25; need to normalise 36; normalising 13, 73–74, 94, 122, 125, 126, 129, 155, 160–161, 173; physical safety 5–6, 9–12, 14; prompted by news events 10–12; sensitive and nuanced approach 15; sharing of PTSD stories 13; stigma and taboos 7, 13–15, 19; threats against journalists' families 13; trauma and stress 7–11, 15; trauma risk management 12; Western-centric perspective 165; younger journalists influencing 17

mental health pressure: burnout caused by 22; economic uncertainty and 24; factors contributing to 21; journalists stepped down from their position citing 22–24

Mexico 3, 6–7, 13, 57, 125

Middle East 15, 26, 42, 43, 68, 173

misogyny 94, 103

moral boundary 89

moral distress 87

moral injury 12, 15, 18, 23, 65, 80–92, 132; covering disasters as risk for 88; debate about 87–88; definition of 80–81; demographic, work-related and clinical factors associated with 82–83; emotional impact of refugee crisis 82–83; inflicted by pandemic 85–86; mitigating risk of 84–85; prevalence of 86; *vs.* PTSD 80; sense of betrayal 85; tools to detect 86

moral wounding 23

Morgan, Emily 123, 144

Nasser, Khaled 14, 39, 41–43, 47, 155

National Union of Journalists of the Philippines 14, 166

Nation Media Group 35

Nazish, Kiran 25, 37

Neason, Alexandria 114–115

Newman, Elana 12, 18, 25, 28, 44, 87

news-gathering, streamlining processes for 26

news industry, conditioning 38–39

news leaders 7, 12, 15, 23, 25, 26, 27, 29, 34, 36–37, 37–38, 68, 69, 70, 72, 73, 85–86, 97, 101–102, 113, 115, 116, 127, 133, 136, 140, 152, 153–156, 158, 160, 167–168, 170; attitude of 36; difficult decision for 37–38; raising awareness 70; role in

mental health 27; stymied by systemic challenge 155

news managers 19, 24–25, 41, 66, 67, 73–74, 84, 85, 88, 99, 101–102, 111–113, 116, 122, 133, 142, 145, 152–161, 172; attitude to mental health 155; coaches to help 153; in deadline-driven news environment 153–154; empathetic 157–158; empathy 154–155, 157–158; inured to violence 155; responsibilities as 160; rethinking workflows around 153; role-play conversations 156–157; skills critical to 161; as 'stress sandwich' 152; support among peers 158; supporting teams 159; ways to help colleagues 154; workshops for 156–158

news media workers, mental health of 1

news organisations 10, 16, 18, 23, 34–35, 56, 58–59, 82, 84, 91, 97–98, 100–101, 109, 111, 129, 139, 145, 152, 160, 170, 173; challenges for 23; as two different companies 23

Newsroom Diversity 18, 122, 156, 165

newsrooms 1–3, 6–7, 9–17, 22–23, 26, 28–29, 34–39, 47, 49, 58, 65, 68–69, 71–72, 80, 84–86, 93–95, 97–98, 100, 102, 112–113, 115–117, 121–122, 124, 126, 128–132, 135–136, 138, 149–150, 154, 156, 159, 166–177; affected by vicarious trauma 68–72; cultures 2, 34–35, 48, 112

New York Times 124

Nowlan, Kate 16

No Woman's Land: On the Frontlines with Female Reporters 58

NUJP *see* National Union of Journalists of the Philippines

office-bound staff, PTSD in 69

O'Neil, Leona 36, 93–94, 163–164

one-on-one meetings 153

online abuse 101

online harassment 13, 93–95, 121, 128, 172; coping strategies 95–97; correlation with physical violence 94; forms of 93; growth in 97; origin of 94; psychological impact 95

online safety 97

online safety editor 98–99

online threats 93, 126, 128

online violence 94–98, 102, 107–108, 121, 126; aims of 96; impact on mental health of women 95; incidence of 94; incited by organisations 98; risk mitigation tools required to reduce 96–97; supporting victims of 97–103; training and resources for addressing 98–100; under-reported 103; against women journalists 94–95, 97, 99–100, 102–107
Owen, John 6, 8, 11, 13

Panama Papers 117–118
pandemic *see* Covid-19 pandemic
Paraan, Weng 14–15
peer support 16, 98–99, 167, 175
people of colour journalists, online harassment of 93, 97
Perera, Amantha 15, 77–79, 89, 114, 125, 139, 165
personal and professional lives, boundaries between 74
personal coaches and management training 27
Philippine Press Institute 15
Philippines 3, 6–7, 14, 121, 166
Philp, Catherine 38, 59–60, 64–66, 100, 102, 155
physical health 2, 24, 109, 138
physical safety 5–8, 18, 35, 82, 91, 93, 97, 170; in dangerous countries 6–7; HEFAT courses 5–6; INSI 6; research 7
physical self-care 135
Picard, Andre 85
policies and reality, disconnect between 167
post-traumatic growth among journalists 61
post-traumatic stress disorder 4, 6, 8–9, 12–13, 18, 29, 32, 42, 43, 46, 48–49, 54–55, 69, 72, 80, 82, 86–87, 91–92, 95, 110; change in criteria for 69; conversations around 58–60; definitions of 54–56; diagnosis 55, 59; hyper-arousal and hyper-vigilance 55; lifetime prevalence among war journalists 8–9; need for education around 56; news organization sued for 29–30; prevalence among journalists 54; risk factors for 46, 57–58; sharing stories of 13; supporting journalists with 60; symptoms of 54–55, 56, 57, 65, 110;

therapy from socio-political context 42; in war journalists 57–58
Poynter.org 22
pre-pandemic 'water cooler' moments 27
primary and secondary trauma 69–70
professional pressures 22, 36–37, 38; *see also* Covid-19 pandemic, pressures of reporting on
Project SIREN 149, 168
psychological burden 23
psychological distress 9
psychological injury 81
psychological safety 1
psychotherapy 144–145
PTSD *see* post-traumatic stress disorder
PTSD model of fear processing 44; in emergency mode 45; 'survival cascade' 44–45
public nature of journalism 26

quality of journalism 24

Ramsay, Stuart 38
Reach Hive 99–100
Reach plc 98–99
refugee crisis, emotional impact of 82–83
relationships in newsrooms 65–66, 68, 84–85, 114, 143, 174
relentlessness of news industry 154
remote working 145
resilience 9, 138
Reuters 10–11, 16, 18, 58, 71–72, 81–82, 84–85, 91–92, 122, 128–129, 139, 155–157, 160, 165, 170, 174–175
Reuters Institute for the Study of Journalism 82, 121
RISJ *see* Reuters Institute for the Study of Journalism
Rory Peck Trust 5–6, 29

Saady, Abeer 94, 127
safety conversations 14, 58, 171
safety demonstrations 136
safety of journalists 6–7, 13; freelance journalists 6, 168; in Mexico 13; women journalists 58
Schlesinger, David 10–11, 15–16
Schofield, John 5, 59
secondary trauma *see* vicarious trauma
Seglins, Dave 38–39, 48, 52–53, 167, 176

self-care 2, 17, 27, 37, 74, 99, 135–151, 157, 169; bearing witness 137; coping mechanisms 144–145; importance of 135–137; integrated into regular activities 135–136; permission to prioritise 136–137; physical 135; psychotherapy 144–145; self-help teaching 144; space for other things 144
self-care tips 138–142; avoiding alcohol 138; breaks 141; breathing 141; ceremonies 140–141; connecting with others 142; control of digital tether 139–140; coping strategies 138, 142; digital boundaries 140; fake commute 140; meditation 141–142; mindfulness 141–142; pastimes 142; physical activity 138–139; relaxation activities 139; running 139; sleep 139; staying hydrated 138; therapy 142
self-compassion 113, 137
Self Investigation, The 17, 120, 152
sexual violence and harassment 58
Shah, Dhruti 111
Shapiro, Bruce 9–10, 12, 87–88
Shay, Jonathan 12, 80–81
'shell shock' 56
sleep workshops 139
social contract 86
social media 26, 68, 72, 93, 95–96, 98, 111, 115, 121, 124–125, 136, 140, 148
social support 28, 47, 49
societal stigma 15, 57
Society for Freelance Journalists 129
solidarity 101, 106, 129, 167, 175
spending on mental health 24–25
spontaneity 27
Sri Lanka 7, 15, 114, 125, 139
staff wellbeing investment, return on investment in 25
stereotype 39
stigma 1–2, 7, 13–15, 19, 24, 32, 34, 37–38, 41, 49, 55–56, 59–60, 69–70, 81, 109, 113, 124, 160, 166, 168, 171, 173, 175; and perceptions, tackling 59; and taboos 37
stress 2–3, 7, 16, 18, 24, 29, 34, 39, 45, 48–49, 69, 99, 110, 116, 120, 148, 175; and burnout 110; management 120; reaction 8, 56; and resilience workshops 16; syndrome 109; and trauma 2, 18, 39, 48
stressful and less stressful jobs, rotating people between 73
stressors 18, 29, 73, 121, 128, 137, 139, 158, 167; and exposure to trauma 29; personal 16; in remote working 73; systemic 2
'stress sandwich' 152
suicide prevention and mental health 126
support to journalists 88–89, 135, 143–146
'survival cascade' 44–46
sustainability 22
systemic sexism 58
systemic stressors 2

taboos around mental health 7
Taking Care survey 86, 95
telecommuting 28
Tiananmen Square protests, coverage of 10–11
toxicity in newsrooms 39
training 6–7, 8, 12, 18, 27, 34, 47, 53, 68, 85, 96, 98–99, 102, 122, 126, 128, 133, 152, 155, 158, 168, 170, 171
trauma 2, 6–7, 10–12, 14–18, 25, 32, 36, 38–39, 44–52, 45, 54–57, 59–70, 72–73, 78–79, 80–81, 84–86, 91, 99, 108, 115, 122, 125, 129–131, 137, 144, 148, 166, 168–169, 174, 176
traumatic events 2, 10, 45, 54–56, 61, 65, 69, 173; covering 34, 36–38; exposure to impact of 46–47
trauma training, at BBC 12
Troubles (sectarian conflict) 36
trust 29, 42, 73, 81, 85, 102, 115, 142–143, 146, 158, 175; in mainstream media 121; and open communication, relationships of 85

UGC *see* user-generated content
UK media 59
Ukraine 21, 66, 127, 138
under-represented in newsrooms 23–24
United States 3, 5, 9, 11, 21, 24, 36, 38, 54, 113, 121, 124, 168
user-generated content 72

values 2, 23, 28, 55, 71, 74, 78, 121, 128, 149–150, 167–168, 175
van der Kolk, Bessel 12, 47
Vassilopoulos, Will 82–84
vicarious trauma 46, 67–79, 87, 127, 130–131, 172–173; definition of 67; impact on journalists 68–72; meaning of 67; and moral injury 132; and primary trauma, difference between 69–70; risk with pandemic 72–73; steps to mitigate 73–75; symptoms of 68; through interaction with distressing material 67–70; ways to mitigate 73
vicarious traumatisation 69
Vice Media 24
violence 52, 89, 95, 98, 107, 129, 136, 155, 169; interpersonal 81; physical 94; sexual 58
virtual threats 94

Walmsley, David 85–86, 158
Ward-Lilley, Sarah 18–19
war journalists, PTSD lifetime prevalence among 8–9
war zones 6, 19, 57, 68, 91, 122–123
'water cooler' moments 27
wellbeing 1–2, 17, 25–26, 32, 36–37, 39, 53, 74, 84, 86, 93, 98–99, 116, 120–121, 125, 135, 139, 141, 152–153, 165, 173–176; as collective effort 135; considered as privilege 25; and mental health 120, 167; and trauma 86, 89
Williams, Sian 46–47, 55, 60, 68, 70–71, 128, 138, 153
women journalists 17, 37–38, 48, 58, 93–95, 100, 102, 108–109, 121; PTSD risk among 57–58; vulnerability to online harassment 93–94
working environments, work design for 115, 116
workloads, unrelenting 111
workplace 24, 38–39, 109, 114, 125–126, 137
work-related traumatic event, exposure to 54, 55
workshops 41, 128–129, 150, 156

Yates, Dean 24, 71–72, 79–80, 84–85, 91–92
yoga 142
Yong, Ed 22–23
young journalists 23–24, 72, 127, 132; concern about 28, 36; lack of education and resources for 23–24; leaving the profession 24; mental health for 24

Zellhuber, Ana 46–47, 125

For Product Safety Concerns and Information please contact our EU
representative GPSR@taylorandfrancis.com
Taylor & Francis Verlag GmbH, Kaufingerstraße 24, 80331 München, Germany

www.ingramcontent.com/pod-product-compliance
Lightning Source LLC
Chambersburg PA
CBHW050536300426
44113CB00012B/2129